THE RETREAT FROM MOTHERHOOD

Books by Samuel L. Blumenfeld

How to Start Your Own Private School—And Why You Need One
The New Illiterates
How to Tutor
The Retreat from Motherhood

THE
RETREAT
FROM
MOTHERHOOD

SAMUEL L. BLUMENFELD

ARLINGTON HOUSE·PUBLISHERS

NEW ROCHELLE, NEW YORK

Library of Congress Cataloging in Publication Data

Blumenfeld, Samuel L
    The retreat from motherhood.

    Bibliography: p.
    Includes index.
    1. Mothers. 2. United States--Population.
3. Mother and child. 4. Women--Psychology. I. Title.
HQ759.B62   301.42'7   75-15764
ISBN 0-87000-304-6

To Janet

who didn't retreat

Contents

Preface

Sigmund Freud once wrote, in a letter to Marie Bonaparte, his loyal disciple, "The great question that has never been answered, and which I have not yet been able to answer despite my thirty years of research into the feminine soul, is: What does a woman want?" Any man who has ever been deeply involved with a woman—and every man has been involved with at least one, his mother—will have asked himself the same question at one time or another. Which merely means that men have been bewildered by women since time immemorial.

But it is also true that women have been bewildered by men. Life is a mystery, and when the race was divided into two sexes—which is one of the more interesting developments in the evolution of higher organic matter—some of that mystery was incorporated in the male, but far more of it in the female. The fact that only the female can actually produce another human being within her body accounts, perhaps, for the greater mystery that surrounds her. In this uneven biological division of labor, she has a capability far superior to that of any male. Is it not ironic, therefore, that women have been designated the "second sex" when in reality they are, in every respect, the first?

Nature has made very clear the female's superior role in the reproductive scheme of things. Only one male is needed to inseminate hundreds of females, but hundreds of females are needed to keep the species going. Yet, in the biological scheme of things, the male is produced in almost as great a number as the female, which makes him far more expendable. That is why millions of men can be destroyed in wars with only a minimal effect on population growth.

This is the harsh reality of nature, although we have so obscured ourselves to it that women have actually accepted the myth of their supposed inferiority for many more centuries than any man could have thought possible.

Another important biological reason why women must be considered the first sex is the length of time the human infant is dependent on its mother. Of all the mammals in existence, the human child requires the longest period of nurturing, caring, and rearing. Thus, out of sheer necessity for survival, the mother becomes the most important person in every human being's life. Her character, her personality, her method of child rearing have more influence on an individual's future development than all other forces combined simply because maternal love is the primary emotional and psychological need in everyone's life. And perhaps that is why there are almost as many men around as women—to enable women to give the inordinate amount of love and attention each human infant needs.

It is because mothers are so important in the lives of human beings that I decided to look into what seems to be the most troubling deterioration of our time: the deterioration of motherhood, not only in terms of quantity, but also quality. In writing this book I have tried to find out why this deterioration is taking place and what can be done to reverse it. On the negative side I discovered that alcoholism and nervous breakdowns are on the increase among women, and that more teenage girls than ever are becoming delinquents, criminals, runaways, prostitutes, drug addicts, and suicides. The negative experiences and influences of childhood have turned them off on maternalism. On the positive side I discovered that there is a small but growing number of women who are indeed trying to reverse the antimaternal trend by rediscovering the natural pleasures of motherhood. But their movement is largely underground and somewhat fragmented. I hope this book will encourage them to do more of what they have been doing and perhaps to see their work in broader social perspective.

To write a book about motherhood is really to write a book about women. To do so I found that I had to delve into areas of which most men would just as soon remain ignorant. John Wayne, whose reputation as a macho can hardly be disputed, once told a newspaper interviewer, "Women have always scared the hell out of me." In a way, every man shares something of that fear, simply because he understands instinctively the power that resides in motherhood.

But if I were asked why did I undertake to write so difficult a book— and it was indeed difficult to write— the answer would be that I did so in order to be able to write the final chapter: "What do you tell your daughter?" The book, in other words, was written for a very practical reason: to enable parents, teachers, doctors, psychologists, jurists, and clergymen to answer some of the many difficult questions girls ask when confronted with Women's Lib, the pill, legalized abortion, sexual freedom, love, and motherhood. I offer some answers, and obviously you will not agree with all of them. But the reasons for my answers are plainly stated. In any case, to write about women is to engage in controversy.

All of which leads us back inevitably to Freud's question: "What does a woman want?" Happiness, I suppose. What does anyone want? I therefore humbly hope that the women who read this book will be the wiser—and ultimately the happier—for it.

S. L. B.

Boston
February 1975

11

THE RETREAT FROM MOTHERHOOD

1

The Retreat
from Motherhood

The symptoms are all around us. *Parents* magazine is down to a meager shadow of its former self. *Cosmopolitan,* the magazine of the liberated single woman, is fat and prosperous, and *Playgirl* features center foldouts of nude men. Few of the women's magazines show pictures of infants. The motherly virtues are ignored; the wifely love-making virtues are played up. Pictures of active glamorous women pursuing careers in the man's world are everywhere. Articles about the woman holding her man with sexual know-how and seductiveness are abundant. Here and there an infant appears. Husband and wife, and unmarried couples, are now so busy making love to each other that they have little time for children at all.

The birth rate for 1972 was the lowest in American history until then, and even the absolute number of babies born in 1972 was the smallest in 27 years. The *New York Times* of March 2, 1973, reported:

Births declined so sharply in 1972, according to Federal statistics published today, that the fertility rate has now fallen to 2.03 children a family, significantly below the "replacement" level of 2.1 children.

A decline in births and rates was evident in 1971 and has already been dubbed "the birth dearth" or "the baby bust." But the new data show that this decline intensified sharply in 1972. . . .

The general fertility rate—births per thousand women age 15 to 44—

15

dropped from 82.3 in 1971 to 73.4 in 1972. The previous low was 75.8 in 1936, during the Depression.

The estimated fertility rate—in effect, the average number of children born to each family—dropped from 2.28 in 1971 to the current figure of 2.03. The previous low was 2.12, also in 1936.

Population grew by a smaller number of persons than in any year since 1945.

Even beyond rates, the actual number of births dropped to 3,256,000 in 1972, a 9-percent decline in one year.

Demographers found this particularly striking for two reasons. One is that the decrease of 303,000 births came despite an increase of 878,000 women of childbearing age—as the post-World War II baby boom continues to mature.

In 1946, 33,290,000 women of child-bearing age had 3,411,000 births. In 1972, 44,340,000 potential mothers—33 percent more—had only 3,256,000 babies—4 percent less.

In 1973 the birth and fertility rates continued to decline, again reaching new lows in American history.[1] There were about 3,140,000 births in the United States in 1973, about 110,000 fewer than in 1972. The fertility rate dropped to 69.3 in 1973. Thus the statistics indicate a very dramatic change in female thinking. Although there were a third more potential mothers in 1972 than in 1946, they produced 4 percent fewer children in absolute numbers than those in 1946. Actually the present decline began in 1958, the year after the post-war baby boom had reached its peak. But instead of leveling off, the decline in recent years has nose-dived, despite the fact that all of those girls born during the baby boom have now reached child-bearing age.

What has turned so many of these potential mothers away from motherhood? We can answer that question by examining current female attitudes. For one thing, women are marrying later and there are more divorces. In 1973 there were 913,000 divorces in the United States, double the number of just nine years earlier.[2] Thus, the basic instability of the family itself is having a dampening effect on the birth rate. Previously the presence of children in a family tended to postpone or discourage divorce. Now, however, some psychologists suggest that a divorce might be better for the children than a family situation full of tension and conflict. Such thinking has encouraged the breaking up of many families.

As for the younger unmarried women, their thoughts about the value of and need to bear children have changed. Caroline Bird, writing in *Signature* magazine of March 1973, described this phenomenon:

> Recently I asked a seminar of women college students what they thought they would be doing in 1982. I was not surprised to hear that less than half expected to be rearing a family. For five years now, college girls have been saying they don't want to settle down and have babies right away. In fact, instead of the traditional job for a year or two, these typical

16

women want to put off having their first child until they are into their thirties.

Is the current retreat from motherhood, then, merely a postponement of motherhood? We shall have to wait five to ten years to find out. Meanwhile, motherhood is no longer an enviable status. The woman who succeeds in business or competes with men in the corporate game achieves more recognition than the one who stays home and bears children. Mothers are looked at more as contributors to people pollution than givers of the gift of life to new human beings. Thus, in the eyes of such organizations as Zero Population Growth, women who bear children are somewhat akin to villains. The *Times* article commented:

> It is the presence of so many potential mothers in the population that impels demographers to warn against optimism. Even a small upward rise in fertility rates could turn the trend lines upward again.
>
> And larger rises could send them shooting up as fast as they have recently gone down. In the view of Philip M. Hauser, a noted University of Chicago demographer, "there is still a population bomb" latent, but armed, in present society.
>
> "The birth rate is notably fluid and capricious—strongly effected by such pyschological factors as the economy or changing attitudes about the role of women," Bickley S. Dodge, a spokesman for the 21,000-member Zero Population Growth movement, said today.

Thus, the 44,340,000 potential mothers in our country have become the target of an immense amount of propaganda urging them not to have children. Not only has this resulted in an increase in the use of contraceptives but also in an increased number of abortions. In fact some authorities believe that the abortions may account for the greater part of the decline in the birth rate. The legalization of abortion has now made an abortion as easy to get as a tonsillectomy. In fact, in 1974 almost 900,000 legal abortions were performed. Tonsillectomy is the only legal surgical procedure for which a higher annual number has been reported—917,000 in 1972.*

The killing of the unborn in such large numbers is no laughing matter. The desire to give life has been replaced by a desire to prevent life, even to snuff it out after it has begun. What this is doing to American women psychologically has yet to be determined. Undoubtedly some pregnant women resort to abortion reluctantly. They would like to bear their children but find that circumstances will not permit them to do so. They may be unmarried. They may not have the means to support a child. The father may not want the child. The child is therefore rejected.

Throughout the country there seems to be a growing rejection of chil-

Boston Herald American, February 3, 1975.

dren of all ages. We see it reflected in the generation gap, in the inability of parents to communicate with their children. We see it in the unhappiness of the children themselves. We see it in the growing teenage drug problem, the increase in young suicides and runaways, in vandalism and teenage crime. We see it in the teenage flight into hippiedom in search of love or its equivalent—something that was missing from their lives at home. The shattered emotional lives of the adults have had their effects on the children.

The increased divorce rate has had a devastating effect on the children involved. If parents cannot love one another, if parents can actually *leave* one another, what faith can a child have in love: its durability, its satisfactions? While we are preoccupied in improving our techniques for sexual love, we have learned very little about improving our techniques for emotional love.

Meanwhile, it is the attitude of the younger women that is determining the birth rate. Caroline Bird writes:

> America's young women are, in effect, going on a baby strike. Why? They explain it in both economic and philosophical terms. One simple fact is that babies now cost too much. The Presidential Commission on Population Growth and the American Future figures that it costs around $60,000 to raise and educate a child from kindergarten through college.

It is, of course, possible to raise a child for much less. But the consumer mentality of the middle class implies that a child must be raised first class or not at all. That is more of the propaganda reaching the young woman.

"Women are changing very fast," says Jacqueline Brandwynne, head of an advertising agency that has done extensive research on what women want. "They're not willing to pretend to play wife or mother when they don't feel like it. They don't feel they have to get married right away, or even at all, and they are willing to postpone pregnancy for years or even do away with childbearing entirely."[3]

But perhaps Caroline Bird hit the nail on the head when she wrote: "It's not so much that these women don't want babies. It's just that for the first time in history, they really are free to consider alternative investments of their energy."

What all of this means is that women are now in a position to experiment with alternate life-styles as never before. It has also given men a chance to experiment in the same vein. Without the responsibilities of fatherhood, men are gaining a greater freedom of movement. This no doubt accounts for why so many men are willing to support the various causes associated with female liberation. If a man is no longer to be tied down by wife and children, he too is free to consider alternative investments of his energies.

Thus it is not hard to see that the retreat from motherhood has as its concomitant a retreat from fatherhood. The childless marriage is now emerging as a new life-style, and such books as Ellen Peck's *The Baby Trap*, advertised as a "devastating attack on the motherhood myth," have been accepted by large numbers of young adults in support of their new experimental view of life.

But some women, apparently out of step with the majority, even prefer unwed motherhood to no motherhood. The growing phenomenon of the unmarried mother bringing up her baby without the benefit of clergy or a husband indicates that the urge to create new life, or at least permit it to grow, is sometimes stronger than the urge to prevent it. Having a child of her own gives a girl an emotional security she may not have been able to obtain with a wandering boyfriend. A helpless child, in need of mother's love and nurturing, is not about to get up and take off as do some of the young men with long hair and guitars when the thought of parental responsibility raises itself.

Whatever the reasons for this phenomenon, the fact is that with each year's decline in the overall birth rate there has also been a yearly increase in the number of illegitimate births. Is this increase caused by our welfare system, by accident, or is it a genuine indication that a growing number of unmarried girls are eagerly accepting the responsibilities of motherhood?

The demands and responsibilities of parenthood *are* great and some young married people simply don't want to accept them. Ellen Peck, advocate of the "childfree" or childless marriage, writes about her own marriage:

> We do not want children. . . .
> What most couples really want is to live life as fully and deeply as possible. That is what we want, anyway. And we do not feel that we can do this and still raise a family. A family would provide its own kind of change and experience, true—but not the kind we want. It would be, when you get right down to it, a repetition of experience—a repetition of the childhood experience. . . .
> I don't want to learn the alphabet again, and learn about creative playthings, toilet training, and playground etiquette again. I went through that once. We all did. Now, I would like some different experiences. I want the Riviera in January. And please give me Berne street festivals, and anniversaries in Liechtenstein, and the chance to step back six centuries by walking onto the grounds of a castle near Saint-Denis-sur-Loire.[4]

It's as if a series of travel posters could replace the profound experience of giving birth to and raising a human being. But why argue with people who do not want to have children? They can even form an organization of their own, as Ellen Peck did when she founded the National Organization for Non-Parents.[5] Ms. Peck is also the author of *How to Get a Teenage Boy and What to Do With Him When You Get Him*. The title apparently sums up her concept of human relationships. Perhaps in ten years her attitude will have changed.

But perhaps it is just as well that people who don't want children not have them. The demands of parenthood are so great—emotionally and materially—that only a minority of parents can be called ideal. Perhaps one of the reasons why so many young people reject parenthood is because of the examples that were set for them by their own parents. Parenting in the last twenty years seems to have undergone subtle changes for the worse. One result is that suicide is now the number two cause of death among the young. The *New York Times* reported on April 16, 1973:

> Researchers estimate that between 70,000 and 80,000 young people, between the ages of 15 and 24, will attempt suicide within the next year and that, of these, between 3,500 and 4,000 are likely to succeed.
>
> In the last 25 years, suicide has risen to what is now considered the second leading cause of death among the young (the first cause is accidental death and many believe that some suicides—the whole area is a murky one insofar as precise statistics are concerned—are erroneously listed in that category).

Why the increase? Some of the answers were given by Dr. Michael L. Peck, a Los Angeles clinical psychologist and director of youth studies at the Suicide Prevention Center and Institute for Studies of Self-Destructive Behavior.

"Stresses today have increased dramatically," he said. "A second, and perhaps more tenable, reason is the fact that people learn to enjoy life at a young age from their parents and they learn to distrust from the same people. Maybe the postwar generation had more general depression to communicate."

It is obvious that today's parents do live under great stress and that the frustrations of modern life are taken out on children whose very presence makes life so much more complicated. Our highly technological society has been with us less than a hundred years. The demands of modern life have changed the environment for child rearing. A hundred years ago a woman was expected to raise many more children with fewer technological conveniences. Today she is expected to raise fewer children with many more technological conveniences, and yet the job of child rearing has apparently become so much more difficult.

Part of the problem is caused by the urbanization of family life in crowded cities. Apartment living provides little room for a family. Suburbia provides room, but sends father further away. In suburbia we find the pressures of social conformity or drudgery and boredom for the housewife. Frustrated mothers take out their dissatisfaction on their children. Fathers, under constant pressure to maintain and achieve a higher standard of living, become impatient with their children. The result is emotional conflict and alienation between parent and child.

It is significant that our present drastic decline in the birth rate was preceded by a growing failure in parenthood. Has the appalling performance of postwar parents soured their children on becoming parents themselves?

The decline in parenthood has taken many forms. Its most outrageous is child abuse. It has been estimated that one in every ten injuries reported for children under two is intentionally inflicted by one of that child's parents. Twenty-five percent of all fractures diagnosed for children under three are the result of physical abuse by a parent. At least two children die every day in the United States as a result of physical abuse by their parents.

One of our leading authorities on child abuse is Dr. Henry Kempe, head of the Pediatrics Department at the University of Colorado Medical Center in Denver and coeditor of *Helping the Battered Child and His Family.* According to Dr. Kempe, 60,000 cases of child abuse were reported during 1971, and the number will no doubt increase each year as more states pass and enforce laws requiring doctors and hospitals to report all cases of suspected child abuse.[6] Most authorities agree that the reported cases are only a small part of the total number. For every case reported, at least five go undetected. Of those reported cases, 3 percent result in death and about 30 percent in permanent injury. The latter include scars from burns or gashes, missing arms and legs, and impaired vision or neurological disorders caused by blows to the head.

Parental mistreatment of children in our society has reached almost epidemic proportions. Such mistreatment ranges from severe physical abuse, including murder, to simple cold rejection, constant nagging, verbal abuse, or parental indifference, impatience, and intolerance. Some of these negative parental attitudes have become the attitudes of teachers and administrators in our school system. All of which might lead us to believe that there is a growing hatred of children not only among parents but among adults in general; that children are no longer considered the value they once were, a symbol of survival. They are now considered a nuisance, a burden, an expense, an intrusion, even a threat to survival. Is all of this a kind of unconscious psychological reaction to overpopulation, overcrowding, overfertility?

According to Dr. Kempe, abusive parents come from every social, economic, geographic, and racial background in our country. They are the people who are unable to control the impulse to burn their children with cigarettes, scald them with hot water, throw them against walls, beat them with pipes. Studies have shown that most abusing parents were once themselves victims of child abuse. In recent years attempts have been made to identify abusing parents and to help them stop mistreating their children. One such attempt is an organization called Parents Anonymous.[7]

Perhaps it is wrong to equate the child abusers in Parents Anonymous with the average modern parent whose failure may be more one of communication than of physical abuse. Psychiatrists who have studied what they call the battered-child syndrome have found that child-abusers are usually emotionally disturbed adults living in an isolated private hell. They were for the most part abused themselves as children. They have been taught not to trust people or institutions. They have a harsh, low opinion of themselves. They expect their babies to do the impossible—to give them the love and acceptance they did not receive from their parents. They usually pick one child as scapegoat and do not abuse others in the family.

Is our society in general guilty of child abuse? Is there a kind of general parental negativism pervasive in our society that tends to put down children? Do the crowded, pressurized conditions of modern urban life make such parental negativism inevitable? It is obvious that in an underpopulated society where the species is threatened with extinction the birth of a child is greatly welcomed and its life is cared for. It is loved as a value. But in a society where children represent economic sacrifice, drudgery, great wearying responsibilities, their value to the parents is called more and more into question, particularly if the spirit and will to sacrifice are dampened by the values of a hedonistic culture.

There was a time when a child was considered a potential economic asset to a family. He was expected to contribute to the family's economic sustenance and to care for his parents when they grew old. Now all of that is gone. Parents no longer depend on their children for care. Parents are now delighted when children can simply take care of themselves and cease to be a drain on their parents' reserves. They no longer expect children to contribute to the family's economic welfare. Children, in our society, have become an economic liability. It is difficult to love a liability that requires sacrifice, a lower standard of living, deferred pleasures. In fact it is difficult *not* to resent such a liability. Such resentment is easily communicated to a child, who begins to feel unwanted, unloved, rejected. Children run away from home by the thousands in search of people to whom they will be an asset, people who might love them for existing, people who are hard to find. In 1972 alone there were one million runaways in the United States.[8] Today more girls run away than boys, and the average age of the runaway keeps dropping, which means that home situations have become steadily worse. In 1970 the average age of the runaway was sixteen. In 1974 it was fifteen. What makes home so unbearable to so many youngsters? Abusive stepparents, fathers who make sexual advances to their daughters, overcrowdedness, lack of privacy, poverty, neglect.[9]

All of modern industrial society becomes afflicted with this problem as children become liabilities instead of assets to their parents. Of course this is not the case in every instance. In small persecuted or religious minorities where survival of the group depends on the birth of children, the latter are considered assets—badly needed assets, highly appreciated assets. This is one of the reasons why, for example, the Mormon church has been so successful in recruiting the young to do its missionary work. It gives the young, who so badly want to be needed, a tremendous sense of value.

There are a few industrial countries in the world in which children are still appreciated for their survival value. One of them is Israel, where physical survival of the adult population depends on a healthy crop of children. Because Israeli young people are aware of their importance to their society, they have higher self-esteem, a higher sense of purpose about their lives. Thus, in Israel, juvenile crime and delinquency, drug taking or suicide are much lower than in countries where children are considered liabilities. In other embattled societies where survival depends on the younger generation, children are accepted and appreciated as an important value to the nation as a whole.

In societies where children have survival value a higher birth rate is officially encouraged. In other societies, where children have become liabilities, there is general discouragement against large families. It should surprise no one that the Communist countries have had the lowest birth rates of all. Since the state superseded the family unit, and since children no longer represent survival value, they represent a liability in an economy of shortages and scarcity. Commenting on this situation, Charlotte Salisbury wrote in her book, *Russian Diary*, published in 1974:

> In Russia "family" doesn't always mean children. In fact, many Russian women don't have children and don't want them. There is a lot of feeling against bringing children into this world when life is so uncertain.

Yet the Russians love children. According to Mrs. Salisbury:

> I never saw a tired mother yanking a balking child; I never heard a yell or a cross word from an adult to a child; I never saw or heard one cry. Children are special, and are loved, indulged, and protected. Grown-ups seem to want to make a child's life as happy as possible, knowing childhood will soon be over and the grim unending realities of Russian life will begin.

As American society becomes more socialistic and the state takes on more and more of the functions of the family, children will have even less survival value than they might have had in a free society. In a free society children are expected to inherit their parents' wealth and property. They are expected to carry on the family business. In a socialistic society children are not needed to ensure a family's economic future; thus their value is depreciated.

Also, in societies where children are encountered in large numbers, such as in large public schools, society tends to resent them. Children are appreciated more as single individuals than in the mass. But our society forces us to deal with children in the mass. The result is that teachers become more interested in manipulating an entire classroom of students than getting to know and appreciate single students. Children feel especially alienated when treated in the mass. They hunger for one-to-one relationships with adults of value. They can rarely get them in our society. Thus the increase of child frustration and unhappiness.

It is obvious that the retreat from motherhood is part of the general American retreat from parenthood, a growing emotional rejection of children by adults on a national scale. This doesn't mean that all American parents and childless adults dislike children. It merely means that the dislike and rejection of children is now so prevalent that it is beginning to have deleterious effects on our society as a whole as manifested in the drug problem, vandalism, juvenile crime, runaways, and suicide. The situation has become so obvious that *Esquire* magazine devoted its entire issue of March 1974 to the theme, "Do Americans Suddenly Hate Kids?"

Can a nation that dislikes and rejects its children survive? Does it deserve to survive? The answer, of course, is no. Every nation's future is in its children—no matter how many of them we have, no matter how well they are loved or how badly they are abused, no matter how many fetuses are sent down the drain, no matter how urgent are the cries to curb population growth. It is a great mistake to translate a growing desire for female independence and a concern for population growth and ecology into a rejection of children. But this, unfortunately, is what has happened.

2

The Population Panic
and Birth Control

Every nation has its own demographic peculiarities, and the one that seems to distinguish the United States from so many other nations is our very high rate of marriage. In other words, it isn't because of large families that our population is expanding but because we have so many small ones. According to one book on the population explosion, *Too Many Americans* by Lincoln and Alice Day:

> With the average American couple having fewer than three children, the present situation in this country is a dramatic illustration of a new and tremendously significant fact: no longer is the large family a requisite of population increase. The low mortality rates of today permit a rapid sustained population growth when average family size is of only moderate dimensions.[10]

The fact is that nearly 95 percent of all adult Americans marry at some time in their lives, which makes us the "marryingest" of the racially European peoples. The British have a marriage rate of 88 percent, the Irish a marriage rate of only 75 percent. What is interesting is that it wasn't always this way. There was a time when it was perfectly respectable in America to be a maiden aunt or a bachelor uncle. Upwards of 20 percent of American women born before 1910 had no children; today that figure is about 10 percent, which is extraordinary when you consider that about 7 percent of all women are incapable of

25

having children. Also, during the last century, more women, about 25 percent of them, had six or more children. Today, only 7 percent have families of such size. Seventy-five percent of our women have four or fewer children. Thus there has been a growing conformity among our people concerning marriage and the size of family. Women have fewer children but, until only recently, more American women have tended to marry, and at an earlier age, than in previous times.

Have the conformist pressures of our modern mass media, particularly with the advent of television after World War II, led a lot of people into marriage who should not have married? Did a lot of women after World War II become mothers because it was the thing to do? The increase in parental failure and divorce in that postwar group seems to indicate that many people who should not have married did so, and many women who should not have had children had them. The result has been a large crop of unloved, unwanted children.

But we have become a very conformist people: marrying when we are supposed to marry, having as many children as we are supposed to have. This conformist pressure has undoubtedly led to the various liberation movements encouraging variant life styles, in opposition to some of our most cherished mass-media concepts of what people are supposed to do with their lives. Actually, our conformist mentality is of recent creation. Prior to the advent of the mass media, our people were much more individualistic. People were expected to be different. Eccentrics were not only tolerated but appreciated. Today, conformity is a national obsession. Even among those who supposedly don't conform, there is conformity. A variant life-style is supposed to conform to a kind of mass-media stereotype of that life-style. In our society an individual tries to find out what he is supposed to want instead of looking within himself to discover what he does want. Of course, it is not easy to know oneself, which is why conformity is so popular. Conformity is the path of least resistance. It saves you the effort of thinking. But it deprives you of the experience of being a complete human being.

The latest conformist pressure as far as women and childbearing are concerned is coming from the population lobby. The population-bomb panic button has been pressed, and women are now being told how many children they are supposed to have. It is quite possible that in the last few years the population lobby has had more to do with the current retreat from motherhood than any other single factor. How did it all start?

The first European to look at population growth as a social problem was Thomas Robert Malthus, an English economist. He contended, in 1798, that the "power of population is indefinitely greater than the power in the earth to produce subsistence for man." He argued, "Population, when unchecked, increases in a geometrical ratio. Subsistence increases only in an arithmetical ratio. . . . By that law of our nature which makes food necessary to the life of man, the effects of these two unequal powers must be kept equal. This implies a strong and constantly operating check on population from the difficulty of subsistence. This difficulty must fall somewhere and must necessarily be severely felt by a large portion of mankind."[11]

Although Malthus wrote this in 1798, it is essentially the same point of view of our present-day population alarmists. They contend that Malthus was never proven wrong. The industrial revolution, plus the open frontier of the new world, permitted man to expand his food supply and thus to support a much larger population. They believe, however, that we have now reached the point where the food supply cannot any longer keep up with the rate of population growth. The result, in the next few decades, will be widespread famine.

Of course the population alarmists are looking at the world as a whole. They have nightmares about the exploding populations in India and China. Even for the United States, where the means to grow sufficient food to sustain a larger population is certainly not lacking, they contend that our country is too crowded and that our population growth must not only be checked but reversed. They contend that although we only make up 5 or 6 percent of the total world population, we consume about one-third of its raw materials production each year. They forget that it is our high consumption of raw materials that permits so many others in less developed countries to live off the revenues they earn by selling to us. Nevertheless, the population experts contend that a stabilized American population, one of zero population growth, would have a beneficial effect on the world population problem as a whole. Economically, this argument doesn't make sense. As the richest, most productive country in the world, our consumer needs have made it possible for others to live and to prosper. The size of our consumer market has made it possible for even such industrial nations like Japan and West Germany to grow rich merely on selling us cars and cameras and other finished goods.

Because of the shakiness of their economic arguments, the population alarmists have appealed to Americans to stop growing because too many people supposedly are spoiling our quality of life. They contend that America is simply too crowded. They gloss over the fact that 70 percent of our people, through their own free choice, prefer to live in urban and suburban areas comprising about ten percent of our total land.[12] Most Americans like to live where there are lots of people, not only for economic reasons, but because they like to be with lots of people. Even when Americans go on vacation, most of them go where the crowds are. If our population were half its present size, most of our people would still live in crowded areas. No one likes to sit in a half-empty movie house, or dance in a half-empty discoteque, or walk around a half-empty amusement park. People have a tendency to judge the quality of something by how many other people want it. Most people are only too happy to stand in line to enjoy a good restaurant, to see a good movie or other amusement, their complaints notwithstanding.

We live in a world where being among large numbers of people has become for many a psychological necessity, regardless of the inconveniences and dangers of such crowding. People like lots of other people because their happiness for the most part comes from other people, not from pine trees and snowcapped mountains. Most people are looking for someone to love and someone to love them, and the more people there are, the more chances one has of being loved. Have you ever tried to make love to a pine tree? Perhaps Thoreau did, but he was peculiarly lacking in the ability to relate to other human beings with any great degree of intimacy.

People put up with smog, traffic jams, crowded mass transit, and other inconveniences and discomforts because of the emotional, psychological, and economic advantages our technological society affords us with its division of labor and high degree of specialization. For most people, the excitement of crowded urban life is preferable to the stillness and beauty of the Canadian wilderness. The amount of nature people get is about as much as they want. Those who want a lot of it can certainly find it in North America.

Nevertheless, the population alarmists have pushed the panic button and the word is out in the women's magazines and elsewhere to "stop having babies." But before women can stop having babies they must accept the idea of birth control. And so the movement for birth control goes hand in hand with the movement to curtail American population growth.

Which came first, the desire for women to gain control over their own bodies or the desire of the social scientists to curtail population growth? Both seem to have arisen at the same time. Many women do not want the burdens of motherhood, regardless of the population problem. Others want only a few children. Some women do not want to marry at all. The population alarmists encourage women to espouse those views that turn them away from having babies. In other words, they tacitly approve of the women who don't want to marry and openly approve of the women who want to have only one or two children. They disapprove of women who want to have more than two children of their own. They would consider a woman who wants six children as a sort of potential social criminal.

Women tend to do what men want them to do. They want the approval and love of men first and of society in general second. If men want them to have lots of babies, they will do so. If men want them to have few or none, they will do that too. Since virtually all of the population alarmists are men, American women are simply beginning to conform to a new set of dictates from American men.

Who are the population alarmists who now seem to exert such enormous influence over the childbearing decisions of American women? Chief among them is Stanford University biologist Dr. Paul R. Ehrlich, whose book *The Population Bomb*, published in 1968, has become the gospel among the alarmists and has had an enormous influence in our country. How did Ehrlich, who started out as an insect biologist, become interested in the population problem? It started, we are told, when he was a graduate student at the University of Kansas, working on the genetic problems of flies and how they had become resistant to DDT. "In 1954," he explains, "this led me to study the general properties of animal populations, which in many cases are very similar to those of human populations. Biologists soon find out that you can't tug on the web of nature at one point without changing it at many other points."

This led Ehrlich into many arguments with the U.S. Department of Agriculture during the 1950s about pesticides. He didn't get very far until Rachel Carson's book, *Silent Spring*, made its impact on the public.

Ehrlich wrote *The Population Bomb* in about three weeks in 1968, at the request of the Sierra Club, which hoped it might influence the election at the time and make the public aware of the population issue. It was written as a polemic, to arouse public concern. His later book, *Population, Resources, Environment*, written with his wife Anne, is a much bigger book. The first paragraph of that book instantly gives you an idea of how seriously, and perhaps hysterically, Dr. Ehrlich views the population issue:

> The explosive growth of the human population is the most significant terrestrial event of the past million millenia. Three and one-half billion people now inhabit the Earth, and every year this number increases by 70 million. Armed with weapons as diverse as thermonuclear bombs and DDT, this mass of humanity now threatens to destroy most of the life on the planet. Mankind itself may stand on the brink of extinction; in its death throes it could take with it most of the other passengers on Spaceship Earth. No geological event in a billion years—not the emergence of mighty mountain ranges, nor the submergence of entire subcontinents, nor the occurrence of periodic glacial ages—has posed a threat to terrestrial life comparable to that of human overpopulation.

In other words, too many people are a threat to life. The desire of too many people to live will utlimately lead to our extinction. Therefore, birth control is the highest good, because it is in the interest of survival. With that kind of moral sanction, women are now free to discard all of the teachings of religion and to practice birth control as a moral duty.

29

Thus every abortion becomes a deed of honor in the heroic struggle to save us from overpopulation, an act to be proud of. Many women do not yet quite see things in this way, but they are fast approaching that state of mind.

Dr. Ehrlich was interviewed by an eighteen-year-old girl for *Seventeen* magazine (January 1971). She asked him if there was any hope for her generation to find a solution to the population problem. Ehrlich's answer:

> If your generation doesn't, there's not going to be one. I think today's generation of students is the greatest we've ever had. Yet even among them I'd estimate about 60 percent are apathetic. That's only 40 percent activists.
>
> Young people can join ZPG (Zero Population Growth). Last year there were about eight chapters and six hundred members. Now there are about 150 chapters and 21,000 members, all concerned with focusing attention on the population problem.
>
> Certainly power plants should be fought wherever they are because power itself pollutes. Power use doubles about every ten years now. It is a fundamental source of pollution. When you generate power you create heat at the site. Then every bit of that power ends up as heat somewhere else. And the world is in danger of overheating from power use in seventy or eighty years if we don't stop. Anyway, power plants do all kinds of bad things: encourage industry, more population, more use of power. Utilities people say we've got to increase our supply to meet the demand. . . . What we have got to do is not increase the supply but reduce the demand.

The astute young interviewer then asked Ehrlich if he practiced what he preached. He replied:

> We certainly try. My wife and I attempt to minimize our use of power and of gadgets as much as possible, although it's difficult the way society is structured. For instance, we don't buy a new car every year. We have the smallest car we feel safe in, and we drive it until it practically disappears. Then we hope someone will find a way to recycle it. We find that having a plain white refrigerator is just as good as changing to a different colored one each year. I don't use elevators when I can walk up, in order to save power.
>
> We feel our most significant individual action is that we have only one child, our fifteen-year-old daughter Lisa Marie.

One of these days Lisa Marie is going to ask her father, "Daddy, wouldn't it have been better if I hadn't been born at all? Think of all the power you could have saved without me. I feel so awful contributing to the pollution of the world."

The young interviewer, a Roman Catholic, was in a dilemma. She asked: "What can I do though? I still want to follow the Pope."

Dr. Ehrlich's answer was quite interesting:

> I feel my Catholic friends are doing a marvelous job of working on the problem within the church, attempting to influence the Pope through their local archbishops. It would be presumptuous for me, a non-Catholic, to suggest that they ought to do anything else. Actually the birth rate among Catholics is not significantly different from that of non-Catholics, and the population explosion is not merely a Catholic problem.

Which brings us to a significant point. Women, including Catholics, have been practicing birth control long before they ever heard about the so-called population crisis. Ireland, a Catholic country, has had a declining birth rate and a declining population for years. France, a Catholic country, had a declining birth rate prior to World War II. Other factors beside religion influence birth rates. In French Canada, for example, the very survival of French identity required a high birth rate. In this case the Church doctrine merely reinforced this survival need. The result is that French Canadians had the highest birth rate of any ethnic group in the world, with some women having as many as twenty children. That birth rate is now leveling off, Church doctrine notwithstanding.

The population scare, however, is making birth control a moral virtue, and this is the message that is now being given to American women through the publications that cater to them. The "new morality" includes a concern for the population crisis. Thus *Seventeen* could tell its impressionable young readers in October 1971:

> Apart from a general swing toward liberalization, two major factors have contributed to a change in sex attitudes. One is a dawning public recognition of the dangers of overpopulation. The biblical imperative to "be fruitful and multiply" no longer enjoins our society. . . . New efforts to curtail birth seem to have become a necessity for universal welfare, although the concept is not accepted by all.
>
> Perhaps more significant is the timely development of easier and more effective contraceptive methods. The guilt and fear surrounding sex were doubtless created in previous generations partly by antisex mythology and partly by the rationally based probability that intercourse would result in pregnancy. Today, making love can be regarded as something apart from making babies. Recreational sex has become both feasible and socially acceptable, and, in some quarters, the only form of sex.

To help their young readers enjoy their "recreational" sex, the January 1971 issue of *Seventeen* carried a very thorough, well-written article on birth control devices and techniques. If your teenage daughter was going to engage in recreational sex, which *Seventeen* then proclaimed to be "socially acceptable," she might reasonably have been as well prepared as possible. The article discussed the rhythm method, the pill, intrauterine devices, condoms, contraceptive jellies and foams, diaphragms, coitus interruptus, and abortion. The safest method of all, abstinence, was only lightly touched on. The letters in response to the article supposedly represented a sampling of readers' opinions. Two were for it, one against it.

The point is not that such an article is bad or even morally dangerous. It may indeed be very morally dangerous, but as hygienic information it is certainly useful. If I had a daughter I would hope that she would know as much as possible about her body for her own protection. But the fact is that most of the contraceptive devices described in the article require the help of a physician and a rather cool, sober adult approach to sex. They require as much psychological preparation as physical preparation. To give this information to a young girl means that she has to think about her basic approach to sex before she has even had her first experience. Is she going to indulge in casual recreational sex or passionate emotional sex, steady sex with one boyfriend or one-night-stand promiscuous sex? How can a teenage girl decide this for herself before she has had any love experience with boys? Therefore, how can she apply her contraceptive knowledge if she hardly knows what sexual or emotional intimacy are about?

The result of the new premarital sexual freedom without the benefit of adult knowledge, of course, has been a sharp increase in unwanted pregnancies, and a rampaging epidemic of venereal disease among teenagers. The connection between sex and love has been lost in the revolution.

Seventeen magazine reaches about a million teenage, high-school girls every month. Its pages are full of ads for clothes, cosmetics, perfumes, shampoos, menstrual aides, silverware, and diamonds. The vast majority of the readers are headed for romance, marriage, and motherhood, yet the editorial content offers the moral guidance of a permissive social scientist, with a little popular psychology thrown in. Although, for many of these girls, motherhood may be only a year or two away, the reader is given no advice whatever on how to prepare herself for such responsibility. In four years of issues—1971, 1972, 1973, 1974 —I found only one major article on marriage: in the August 1971 issue, entitled "The Ups and Downs of Young Marriage." Its message could be summed up in this quote:

> Too many teens are getting married too soon and for the wrong reasons. The results are often divorce, broken homes, babies without fathers, health breakdowns mentally and physically. Divorce rates for those who married in their teens are estimated to be three or four times higher than for any other age group. In fact, it's estimated that in five years, approximately fifty percent of teenage marriages will end in divorce.

The solution? The writers recommended premarriage counseling. Another article, a one-pager in the July 1971 issue written by an eighteen-year-old girl, entitled "Marriage and Motherhood Aren't for Everyone," had this to say about motherhood:

> Is motherhood really fulfilling? I have seen many cases where it is not. I baby-sit for several young mothers in my neighborhood. For some, motherhood is creative, but for most it tends to be intellectually stifling and routine. As child after child appears, once cheerful and lively women become increasingly bitter, exhausted and resentful of lost career opportunities. They complain, "If I have to change one more diaper today I am going to go stark raving mad!"

32

It took three years before *Seventeen* published another piece on marriage, an October 1974 article entitled "Marriage in the Classroom." It dealt with a gimmicky high school marriage course given near Portland, Oregon, in which students were fictionally coupled off so that they could work on a variety of marriage problems in the classroom. The teacher was quoted as saying:

When I first started teaching marriage I found that students were pretty much aware of the psychological problems, because people are always talking about them. No one ever talks about financial problems. We're also not encouraging having babies, as some population-control people worry. We want students to gather information about having babies as a learning experience.

It's as if there were a taboo against motherhood in *Seventeen*, whose readers are permitted to know about babies as a "learning experience" but not as a potential doing experience. The only article on motherhood I found in four years of *Seventeen* was one on how "two unwed girls faced the agonizing dilemma of teenage motherhood," in the January 1973 issue. The article commented:

Why in these days when everyone is supposed to be so sophisticated about sex are so many teens getting pregnant? . . . Many girls shun contraceptives because they do not want to spoil the "spontaneous emotion" of sex.

Of course that's the problem. A teenage girl's approach to sex is emotional and romantic. She is anything but sober and adult at the moment. The emotional preparation for being seduced is quite different from the cold, calculating preparation for contraception. The two states of mind don't go together in a teenage girl as they might in the mature, scientifically oriented mind of a Joyce Brothers. As for the unwed mothers keeping their babies, the article revealed this interesting growing phenomenon:

But a disturbing development is emerging from this trend to keeping the child. The young mothers who thought babies were cuddly and "groovy" at first are now beginning to give them up for adoption two or three years later because they can no longer handle the situation.

The truth is that our teenage girls are being prepared for nothing but wearing pretty clothes, applying makeup, and enticing boys. Ellen Peck perhaps sums up *Seventeen's* philosophy with the title of her book, *How to Get a Teenage Boy and What to Do With Him When You Get Him*. We are teaching our teenage girls to do only two things: entice boys and stimulate them sexually. And what do teenage boys do when they are stimulated sexually? They knock up teenage girls. So much for "recreational" sex.

Thus the teenage girl is being encouraged to seduce the teenage boy, instead of vice versa. Motherhood? That's a kind of inconvenience, like venereal disease. You try to prevent it with contraceptives. If you don't succeed, you get an abortion. If you must have the child, you can give it away at birth. If you decide to keep it, you can give it away later on when you "can no longer handle the situation."

It is interesting how the potentially nightmarish life of the American teenage girl begins to emerge from between the bright, colorful ads for new clothes and eye makeup and hair preparations. In one article on VD (April 1972) we read about how "gonorrhea is now soaring out of control in the U.S." and how it is increasing faster for teenagers than for any other group. In another article (March 1973) we read about a hotline for teen suicide prevention. One such hotline receives 500 calls a month, two-thirds from girls. "Their biggest hangup is still sex. They think they may be pregnant and want an abortion, or they're sleeping with their boyfriends and their parents have disowned them, or they're worried about VD." In another article entitled "Is Virginity Outmoded?" (October 1971) we read that "In this confusing era of the New Morality every girl must ultimately make up her own mind about what value she's going to place on sexual intimacy. Outside the church, there is no single, dominating moral code to set guidelines. Thus, every girl has to make up her own mind and work out her own standards."

Pray tell, when does the average teenage girl get a chance to "work out her own standards"? Under whose guidance does she work them out? Or is she expected to know the consequences of sexual intimacy before experiencing such intimacy or discussing it with someone who might have experienced it? Why should we expect every teenage girl to be an Aristotle or a Moses writing her own Ten Commandments? Girls with enlightened parents may get adequate guidance. Girls without such parents will get their guidance from other girls.

Seventeen finally got around to the subject of premarital sexual restraint in a June 1974 article provocatively entitled "The Right to Say No." The arguments given against premarital sex were very weak indeed. Clearly the author had no intention of throwing cold water on premarital sex, and the issue was not whether a girl should or should not engage in it. The message seemed to be that a girl had the right to say "no" until the right guy came along. The only example the article gave of a girl who was against premarital sex on principle was that of a sixteen-year-old who had joined a Youth for Christ group. She was quoted as saying, "My outlook on sex is different from most. I really don't want to go to bed before I'm married. Giving a part of myself and knowing it's not going to last is just not for me." The impression given by the total content of the article was that you had to be a religious freak to be against premarital sex on principle. The author's true sympathies were obviously with the other girls she interviewed:

When I spoke with a group of high school juniors and seniors, a seventeen-year-old with dark snapping eyes took the lead. "Pressures?" she said. "I don't feel any. I don't have sex to please my boyfriend. It's kind of like a partnership. I feel it's right at this point, that it brings a special tenderness to our relationship."

Yet for many nonvirgins, the real reason for making love is not a mutual search for tenderness but a groping for ego gratification that often doesn't come off.

Note how cleverly approval is given to premarital sex as long as it is a "mutual search for tenderness." It all sounds so right, so moral, so syrupy. Forget about such unpleasant possible consequences as venereal disease, unwanted pregnancy, abortion, emotional turmoil, breakups, parental ostracism, etc. Yet, believe it or not, some girls are actually inhibited by these possible consequences. The author wrote about two such girls:

Two high school juniors with whom I spoke, pretty girls with long, silky dark hair, impressed me with their instinctive sense of where the scene was at for them. Both Marian and Sally (not their real names) quickly assured me that they believed in premarital sex. "I just feel sex is a natural human need," Sally said. "My sister at college sleeps with her boyfriend, and I think that's good. I don't intend to marry until I've lived with the guy at least a year."

Both girls had boyfriends with whom they had been going steady for some time. . . .

How long do they intend to wait? "Until I'm ready," Sally said. "If I was prepared to face the consequences of pregnancy that would be ready." They explained that there was no contraceptive clinic where they lived and that they'd be too embarrassed to go to the family doctor. "The girls we know are deathly afraid of having an accident," Marian said. "That's what holds us back."

Thank heaven some girls use their heads. In any case, *Seventeen* may have a taboo against *wanted* motherhood, but it has none against premarital sex which inevitably leads to unwanted pregnancies. But *Seventeen* is not the only magazine for women through which the population alarmists are spreading their message. Since the message in *Seventeen* is aimed at teenage girls, the emphasis is on postponing marriage and developing a positive attitude toward birth control, but not encouraging sexual abstinence and restraint. In the other women's magazines, primarily aimed at married women, the message is to limit the number of children to the currently acceptable number. Thus *Redbook*, which caters to young marrieds, carried an article in its March 1971 issue entitled "How Many Children Are We Entitled to Have?" It's the story about a couple who had dreamed of having twelve children when they married and how they changed their minds after having two children and reading two books on overpopulation, *Famine—1975* by William and Paul Paddock and *The Population Bomb* by Dr. Ehrlich. The couple decided to revise their plans. They decided to have only one more child of their own and adopt the others. Wrote Ann Goodstadt, author of the article:

"Personally I don't feel I have a right to have children just because I enjoy mothering. I would be quite happy to apply for a license to have a child as long as I know that these were given fairly, on a one-couple-two-children basis."

On the basis of the reasoning in those two sentences alone, Mrs. Goodstadt indicates that she is not fit to raise anything above the intelligence of a chimpanzee. In the first place, any married woman who actually feels that she has no right to have children because of the current emotional climate created by hysterical and fallible social scientists and misplaced biologists hasn't much of an ego nor the slightest hint of independent judgment. The arguments of the population alarmists are open to serious question, but Mrs. Goodstadt apparently accepts them as gospel and is ready to relinquish her inalienable freedom to bear as many children as she wants for a social scientist's dictatorship and some bureaucrat's permission to bear children on a license basis. It is obvious that Mrs. Goodstadt has no love of freedom, and not much pride. After all, if she really loved children more than she does obeying social scientists, she and her husband could go to Australia where they need babies. But she is put forth as an example of the new feminine virtue by a respectable mass-media publication.

So the message is two children per couple as per Zero Population Growth. Even if you're a good mother and love children, two children per couple is the limit—only for replacement. What about all of those people who have no children at all? Dr. Ehrlich wants our population growth to be reversed to a population decline, and that can only take place if more people have no children, and more couples have fewer children.

All of this requires a new kind of conformity, a conformity to a new set of rules created for society by a group of self-styled "planners," which is then propagandized through the mass media as if handed down from Mount Sinai. A good example of such propaganda appeared in *Good Houskeeping* in May 1971. The article, by Jean Libman Block, was entitled "The Population Bomb and How To Defuse It." It started off with a statistical view of our planet's "terrifying people explosion," finally leading to the question: "What can we in this country do to stop the population spiral?" Answered Miss Block:

> Many solutions are being offered: voluntary limitation of family size to one or two children, more freely available birth control, easier abortion, voluntary sterilization, a severe tax on large families—all the way to compulsory limits on family size.

36

However, the writer then recounted the story of one young couple, Tom and Nancy, whose solution to the population problem she considered highly commendable. The couple had had one natural son of their own, had adopted a second son of mixed racial origin, and they intended to adopt a third child, probably a Vietnamese orphan. "Nancy employs an intrauterine device as her form of contraception," Miss Block informed us. "She intends to have no more children of her own." Goody gumdrops for Nancy. There was no small amount of altruism in the decision of this couple to have no more children of their own. Nancy said: "Those who want lots of children can satisfy their desire for a big family through adoption." Tom said: "I think it is one of the most exciting and rewarding decisions of a lifetime, the decision to raise another person's child." Who could quarrel with two young people willing to give so much of themselves to the homeless children of others? The only problem with this is genetic. Tom and Nancy may, in the process, phase out their own genetic line, which, after all, produced Tom and Nancy, two pretty good people. If all young couples in America started importing and adopting all of the homeless waifs of Africa and Asia, we might end up with an America looking more like India than America.

After telling us about Tom and Nancy, Miss Block then goes on to offer other approaches to the population problem. She writes: "The objective of most planners is to stabilize population—that is, to arrive at a total that remains about the same." Who are these all-knowing, omnipotent planners who have decided that the American nation shall not grow any larger than it is and whom we must now obey without question? One of them is Dr. Alan Guttmacher, president of Planned Parenthood–World Federation. Dr. Guttmacher advises, "We must disregard taboos and offer birth control on humane, empathetic terms to all who need and desire it. The reticence of some members of the medical and religious communities to do this must be vigorously overcome."

The article then discusses abortion, quoting Lawrence Lader, chairman of the executive committee of the National Association for Repeal of Abortion Laws: "The right to abortion, an inalienable right of all women, is an integral part of population control." Next, we are told about the Association for Voluntary Sterilization, which is "now conducting an educational drive to make both the public and medical authorities aware of this no-fail form of contraception—especially couples who have completed their families." As for permissible family size, Miss Block writes: "Assuming that couples are free to practice any kind of birth control they wish, or none, what size family should they aim for? 'Stop at two' has been the slogan of many population activists. But some experts say even two are too many." So she goes on to quote another planner whose dictum is to "stop at one." She writes:

Awareness of the threat of overpopulation is permeating every level of society and major religious denominations have aligned themselves with the most forthright of population-control activists. Most significant, a concerned young generation shows signs of pursuing its anxiety about the environment right up to the deliberate limitation of family size to two or under.

She ends her article by quoting Canon Michael Hamilton of Washington, D. C., Cathedral, who told his congregation: "Couples now have a moral duty to limit their families to two children or less. Population pressures and the earth's resources have reached the point where none of us is morally free to have as many children as we wish."

One would think from the tone of Miss Block's article that her views were the only possible ones *Good Housekeeping* could promote. Could not a dissenting opinion be permitted in its pages? Weren't there any valid arguments to counter the views put forth so authoritatively by the population "planners" and promotors of recreational sex? Not everyone agreed that the population crisis was exactly as Dr. Ehrlich said it was. Jane Jacobs, author of *The Death and Life of Great American Cities*, expressed rather strong opposing views in an interview published in *Vogue* in August 1970, entitled "More Babies Needed, Not Fewer." The interview, written by Leticia Kent, is important because it offered some very sound arguments against the population alarmists that the other magazines preferred to ignore. The interview started with a question about the current programs of population control. Here's Miss Jacobs' answer, followed by most of that interview:

JACOBS: In my generation women were made to feel guilty if they didn't stay home and devote themselves to being wives and mothers. If we worked at jobs or at a profession, we had to struggle against regarding ourselves as irresponsible, selfish, and willing to jeopardize the future.

The more things change, the more they remain the same. Now America has its theme for making *this* generation of women feel guilty: "People pollute." "Voluntary sterilization." "Population Growth Zero." Women who want children are obviously now going to have to struggle against regarding themselves as irresponsible, selfish, and willing to jeopardize the future. Another generation of women afraid to be themselves, manipulated by guilt—if they let themselves be.

KENT: But don't you believe in birth control?

JACOBS: Of course. It's a major human right. But there's a vast difference between voluntary, individual choices as to family size and compulsory public policies—which are implicit in the present campaigns.

KENT: But according to statistics, the country will be overcrowded with people if we don't do something drastic about controlling population.

JACOBS: Ben Wattenberg, the American demographer, reports that we are not, by international standards, a crowded country. Holland is eighteen times as dense in population as the United States. England is ten times as dense. And even Switzerland, with all its mountains, is seven times as dense. One out of every three American counties has actually been losing population to the suburbs of cities so that vast areas of the country are more sparsely populated than they used to be.

KENT: But how can the world feed itself if people keep on multiplying?

JACOBS: By industrializing more. You see, productive agriculture depends upon tools and other industrial products. That explains why the most industrially advanced countries—Japan, Western Europe, the United States—are also the most reliable and abundant food producers. And that's why underdeveloped countries like those of South America have very unproductive agriculture. But underdeveloped countries can change. Colin Clark, the English economist, estimates that if other countries were as productive in their agriculture as Holland, the world could support ten times its present population. And even Dutch agriculture is increasing. The total amount of food that could be produced in this world—without harm to the planet—is incalculable.

KENT: But if we don't control population, won't we run out of resources?

JACOBS: That's like saying too many people cause too many automobiles so the people have got to go. Whether or not we run out of resources depends on whether or not we keep wasting them as we do now. In the United States, lack of progress in dealing with wastes and overdependence on automobiles are becoming very destructive of water, air, and land. Whether or not we run out of resources also depends on our learning to use a wider range of resources than the few we now exploit. The issue of population control diverts us from facing the real changes and improvements we need to make.

KENT: Still, isn't our increase in population destroying the ecology of the country? Biologists say that excessive increase in any species signifies that the natural ecology is out of balance.

JACOBS: The ecology of people is just *not* like the ecology of other animals. Other animals live on what nature provides more or less ready-made. People develop new goods and services, new resources, new means of abundance. And people might pretty well have died out by now if they had continued to exploit natural wildlife for their food instead of developing agriculture. Think of all the land modern economies have released for food production by inventing tractors to replace millions of hungry draft animals and by developing synthetic fibers to replace flax and cotton. And think of the forests that were saved when modern economies started using coal and oil for fuel. My point is that along with natural ecology we also have a human ecology and there is nothing to be gained by pretending that people are like deer or insects.

KENT: But we *are* hurting the natural environment. Look at how bad pollution is right now.

JACOBS: Sure, because for the past thirty years we have utterly neglected the work that would prevent pollution. Our problem is the undone work—not the numbers of people. It will take a lot of ingenuity and a lot of people to solve the problems we've let pile up. Limiting future generations will not eliminate existing pollution. It will not develop new kinds of nonpolluting vehicles, new waste-recycling enterprises, or new methods of handling sewage. To say "people pollute" and to think you've said anything is to evade all the hard problems. . . .

KENT: But certainly population control would not interfere with solving other problems and might make it easier. What harm would it do?

JACOBS: It might do enormous harm to the human ecology.

KENT: How?

JACOBS: Who knows whether it isn't extremely important for some human beings to come from large families and some from small ones? We ought to be wary of anything that tends to destroy human diversity. We surely need diversity in sizes and kinds of families just as much as we need diversity of talents, occupational preferences, and personalities. In fact, so far as the family is concerned, we've probably already tended toward too much standardization. I mean the standardized American family.

KENT: Are you suggesting communes or the abolition of marriage, or what?

JACOBS: We have adopted wholesale a very strange sort of family when you come to think of it: just one or two parents and the children, no one else, in the household. This is entirely different from households and families of the past and different from families in most of the rest of the world right now. For one or two adults, by themselves, to take on the whole responsibility for the family unit may have worked out in some cases, but it has proved to be an abysmal failure in many others. By and large, this family may be an experiment that has failed. The middle-aged don't even want to think about that possibility, but the young are considering it. Their communes may forecast an important change in the future American family, or, anyhow, an alternative. We don't know much about human ecology and, unfortunately, the ecologists instead of applying their insights about the interdependence of diverse organisms and activities, are behaving as if human ecology were not even worthy of respect. Worse, concern for ecology has become a cloak for antihumanism.

KENT: Can we at least agree that the underdeveloped countries need population control to overcome their poverty?

JACOBS: No. People are producers as well as consumers, and wherever poverty is deep and persistent, it is because a great deal of work is just not being done, because people are not producing. Whatever the particular causes of this stagnation, "overpopulation" is not one. Take a look at the world. Some of the poorest countries, like Colombia, are very thinly populated. If densely populated Japan and Western Europe were poor, and thinly populated Colombia and the Congo and Brazil were prosperous, a nice case might be made that people reinforce their poverty by their own numbers. India's trouble is that its people are not productive enough to provide for their own needs. When India had fewer people a generation ago, and still fewer two or three generations ago, it wasn't correspondingly more prosperous. If India were to have fewer people in the future than it has now, but nothing else were to change radically, the fewer people would continue poor and unproductive. Again, population control is an evasion.

Let me ask you a question suggested by yours about underdeveloped countries. Does it strike you as ironic that a country with as many unsolved social and practical problems as ours is so ready to tell the rest of the world how many children it ought to have? The Population Growth Zero campaign tells us some things about our national character, most of them unpleasant.

KENT: What, besides women's guilt complexes?

JACOBS: We seem to have a messianic compulsion to settle the prob-

40

lems of the whole world and population control may be another vehicle for that. We also seem to have a need for apocalyptic crises and I think that population control is our new crisis fad. The idea that there is a population crisis is convenient for a lot of special interests, too. For instance, it provides a persuasive extra argument for women's groups that want abortion laws liberalized even though "need for population control" isn't really the reason women oppose current abortion laws. They oppose them for private, not public, reasons. And I am afraid that many of the people worrying about the rising welfare rolls or the increase in crime see population control as a way of cutting down crime and welfare. But the spiralling welfare rolls, like the crime, are symptoms of profound troubles in our economy and society—not causes of these troubles.

It is obvious from the interview that Jane Jacobs is hardly a traditionalist. Nevertheless her views on the population issue vary considerably from those being directed at the millions of women who read the mass circulation magazines. Why do all of the magazines insist on parroting only one point of view? Why do they make no effort to present variant views? Probably because of the basic conformist nature of the American mass media. The mass media seems to adopt or reflect the general world view as conveyed to them by a handful of leading academic thinkers. If the leading academic thinkers are swept up in the population crisis, then the leading editors of the leading magazines take up the chant. If the majority of the thinkers think there's a population crisis, then there is a population crisis. The majority may be wrong, but the loudness of their voices, the insistence of their arguments, and the weight of their credentials make it difficult for the minority to be heard, even if the minority is right.

Also there may be another reason why the mass media is so one-sided. Most of the editors and television producers live in New York or Los Angeles, two of the most densely populated areas in the world, aggravated by well-publicized pollution problems. To them "overpopulation" is a daily fact of life. Their empathy with Americans who live in the roomier towns and hamlets between New York and Los Angeles is somewhat limited.

It is obvious to anyone who has traveled across the United States that this country is very far from overpopulated. The fact that so many of our people like to live on top of each other in urban centers does not alter the fact that there is much room in this country for many more people and much more development than any of us can conceive. In fact, the solutions to the pollution problems will only come about when there are enough people in this country to make those solutions economically imperative. It is no doubt true that an America with 400 million people will not be quite the same as an America with 200 million people. It might be better or it might be worse, depending on what Ameri-

41

cans do with their productive energies and ingenuity. I prefer to think that it would be better for the simple reason that a commitment to create more human beings would have to be accompanied by a commitment to make life better for everyone. I don't think that 200 million more Americans would be a blight on the planet. I think it would be a blessing—only, however, if those people were politically and economically free enough to use their energies in making their world better.

3

The Rise of
Women's Lib

People pollution did not give rise to Women's Lib, though Women's Lib has certainly contributed to the current retreat from motherhood. But is feminism necessarily anti-maternal? Only a knowledge of the movement can tell us.

Popular revolts reflect popular discontent. And who can doubt by now that the Women's Liberation movement represents very widespread discontent on the part of most women, even those women who prefer to remain somewhat quiet? For after having read a great deal of feminist writing, it is difficult for me not to conclude that these anti-male sentiments, justified or unjustified, and sometimes expressed in language that would make a sailor blush, express the true feelings of the majority of women. These women write with a power, a vividness, an anger seldom found in the writings of men. Female fury, female anger makes the male version pale in comparison. When they rake Aristotle or Freud over the coals, there are just a few charred bones left. Sometimes a man is tempted to respond: "Why didn't you tell us that being a woman in a so-called man's world is so horrible?" But as one young women's-libber wrote: "I never realized how oppressed I was until someone brought it into the open."

The trouble with that kind of statement is that the young lady may be attributing to males the oppression that life in general forces all of us to bear. Reality is oppressive in the demands it makes on all of us. But most men have learned how to bear that oppression with a minimum of complaints. They don't blame the oppression on women, or children, or any particular scapegoat. In their daily confrontation with the world, these men learn that reality is a hard taskmaster and that it has no gender. It is not surprising that a young woman might say that she had never realized how oppressed she was until someone awoke her to it. Personally I don't think it's possible to be oppressed and not know it. If you don't know it, then it's not oppression; it's something else. Oppression, like physical pain, has a way of making itself felt.

But, of course, the oppressor is the last—or maybe the first in some cases—to understand the feelings of the oppressed. Also, some people have a higher tolerance for oppression than others. For example, prior to the building of the Berlin Wall, East Germans could easily escape Communist oppression by taking a subway to West Berlin. Millions did exactly that. But other millions didn't. They were quite willing to live under an oppressive dictatorship and were not at all tempted by freedom.

Who are those who must have freedom, who find oppression intolerable, who risk their lives to escape? They are generally the young, the ambitious, the rebellious, the proud, the self-motivated, those with strong egos, a strong sense of self-esteem, a sense of individual sovereignty and independence. They are the individuals who are the most sensitive to oppression, willing to take risks to be rid of it, to gain freedom.

Then there are those who rebel for masochistic reasons, because they want to be beaten down by authority. Sometimes they strike out against an oppression that is not there. Their rebellion is often irrational, violent, emotional, and self-destructive.

And sometimes oppression can be so institutionalized, so readily accepted by the oppressed—like the income tax—that obedience for many becomes a way of life; though mere compliance for others may be a painful ordeal. There is also the need to separate the idea of oppression from that of authority. All authority is not oppressive. Yet, authority implies a curtailment of freedom—if that authority is represented by a human being or an institution run by human beings. In general, as we mature, we learn to control our own behavior in the interest of survival. We give up impulsive behavior because we know it might kill us. We impose our own authority over ourselves, and do not need the authority of others. We learn that individual sovereignty is indeed based on self-control. But what are the obstacles to the development of self-control? Why do so many people need the oppressive hand of authority to impose control over them? The greatest obstacles to self-control are the emotions: anger, rage, and fury directed against those who frustrate us. It is our inability to control those who have the power to frustrate or satisfy us that enrages us. Because we are at their mercy during infancy, we tend to want to control them rather than ourselves.

The Women's Liberation movement is, in the simplest terms, a rebellion against male domination. It is basically the expression of women who no longer want to do what men want them to do or to be what men want them to be. In its most benign form it agitates for women's rights in the form of equal pay for equal jobs, equal entrée into all of the professions. It is a continuation of the fight to change the legal structure, which has sanctioned male dominance with governmental force. In this struggle women have already won the vote, equal education in most areas of learning, the right to own property even though they may be married, etc. The present drive for the Equal Rights Amendment is an attempt to nullify all legal supports to male dominance. In its most extreme form the movement calls for the destruction of the traditional family and even a self-imposed ban against falling in love with men. Is there a middle ground? Yes. The middle ground calls for an end to sexism, which like racism is a form of prejudice and discrimination, but based on sex rather than color. However, on the whole, women's libbers seem to have a rather vague idea of what they really want their relationship with men to be. One feminist wrote: "We will not be able to sort out what we do want from men and what we want to give them until we know that our physical and psychological survival—at home and at work—does not depend on men."[13]

Thus, women have to be fully liberated before they can decide what their new relationship with men can be. But what happens in the meantime? Men and women will have to continue to live together. Children will continue to be born, and they will have to be cared for and raised.

Is equality between men and women possible? Are the differences between them so great as to make equality impossible? Dr. Naomi Weisstein writes:

I don't know what immutable differences exist between men and women apart from differences in their genitals; perhaps there are some other unchangeable differences; probably there are a number of irrelevant differences. But it is clear that until social expectations for men and women are equal, until we provide equal respect for both men and women, our answers to this question will simply reflect our prejudices.[14]

The "social expectations" are crucial to Women's Libbers. They resent the fact that girls are programmed for motherhood and an acceptance of male domination. They resent the fact that little girls are given dolls to play with instead of erector sets. Yet, how do we teach girls to be mothers unless we show them how? According to Dr. Vincent J. Fontana, an expert on child battering, mothering is not instinctive.[15] It must be developed early in life from watching and imitating a model. The epidemic in child abuse is a cold indication that the mothering instinct is not what so many think it is—a natural expression or development of femaleness. Mothering, it turns out, is a learned skill.

We have observed that the Women's Liberation movement is a manifestation of women who don't want to do or be what men want them to do or be. This leaves women in the peculiar situation of trying to find out what it is they do want to do and be. But is it possible for women so to separate themselves from men as not to reflect male expectations to some extent? The manufacturers of cosmetics don't seem to think so. Men, of course, are not too sure these days what they want from women besides sexual pleasure. Many of them want a woman to take care of the home and kids, to cook and clean, to comfort them. Some women accept this domestic role quite willingly. Others are in open revolt against it. Some of the latter see the domestic scene as an oppressive capitalist plot. Writes Roxanne Dunbar:

> The present female liberation movement, like the movements for black liberation and national liberation, has begun to identify strongly with Marxist class analysis. . . . Our analysis of women as an exploited caste is not new. Marx and Engels as well as other nineteenth-century socialist and communist theorists analyzed the position of the female sex in just such a way. Engels identified with family as the basic unit of capitalist society, and of female oppression. "The modern individual family is founded on the open or concealed domestic slavery of the wife, and modern society is a mass composed of these individual families as its molecules." And "within the family, he (the man) is the bourgeois and the wife represents the proletariat."[16]

Thus the destruction of the family is part of the program of some Marxist-oriented women's libbers. How many go along with this radicalism? It would be hard to say. But virtually all women's libbers see the family and child rearing as great sources of oppression. Writes the same Marxist feminist:

> How will the family unit be destroyed? . . . The alleviation of the duty of full-time child care in private situations will free many women to make decisions they could not before. . . . Women will feel free to leave their husbands and become economically independent, either through a job or welfare.[17]

In other words, the taxpayer will be expected to subsidize female independence through the support of child-care centers. Apparently, it's all right to impose this additional oppressive burden on the taxpayer who may have no interest in women or children. The tax-payer, obviously, is someone anyone can oppress, including women.

While men tend to see women as the homemaker, the women's libbers see it as just the opposite: "The masculine ideology most strongly asserts home and country as primary values. . . ."[18]

If women have been oppressed for as far back as man can remember, why have they now suddenly become aware of it? The reason is not too difficult to find. Western capitalism has been so successful with its science that it has made possible the swiftest rise in population growth since the beginning of civilization. The population explosion and the development of modern contraceptive technology have suddenly given women the freedom they never had before: freedom from the imperative to become mothers and freedom from unwanted pregnancy. Now they can pursue the careers they've supposedly always wanted to pursue and have all the sex with men they want without the consequences of pregnancy. As Lisa Hobbs writes in *Love and Liberation*:

> Large numbers of children are no longer needed to maintain the human species. Women's sole societal function, so long held in awe and veneration, has become a cursed, destructive power. The only feminine role that was socially imperative and unique to the female genetic nature has lost its societal value. Our bodies are now obsolete in an overpopulated world.[19]

So now women are faced with the problem of what to do with the new freedom technology has given them, the new freedom *men* have given them. For make no mistake about it, women would not suddenly be faced with the problem of what to do with themselves unless men had decided that they no longer wanted or needed to control women. That, perhaps, more than anything else accounts for the underlying bitterness one finds in much of the Women's Liberation literature: the fact that men no longer want to control or enslave them. Men have set them free. But most women's libbers don't see it that way. They find themselves sexually free but still oppressed by the chains of a sexist society, just as blacks, no longer slaves, find their opportunities limited by the organization of a white society.

Of course, the best way to evaluate the Women's Liberation movement would be to examine what the major spokesmen, or "spokespersons," of the movement have written. But first a brief but necessary history of the feminist movement.

It appears that the formation of a patriarchal society for the human species occurred far back in prehistory. There are a variety of theories to explain why men found it necessary to subjugate women in their upward climb toward civilization, and these theories are discussed in the next chapter. Whatever the reasons, it is a fact that human society has been organized along patriarchal lines for as far back as man or woman can remember. That throughout history women have expressed their discontent with this organization there can be no doubt. But it wasn't until the creation of the United States with its philosophy of equal rights for all that women could begin to question and challenge the whole basic patriarchal structure of human society. I stress "human society" because patriarchy has been the rule for all human societies, large or small, Marxist or capitalist, advanced or primitive, in caves or on islands, in the arctic or in the tropics. It is a universal human phenomenon.

But the revolt of the women had to begin somewhere, and it stands to reason that it would start where people in general had the greatest freedom—the Anglo-Saxon world. The first great feminist document, *Vindication of the Rights of Women,* was written in 1792 by Mary Wollstonecraft, an English writer. (Her daughter, Mary Wollstonecraft Shelley, wrote *Frankenstein,* which is not considered feminist literature even though it projects a rather monstrous view of men.) The feminist movement in the United States, however, did not get officially under way until the 1848 convention at Seneca Falls, New York, where Elizabeth Cady Stanton, Lucretia Mott, and others issued a declaration of independence for women.

The basic and underlying theme of the movement was man's unjust and forceful subjugation of women and how that enslavement had given women the sense of inferiority so many of them had. The feminist complaint could be summed up in this excerpt from the Seneca Falls Declaration:

> The history of mankind is a history of repeated injuries and usurpations on the part of man toward woman, having in direct object the establishment of an absolute tyranny over her. . . .
> He has made her, morally, an irresponsible being, as she can commit many crimes with impunity, provided they be done in the presence of her husband. In the covenant of marriage, she is compelled to promise obedience to her husband, he becoming, to all intents and purposes, her master —the law giving him power to deprive her of her liberty, and to administer chastisement.[20]

A stronger and more vivid expression of the same sentiments had been made by Sarah M. Grimke, an activist in the anti-slavery movement, in 1837. She had said:

> All I ask of our brethren is, that they will take their feet from off our necks and permit us to stand upright on that ground which God designed us to occupy. . . .
> The lust of dominion was probably the first effect of the fall; and as there was no other intelligent being over whom to exercise it, woman was the first victim of this unhallowed passion. . . . All history attests that man has subjected woman to his will. . . . He has done all he could to debase and enslave her mind; and now he looks triumphantly on the ruin he has wrought, and says the being he has thus deeply injured is his inferior.[21]

It is interesting to note that from the very beginning, men have been involved in the feminist movement. The convention at Seneca Falls, for example, was chaired by a male. Subsequent conventions and meetings had their male participants. In fact, feminist meetings from which males were excluded were quite rare. The point I wish to make is that the feminist movement could never have gotten started unless there were enough males ready to accept it, sympathize with it, and even promote it. Female liberation has always received a powerful assist from members of the oppressor class. The reason for this is obvious: just as in a society permitting slavery not everyone wants to be a slaveholder, so it is that not all men want to subjugate or control women.

The thrust of the·feminist movement in those early days was to change the laws that held women in such strict subservience to their husbands. Said Elizabeth Cady Stanton to the Joint Judiciary Committee of the New York State Legislature in 1854:

> The wife who inherits no property holds about the same legal position that does the slave on the Southern plantation. She can own nothing, sell nothing. She has no right even to the wages she earns; her person, her time, her services are the property of another. She can not testify, in many cases, against her husband. She can get no redress for wrongs in her own name in any court of justice. She can neither sue nor be sued. She is not held morally responsible for any crime committed in the presence of her husband, so completely is her very existence supposed by the law to be merged in that of another. . . .[22]

Feminist pressure finally got the New York State Legislature to pass the Married Women's Property Act of 1860, which represented a considerable advance in the legal status of women. It guaranteed a woman the right to keep her own earnings; the right to equal powers with her husband as joint guardian of their children; and property rights as a widow equal to those her husband would have had, had his wife died before he did.

Prior to the Civil War the feminist movement was closely linked to the anti-slavery movement, but after the war the women became divided over the issue of the Fourteenth Amendment that gave Negro males the vote, but denied it to white females. Feminists like Elizabeth Cady Stanton and Susan B. Anthony, who had wanted women to get the vote through the Fourteenth Amendment, felt betrayed and outraged. Thus began the post-Civil War decade of feminist militancy with sit-ins at polling places, the nonpayment of taxes, and women voting illegally. By 1869, however, the feminist forces had split into two factions: the National Woman Suffrage Association, organized by Stanton and Anthony, and the American Woman Suffrage Association representing the views of Lucy Stone and Julia Ward Howe. The latter organization limited its activities to getting the vote for women and thus acquired a large conservative following. Susan B. Anthony's group, however, was concerned with woman's general position in a man's world. She was particularly concerned with the need for women to gain full equality, economically as well as politically.

By 1871 the idea of "sexual freedom" began to enter the movement through the zealous efforts of the Claflin sisters—Victoria Claflin Woodhull and Tennessee Claflin—who had burst onto the scene in 1870 with the publication of a radical feminist newspaper, *Woodhull & Claflin's Weekly*. Topics such as prostitution, venereal disease, abortion, socialism, and free love were openly discussed. The two women themselves led uninhibited sex lives and were the subjects of much notoriety. The Claflin sisters' views on sexual freedom offended popular morality, including numerous women whose interest in the feminist movement was limited to getting the vote. Nevertheless, those views reflected a great deal of the sexual discontent and frustration women have always felt in their relationships with men. Even Elizabeth Stanton concluded, by the time she was sixty-five, that "the first great work to be accomplished for woman is to revolutionize the dogma that sex is a crime." "A healthy woman," she wrote in her diary, "has as much passion as a man."[23]

In 1890 the two factions of the feminist movement reunited as the National American Woman Suffrage Association, with Elizabeth Cady Stanton as first president. Stanton tried to imbue the new organization with a much broader view of the feminist struggle, but suffrage remained the great rallying point for the movement as a whole.

Finally, in 1919, after a great deal of militancy here and in England, the suffragettes achieved victory with the ratification of the woman suffrage amendment by the last state, Tennessee. With the achievement of suffrage the organized feminist movement collapsed. The great emotionalism that had been necessary to gain the vote was spent. Even though the Equal Rights Amendment was first introduced in 1923, feminist political activity all but ceased. Nevertheless, with the most blatant strictures of the patriarchal system abolished, the 1920s ushered in a new age of female emancipation. Women flocked to colleges and professional schools. Many went into politics and became full professors at universities. Women's fashions became more masculine and practical as women went in for sports and physical activity. Some women even began to enjoy the possibilities of sexual freedom as exemplified by Isadora Duncan and Edna St. Vincent Millay.

During the thirties women like Amelia Earhart and Eleanor Roosevelt continued to expand the horizon of female endeavor. However the social upheavals brought about by the depression, communism, Nazism, and fascism made the issues of female freedom and equality

50

irrelevant. Men were worried about survival in a world headed for political catastrophe. Then, during World War II, with the acute labor shortage, women had a chance to prove that they could perform any man's job. They also joined the WACS and the WAVES. But with the end of the war and the return of our soldiers to civilian life, a new era began, an era that today's feminists call the "counter-revolution," a patriarchal reaction against female liberation. As Caroline Bird describes it in *Born Female*:

> The 1950s saw an unprecedented return to family life. Never had husbands, home, and children been more sentimentalized. Never had so many girls married so young. Not for fifty years had American women been so fertile. Never had so many women defined themselves so exclusively as "mother."[24]

How do we explain this social conformity of the fifties in which women rejected all of the preachings of the feminists and returned to their traditional role as wife and mother? Part of it was probably a renewed affirmation of the values of survival as represented by family and procreation. The war had devastated half the civilized world; nations had been decimated; cities had been wiped out. Western civilization was determined to repair the damage done to its body and spirit by the violence it had inflicted on itself. It returned to the basic values of renewal and regeneration.

In the United States this return to basic patriarchal values was aided by the spread among intellectuals of Freud's psychoanalytic theory of sexuality, which more or less provided the patriarchal system with an objective, scientific, psychological basis. Kate Millett explained it from the feminist point of view in her book *Sexual Politics*:

> Coming as it did, at the peak of the sexual revolution, Freud's doctrine of penis envy is in fact a superbly timed accusation, enabling masculine sentiment to take the offensive again as it had not since the disappearance of overt misogyny when the pose of chivalry became fashionable. The whole weight of responsibility, and even of guilt, is now placed upon any woman unwilling to "stay in her place." The theory of penis envy shifts the blame of her suffering to the female for daring to aspire to a biologically impossible state. Any hankering for a less humiliating and circumscribed existence is immediately ascribed to unnatural and unrealistic deviation from her genetic identity and therefore her fate. A woman who resists "femininity," e.g., feminine temperament, status, and role, is thought to court neurosis, for femininity is her fate as "anatomy is destiny." In so evading the only destiny nature has granted her, she courts nothingness.[25]

Freud, with his theory of penis envy and his view of the female personality as basically passive, masochistic, and narcissistic, was obviously a "male chauvinist pig," whose theories in general insured a continuation of the patriarchal status quo, despite the liberalization of women's legal status. Nevertheless, Freudianism was accepted as the gospel by the intellectual and academic world, and so the editors of the leading women's magazines eagerly spread the message among their millions of readers. The message was basically this: Because of female anatomy feminine fulfillment can only be achieved through marriage and motherhood. Betty Friedan's book, *The Feminine Mystique*, is all about how this doctrine of feminine fulfillment took hold. She writes:

> In the fifteen years after World War II, this mystique of feminine fulfillment became the cherished and self-perpetuating core of contemporary American culture. Millions of women lived their lives in the image of those pretty pictures of the American suburban housewife, kissing their husbands goodbye in front of the picture window, depositing their stationwagonsful of children at school, and smiling as they ran the new electric waxer over the spotless kitchen floor. . . . They changed the sheets on the beds twice a week instead of once, took the rug-hooking class in adult education, and pitied their poor frustrated mothers who had dreamed of having a career. Their only dream was to be perfect wives and mothers; their highest ambition to have five children and a beautiful house, their only fight to get and keep their husbands.[26]

Meanwhile the preachings, arguments, and struggles of Elizabeth Cady Stanton, the Claflin sisters, Susan B. Anthony, and the others were forgotten and discarded. The feminist movement was dead history and there was no more talk of female emancipation. The new view of life was summed up in the word "togetherness," a concept coined by the publishers of *McCall's* in 1954. But by 1960 the world of family "togetherness" was already beginning to come apart. Female discontent and frustration began to rear its persistent head once more. Stories about the trapped American housewife with her symptoms of anxiety and depression began to appear all over the lot. Writes Friedan:

> By 1962 the plight of the trapped American housewife had become a national parlor game. Whole issues of magazines, newspaper columns, books learned and frivolous, educational conferences and television panels were devoted to the problem. . . . They got all kinds of advice from the growing armies of marriage and child-guidance counselors, psychotherapists, and armchair psychologists, on how to adjust to their role as housewives. No other road to fulfillment was offered to American women in the middle of the twentieth century.[27]

These were symptoms of the same malaise that had afflicted women from the time they had begun to feel the oppression of patriarchy. It was the beginning of the latest phase of the rebellion against male domination. Men, for the most part, could not understand it because they assumed that women had indeed achieved emancipation and were satisfied. They had the vote, didn't they? Men assumed that women wanted to marry, have kids, and live in the suburbs. Women, too, assumed that that's what they wanted. In fact the women had been quite aggressive in getting men to give them exactly the life they had. So how come it wasn't working?

Friedan tells us it wasn't working because no human being with any intelligence could limit herself, or himself for that matter, to the tedium, boredom, and inanity of housewifery without going stark raving mad. The world of the housewife simply did not permit enough human growth to satisfy a normally intelligent adult. But it wasn't the dissatisfaction of suburban housewives that rekindled interest in the feminist struggle.

Which brings us to the current Women's Liberation movement. Although the current movement began to make waves in earnest in the late 1960s, one must go back to the early fifties and the publication of Simone de Beauvoir's monumental study of women, *The Second Sex*, to understand the intellectual force behind the current drive to overthrow patriarchy. First published in Paris in 1949, the first English edition of *The Second Sex* was published in the United States in 1953 during the height of the sexual counterrevolution. At the close of World War II, Simone de Beauvoir had achieved considerable fame on both sides of the Atlantic as a writer and a colleague of Existentialist philosopher Jean-Paul Sartre. But *The Second Sex* revealed that she was a lot more than merely the fashionable subject of gossip at literary cocktail parties in Paris and New York. She was, without dispute, the world's most scholarly, erudite, literary, and passionate spokesman (or spokeswoman) for the feminist cause since its collapse in 1920. *The Second Sex* was an incredibly ambitious attempt to analyze in virtually encyclopedic manner every aspect of the feminization process—that process whereby the patriarchy transformed female human beings into the feminine, submissive, inferior caste they were. Clyde Kluckhohn, reviewing the book for the *New York Times*, wrote:

> Essentially this is a treatise which integrates the most variegated strands of history, philosophy, economics, biology, belles-lettres, sociology and anthropology. I cannot think of a single American scholar, man or woman, who controls such a vast body of knowledge as this French writer.[28]

The *Saturday Review* assigned six distinguished writers—including Dr. Karl Menninger, Phyllis McGinley, Margaret Mead, Ashley Montagu, and Philip Wylie—to review the book.[29] Their reviews provide an excellent picture of the intellectual climate of the period regarding feminism.

Menninger, representing the dominant psychoanalytic outlook of the time, called it "a pretentious and inflated tract on feminism. Hence it is intrinsically tiresome. . . ."

Phyllis McGinley, representing the women who had accepted housewifery in suburbia as the ultimate in feminine fulfillment, wrote:

"Nothing dates so rapidly as radical doctrine; and *The Second Sex* is both radical and sentimental. . . . All these arguments, brilliant as they sound, are merely sublimations of feminist arguments we all advanced at seventeen. Here is, in short, nothing more than the Great Complaint of Virginia Woolf's 'A Room of One's Own' raised to the nth power and supported by exhaustive but unscientific research."

Margaret Mead criticized de Beauvoir for saying so little about motherhood and maternal love. Nevertheless, she wrote: "Stripped of its personal bias and its over-decorative paraphernalia, the main argument—that society has wasted women's individual gifts by failing to institutionalize them—is a sound one."

Ashley Montagu, the anthropologist, reviewed the book favorably. He wrote:

> There are so many things I want to say about this book. First, that it is a great book, a book that will be read long after most works which have been forgotten. Second, in its qualities of analysis, restrained eloquence, and the influence it is bound to have upon human thought and conduct, it ranks next to John Stuart Mill's *Subjection of Women* (1869). Third, one cannot help being impressed by the skill with which the author has avoided the pitfalls into which so many others have fallen in discussing such thoroughly misunderstood institutions, for example, as matriarchy. Fourth, the balance, good common sense, and profound insight of the author constitute a most refreshing and illuminating experience in an area in which the discussion is usually tendentious and biased. Fifth, the book is beautifully written in all senses of the word. And sixth, while the book could have been written by a man, it took a woman to do it.

Montagu ended his review with some prophetic words: "It will be up to the women of the world fully to emancipate themselves. Some men will help, but for the present women will largely be forced to do the necessary work for themselves. Meanwhile, Simone de Beauvoir's *The Second Sex* may serve them not only as a breviary but also as a call to action."

Of course, it would take another fifteen years before action would be forthcoming.

The most surprising review of all was Philip Wylie's. Wylie had gained tremendous notoriety during the forties with his book *Generation of Vipers*, in which he had blasted the venerated American institution of "Mom," castigated the "Cinderella" mentality of American women, and criticized our sexual hypocrisy. I reproduce the bulk of that review, not only because it gives us an excellent insight into the intellectual climate of the time, but because it clearly points out the importance of the book as a source of intellectual enlightenment—for both men and women—at a time when the dominant intellectual and cultural attitude was clearly anti-feminist. Wylie wrote:

The Second Sex by Simone de Beauvoir is one of the few great books of our era. It flows from a quality men often deny to women: genius—at least by my definition of that lofty capacity. Genius, I think, is the ability to discover or to create a new *category* or a new *dimension* of human knowledge, human understanding, or human experience. Simone de Beauvoir has finally succeeded in adding that much insight to the subject of Woman and the twice-larger subject of human sexuality. That is why I feel no one can leave her book unread and still be considered intellectually up-to-date. It makes a fresh contribution to awareness that cannot be missed any more than the contributions of Freud, say, or Einstein, or Darwin—without the onset of a private "cultural lag."

The space accorded me here leaves little room for the detailed acclaim deserved—a reviewer's praise of the erudition, the librarian's patience, the cerebral appetite with which Mlle. de Beauvoir has performed her task. And there is no need to say what it is that she has added to the general awareness; that is in the book. My urgent purpose is but to bring to it what attention I am able.

Perhaps I can do this partly by reminding readers this is the reverence of a male, and of an American long known as the leading critic of females—a dim-viewer and angry-speaker, too. Perhaps I can suggest more by pointing out that my own books, from *Generation of Vipers* onward . . . have concerned in large part the selfsame subject:

What is woman?
What, in correspondence, is Man? And,
What is sexuality?

But probably I can do most in behalf of *The Second Sex* by saying that, while I agree with its brilliant statement of the problem and with its synthesis of the male-female situation (which is where I find a new dimension), I disagree with its principal suggestion for the resolution of the problem. This very disagreement, fundamental to the philosophy of the work, is the proper measure of my enthusiasm for what its author *does* accomplish. (I see the ageless debasement of woman ended by an initial application of other means than the material, the economic, the strictly "social.")

Scientists have a way of saying that every "right answer" is found only after some one asks the "right question." . . . So I think, at infinitely long last, Mlle. de Beauvoir in this book has asked concerning Sex the right questions, and usually in the right terms. Until we have answered her—whether by following her suggestions or not—we shall have not content with our minds or peace in our emotions. . . .

If humanity is soon to enjoy the forward rush which a real understanding of sexuality would assure, the sturdiest first steps will probably be made by Americans "pioneering" as bravely as ever—indeed, more courageously than ever, since it is easier to die for a tradition than to live opposed to one. I believe *The Second Sex* has lighted the scene of modern despair and revealed its "frontier" and its "challenge" as no comparable work has done. Its effects on men and women will be fascinating and they cannot be evil since what this great woman sets forth is the Truth.

Despite reviews like Wylie's, *The Second Sex* had no immediate effect whatever on American women. Nevertheless it became a kind of intellectual time bomb for the feminist movement. Yet, as much as nine years later, *Harper's* magazine (October 1962), in a special survey devoted to "The American Female," could report:

> The American woman of today is not very different from her mother or grandmother. She is equally attached to the classic feminine values— sexual attractiveness, motherly devotion, and the nurturing role in home and community affairs. She is not a great figure in public life or the professions. And like most men, she is repelled by the slogans of old-fashioned feminism.

In 1963 Betty Friedan's *The Feminine Mystique*, called by many of its critics "the feminine mistake," was published. It was the first indication that surburban female discontent *might* rekindle the flame of the feminist movement. The state of female aspirations was put into a rather nonfeminist perspective by Paul Foley in an article in the *Atlantic* of March 1964 entitled "Whatever Happened to Women's Rights?" Mr. Foley wrote:

> In 1963 the average age at which females in America married was 19.8 years.
> What underlies the urgent drive of today's young women to early marriage as an end rather than a beginning? Many things, of course, but we should not overlook a seldom-mentioned fact: America, more than any other enlightened society in this last half of the twentieth century, puts a social stigma—overt or hidden—on the simple fact of a woman's remaining unmarried. . . .
> For public scrutiny of the American woman, 1963 was a banner year. In addition to the very impressive report of President Kennedy's Commission, there was a flood of magazine articles and books, ranging from the best-selling handbook *Sex and the Single Girl* to the virtually fact-free vision entitled *The Feminine Mystique*. Out of it all certain things emerge clearly:
> Women arose as women in the middle of the nineteenth century.
> They demanded, as they should have, certain basic rights.
> Having achieved these rights, they have been almost finicky in the selectivity with which they exercise them.
> Rights to own things are very popular.
> Rights to do things, such as become well-educated, vote, run for office, enter the professions, are handled like old-fashioned jewelry; they are valued but they lie unused in the drawer.
> The one "right" which women have always had, frequently scorned, never fought for, is the one to which they now rush in fevered haste, the right to get married.

Nevertheless, by 1966, Friedan was able to round up enough feminists to get the National Organization for Women (NOW) started. It represented a formal resumption of the feminist movement after a lapse of about forty-five years. Its program was "to bring women into full participation in the mainstream of American society . . . exercising all the privileges and responsibilities thereof in truly equal partnership with men." It was a fairly conservative program, hardly a battle cry against the patriarchy, hardly reflecting the tremendous fermentation that was already taking place on campuses all over the country among student radicals as drugs started to make their way into the culture and the sexual revolution was beginning to sweep away all moral restraints. Friedan had explained in her book what kind of a program was needed, and by 1966 it already sounded obsolete:

> A massive attempt must be made by educators and parents—and ministers, magazine editors, manipulators, guidance counselors—to stop the early-marriage movement, stop girls from growing up wanting to be "just a housewife," stop it by insisting, with the same attention from childhood on that parents and educators give to boys, that girls develop the resources of self, goals that will permit them to find their own identity.[30]

Meanwhile, Simone de Beauvoir's time bomb was still ticking away. It had a few more years to go before it would explode into what we now call the Women's Liberation movement, with its direct assault on the entire patriarchal, "sexist" structure of our society.

This more radical form of feminism seems to have arisen in the mid-sixties among the already sexually liberated women working within the New Left in such groups as Students for a Democratic Society (SDS), the Student Non-Violent Coordinating Committee (SNCC), and the various anti-war groups. The women found that they were being relegated to doing the "shitwork" for their male superiors who paraded about pretentiously as "professional revolutionaries."[31] In their sexual relations with the men within the movement, they found the same chauvinistic attitudes among their revolutionary lovers as they had found among their fathers and brothers. Writes Robin Morgan about that period:

> Thinking we were involved in the struggle to build a new society, it was a slowly dawning and depressing realization that we were doing the same work and playing the same roles *in* the Movement as out of it: typing the speeches that men delivered, making coffee but not policy, being accessories to the men whose politics would supposedly replace the Old Order. But whose New Order? Not ours, certainly.[32]

When the women complained about their position in the New Left movement, they were laughed at and dismissed. Stokely Carmichael, leader of SNCC, was reported as saying: "The only position for women in SNCC is prone."[33] The result was that women began to form their own caucuses within the movement. Men's reactions ranged from fury to ridicule. In 1966 women who demanded that a plank on women's liberation be inserted in the SDS resolution that year were pelted with tomatoes and thrown out of the convention. All of this infuriated the women, who began to form their own groups with the growing realization that women's liberation would have to become a movement all its own. They were vindicating what Ashley Montagu had said in 1952, that "women will largely be forced to do the necessary work for themselves." The women were learning—the hard way. What is interesting is that these women realized that merely having the freedom to sleep with any guy they wanted did not mean they had achieved female liberation or personal happiness. In fact it was their very sexual freedom that led them into the nitty-gritty of the male-female confrontation.

All of this radical feminist activity went on underground until September 7, 1968, when a women's liberation group had decided to demonstrate in Atlantic City against the ultimate symbol of femininity, the Miss America pageant. This was news, and the national media took it up, especially because it all had such high entertainment value. The rating-conscious media have a tendency to confuse news with show biz, and this first Women's Lib demonstration was a perfect combination of both. In any case, it was the first inkling America had that there was a new radical feminist movement afoot. The group's planning manifesto read:

> We will protest the image of Miss America, an image that oppresses women in every area in which it purports to represent us. There will be: Picket Lines; Guerrilla Theater; Leafleting; Lobbying Visits to the contestants urging our sisters to reject the Pageant Farce and join us; a huge Freedom Trash Can (into which we will throw bras, girdles, curlers, false eyelashes, wigs, and representative issues of *Cosmopolitan, Ladies' Home Journal, Family Circle*, etc.—bring any such woman garbage you have around the house); we will also announce a Boycott of all those commercial products related to the Pageant, and the day will end with a Women's Liberation rally at midnight when Miss America is crowned on live television. . . . In case of arrests, however, we plan to reject all male authority and demand to be busted by policewomen only. . . .[34]

The next noisy demonstration that attracted the attention of the media was staged a few months later at the New York Marriage License Bureau by a group called the Feminists. The group was led by Ti-Grace Atkinson, a tall blonde from Louisiana, a doctoral candidate in philosophy, a long-time radical feminist who had broken away from NOW because the Friedan group was too conservative. Ms. Atkinson's brand of radicalism was something quite new for America. She told an interviewer: "Love has to be destroyed. It's an illusion that people care for each other. Friendship is reciprocal, love isn't."[35] Meanwhile, in the fall of 1968, the new feminist liberation movement had held its first national conference, bringing together about two hundred women from twenty states and Canada.

Of course, all of this tended to confuse Americans who had been taught in school to believe that the American woman was already emancipated. However, by late 1969 *Life, Time,* and other mass media publications were doing long, detailed articles about the new feminism. A female journalist, writing in *Life* (December 12, 1969), reported:

> Today women's liberation has become a serious national movement. In less than two years, it has grown in numbers and militancy, embracing a wide spectrum of women. . . . The movement, which some say is 10,000 strong, has no national organization, no formal title, but "women's liberation" is the collective name most often used to describe it. . . .
>
> As I read more about the movement, I felt certain chords in my own experience were being hit. Almost every woman, even if she is happy in her role, has buried within her rankling resentment. From our earliest years, we were taught our lives would be determined not by ourselves but by the men we married. . . .

Meanwhile the public was titillated by the grosser antics of the Women's Libbers and the names of some of their groups, such as WITCH (Women's International Terrorist Conspiracy from Hell), Redstockings, WRAP (Women's Radical Action Project), Keep on Truckin' Sisters, and SCUM (Society for Cutting Up Men) founded by Valerie Solanis, the film writer who took a shot at Andy Warhol. It wasn't until 1970, however, that the country began to realize how serious the movement was. It was the year in which Simone de Beauvoir's intellectual time bomb went off.

4

The Subjugation of Women: Was It Necessary?

How do we know that by 1970 the Women's Liberation movement was more than a passing carnival for female exhibitionists satisfying the insatiable hunger of talk shows, columnists, and mass media peddlers of literary excitement? We know it by reading their books; and in the year 1970 America saw the publication of four important books by the enraged ladies. This was the intellectual explosion caused by Simone de Beauvoir's time bomb. The four books were Kate Millett's *Sexual Politics*, Germaine Greer's *The Female Eunuch*, Shulamith Firestone's *The Dialectic of Sex*, and Robin Morgan's *Sisterhood is Powerful*, an anthology of writings from the Women's Liberation movement. All four books represented an impressive intellectual labor, and a reading of them by any man shattered all the preconceived notions he had ever had about women, about sexuality, about the human race.

The four books represent the most concerted and powerful intellectual attack ever launched against patriarchy, attacks of such emotional force that I found myself questioning for the first time the entire basis of our patriarchal social structure. I venture to say that most people don't even realize that we live in a patriarchy. They might think that the feudal Saudi Arabians or the primitive Ethiopians live in one, but they

61

would hardly apply the term to American society, which is supposedly democratic, pluralistic, egalitarian, capitalistic, and republican. Some people may even think we live in a matriarchy, considering the amount of power and influence women do have in our society. But the truth of the matter is that patriarchy is a universal human phenomenon, an outgrowth of the fact that whenever people organize any sort of society, the men dominate the women. In America we don't call this state of affairs a patriarchy; we call it a "man's world."

The form that male domination takes may vary from culture to culture, society to society, but the end result in all of them has been the same: to make of the females, through a well-programmed feminizing process, a subordinate class, an inferior caste devoted mainly to the task of bearing and rearing children and providing men with a modicum of sexual satisfaction. As we have already noted, Simone de Beauvoir's *The Second Sex* was the first attempt to describe in encyclopedic detail and thoroughness that feminizing process as practiced in Western society. The four books published in 1970 were further attacks on this male-inspired "feminization" process—in words that Simone de Beauvoir would have been too modest, too "ladylike," to use. But then we must understand what it is the women are trying to overthrow and what it was the men were subjugating when they created the patriarchal system. All of these new books are therefore quite useful in getting us to think about the basics of the male-female relationship.

The true feminists have always seen the subjugation of women as a brutal, oppressive, sadistic action of the male sex over their own. Since most men do not consider themselves brutal, oppressive, or sadistic toward women or anyone else, it is hard for them to empathize with feminists or understand what they are talking about. But the historical record is clear. Somewhere back in prehistory, when human beings began to organize into societies, the males found it necessary to impose their will over the females and to institutionalize that domination so that it became an accepted, unquestioned way of life. That the initial subjugation required harsh, brutal, and oppressive measures seems obvious considering who it was the men were subjugating. As men well know, women are neither emotionally nor physically weak. Their wills can be as strong as men's, and often stronger. However, men had one decisive advantage, an edge in sheer physical strength—and a strong enough justification to use it.

Was the subjugation of women necessary? Was it indeed justified? Could civilization have come into being without it? Did women secretly welcome this symbiotic, potentially sado-masochistic arrangement? Or have they burned with resentment from the very beginning? These are questions worth answering because they might tell us if what the Women's Liberation movement wants might destroy civilization or force us to create an entirely new kind of society based on an entirely new relationship between the sexes, assuming that such a new relationship is even possible.

There are a number of theories which attempt to explain why men found it necessary to bludgeon women into submission. The most interesting theory involves the nature of female sexuality. It holds that women are basically unable to control their own excessive sexuality in the natural state, and that it was this uncontrollable sexuality that men had to suppress in order to make civilization possible. This view has been advanced by one of the leading feminists herself, Dr. Mary Jane Sherfey, a psychiatrist whose paper on the subject, entitled "A Theory on Female Sexuality," first appeared in *The Journal of the American Psychoanalytical Association* and was later reprinted in the feminist anthology, *Sisterhood is Powerful.*

The paper is worth examining in detail because it tends to justify on sound biological grounds primitive man's subjugation of women. It also lends credence to all of those lurid stories one heard as a youth about the legendary local nymphomaniac who could take on the whole high school football team. Dr. Sherfey, however, puts the matter in the serious language of the scientist. She writes:

> No doubt the most far-reaching hypothesis extrapolated from biological data is the existence of the universal and physically normal condition of women's inability ever to reach complete sexual satiation in the presence of the most intense, repetitive orgasmic experiences, no matter how produced. Theoretically, a woman could go on having orgasms indefinitely if physical exhaustion did not intervene.

It is this fact of female insatiability that is at the heart of female sexuality. Unlike the male, whose sexual arousal can be temporarily ended by an orgasm with its ejaculatory release, the female is incapable of experiencing this kind of satisfying climax. She can go on having what Masters and Johnson call "multiple orgasms"—as many as fifty in one hour!

But what about all of those frigid women we hear so much about who never have orgasms at all? "It seems," writes Dr. Sherfey, "that the vast majority of cases of coital frigidity are due simply to the absence of frequent, prolonged coitus." In other words, the husbands of frigid wives simply can't do it long enough and often enough. Dr. Sherfey then cites as corroboration an experiment Masters and Johnson conducted in treating couples with severe chronic frigidity. The husbands were trained to use the proper techniques that are necessary to arouse all women and the specific techniques required by their wives. In many cases this alone was sufficient to bring the women to orgasm. In the more stubborn cases, daily sessions of marital coitus were prescribed followed by prolonged use of an artificial phallus for as many as

63

three to four hours. Of the fifty women treated most responded within a few days and all but one responded within three weeks at the most. Reports Dr. Sherfey: "They began to experience intense, multiple orgasms; and once this capacity was achieved after the exposure to daily prolonged coitus, they were able to respond with increasing ease and rapidity so that the protracted stimulation was no longer necessary."

What all of this seems to suggest is that any woman is a potential nymphomaniac. It also suggests that few men have the staying power to satisfy women, if indeed women can be satisfied, for after a man has "shot his load," so to speak, and is ready to turn over and go to sleep, his wife or sweetheart may be on the threshold of her multiple orgasms that could go on for another hour or so before she may be willing to give up from exhaustion. At this point one can see the practical uses of the gang bang or a battery-operated vibrator as possible solutions to the problem. I realize that this sort of jesting about female sexuality infuriates women, particularly Lesbians, who have a much deeper understanding of female sexuality than men can ever have. Martha Shelly, one of the feminist Lesbians, put it very bluntly when she wrote: "Freud founded the myth of penis envy, and men have asked me 'But what can two women do together?' As though a penis were the *sine qua non* of sexual pleasure! Man, we can do without it, and keep it going longer, too!"[36]

But the fact is that men have needed a certain sexual and emotional stability in order to build civilization, and the first problem they had to deal with was female sexuality. Dr. Sherfey suggests that the female's "inordinate orgasmic capacity" did not evolve for a monogamous, sedentary way of life. In fact, she doesn't think that either men or women were built biologically for the single-spouse, monogamous marital structure of our society. "However," she writes,

> if the conclusions reached here are true, it is conceivable that the *forceful* suppression of women's inordinate sexual demands was a prerequisite to the dawn of every modern civilization and almost every living culture. Primitive woman's sexual drive was too strong, too susceptible to the fluctuating extremes of an impelling, aggressive erotism to withstand the disciplined requirements of a settled family life—where many living children were necessary to a family's well-being and where paternity had become as important as maternity in maintaining family and property cohesion. For about half the time, women's erotic needs would be insatiably pursued; paternity could never be certain; and with lactation erotism, constant infant care would be out of the question.

When did all of this subjugation take place, and how long did it take? Historical data indicates that precivilized women enjoyed the full sexual freedom they now want to regain. Dr. Sherfey estimates that the subjugation took about 5,000 years to accomplish and that it took place between the time of the establishment of the earliest agricultural settlements and the rise of urban life, which marks the beginning of advanced civilization. "Not until these [sexual] drives were gradually brought under control by rigidly enforced social codes," she writes, "could family life become the stabilizing and creative crucible from which modern civilized man could emerge."

Thus, when Roxanne Dunbar, another women's libber, wrote: "The masculine ideology most strongly asserts home and country as primary values, with wealth and power an individual's greatest goal," what she was saying is that civilization is a masculine invention. She added: "The same upper class of men who created private property and founded nation-states also created the family."[37] In other words, father, not mother, is the inventor of the family.

Apparently the pressures of female sexuality are so strong that the female liberationists now want to remove the restraints placed on it by the family structure. Writes Dunbar: "How will the family unit be destroyed? . . . The alleviation of the duty of full-time child care in private situations will free many women to make decisions they could not before. . . . Women will feel free to leave their husbands and become economically independent, either through a job or welfare."[38]

Dr. Sherfey recognizes the dangers to present society if female sexuality is permitted to awaken fully and freely after thousands of years of suppression. Yet, as we all know, the awakening is well under way. Sherfey writes:

> It is hard to predict what will happen should this trend continue, except one thing is certain: if women's sexual drive has not abated, and they prove incapable of controlling it, thereby jeopardizing family life and child care, a return to the rigid, enforced suppression will be inevitable and mandatory. Otherwise the biological family will disappear and what other patterns of infant care and adult relationships could adequately substitute cannot now be imagined.

Some of the feminists, however, are clearly ahead of Dr. Sherfey. They are already thinking of alternative social arrangements that would enable them to bear and rear children as well as enjoy full sexual freedom. Modern contraceptive technology makes sexual freedom possible, and the "nuclear family," which Germaine Greer considers to be the incubator of all our Freudian neuroses, can be replaced with what she describes as a communally oriented "organic family." Greer writes:

> The institution of self-regulating organic families may appear to be a return to chaos. Genuine chaos is more fruitful than the chaos of conflicting systems which are mutually destructive. When heredity has decayed and bureaucracy is the rule, so that the only riches are earning power and

mobility, it is absurd that the family should persist in the pattern of patriliny.[39]

However primitive man did not have our modern contraceptive technology, and without it female sexuality was a problem that had to be dealt with if men were to expand the scope of their lives beyond the confines placed on them by unstable female erotism. The solution was simple: force women into a pattern of responsible, disciplined behavior that would make the creation of a family unit possible, establish paternity and marital fidelity, and free men to pursue preoccupations more interesting than sexual pleasure. Sexual pleasure alone, carried beyond its intense momentary excitement, is a bore for most men. Deeper, more lasting emotional and intellectual pleasures are only possible when sexual desire has been disciplined. That men had to impose sexual discipline on women tends to indicate that women had no desire or necessity to impose such discipline on themselves. It also tends to indicate that male sexuality, with its satisfying climactic release, lends itself much more readily to self-control than does female sexuality. However, much research remains to be done on the nature of human sexuality before we can place the blame for female subjugation entirely on her sexual nature.

Other feminists see the subjugation of women as a pure drive for power on the part of the male, without any compensating altruistic or idealistic visions of great civilizations to be built on the sacrifice of women's sexual freedom. This is certainly the view of most feminist Marxists who see the suppression of women as the prerequisite for the development of the private property system for which paternal lines of inheritance through male progeny had to be established. This, of course, is true. The patriarchy established the father not only as the ruler of his women but also of his sons. Thus that affectionate but sometimes conflicting relationship between father and son was only possible if the female could be made subordinate to her husband. She bore *his* sons. And his sons bore his name and inherited his property and his wealth. But it was all done by courtesy of the woman who bore the children. Germaine Greer writes:

> The patrilineal family depends upon the free gift by women of the right of paternity to men. Paternity is not an intrinsic relationship: it cannot be proved, except negatively. The most intense vigilance will not insure absolutely that any man is the father of his son.[40]

Of course Ms. Greer underestimates the sense of loyalty that some women have toward their husbands. But obviously the nature of female sexuality makes the whole idea of loyalty problematic for many women. Greer states:

> When there was property to pass on and legitimacy to be upheld, it was imperative to surround women with guards, to keep them in one

66

place, keeping their natural curiosity and urge for movement and expression as undeveloped as possible. The chastity belt which warrior barons clapped around their wives when they went to war was the outward emblem of the fruitlessness of the struggle, the attempt to provide a barricado for the belly. Nowadays women demand trust and offer their free assurance about paternity, honoring the contract that they have made, to be protected, fed and housed in return for insuring immortality in legitimate issue.[41]

In short, the patriarchal family is a male invention to serve male ends, and the security that a woman gets in exchange for her enslavement is obtained at the cost of her "natural curiosity and urge for movement and expression."

The early Marxists saw the patriarchal family as the purest instrument of economic exploitation. Friedrich Engels wrote in his *The Origin of the Family*:

> The modern individual family is founded on the open or concealed slavery of the wife. . . . Within the family he is the bourgeois and his wife represents the proletariat.[42]

Thus, to the Marxists the subjugation of women was essentially an economic act. Yet, today, there isn't a Communist country that is any less patriarchal than the capitalist ones. Men still dominate women in the Communist states. Theoretically a female Communist could become chairperson of the Communist Party. But it will never happen. Which brings us to an even more interesting approach to the subject of female subjugation. While Dr. Sherfey contends that it was the uncontrollability of female sexuality that led to the subjugation of women, Kate Millett contends that it was the power drive of male sexuality that was responsible for the brutal and sadistic suppression of women. Her often-brilliant book *Sexual Politics* views the subjugation of women as primarily a sexual act, in which the male's sado-sexual impulses were given free reign and resulted in the creation of a patriarchal society based on power, dominance, and coercion. "Sexual dominion," Millett writes, "obtains . . . as perhaps the most pervasive ideology of our culture and provides its most fundamental concept of power."[43]

To prove her thesis she quotes convincing passages from the writings of D. H. Lawrence, Norman Mailer, and Henry Miller who describe sexual intercourse in the most blatant terms of power and conquest, in which women are humiliated, assaulted, and reduced to contemptible, inferior, animal status. The aim of such misogynist literature, Millett believes, "is to reinforce both sexual factions in their status."[44] Norman Mailer, in *Prisoner of Sex*, took issue with Millett, criticizing her for quoting passages out of the context of complex works of art. It is suggested that one read Mailer after reading Millett.

Actually, Millett does not claim that aggressive male sexuality was the sole impetus behind patriarchy. "There is some evidence," she writes, "that fertility cults in ancient society at some point took a turn toward patriarchy, displacing and downgrading female function in procreation and attributing the power of life to the phallus alone."[45] Perhaps it was this belief in phallic procreativity that led men to the inevitable task of controlling women, the carriers of their seed. Since patriarchy's chief institution is the family and not the brothel, it is obvious that procreation and not sexual pleasure was its central purpose and that female sexuality had to be sacrificed on the altar of male-protected motherhood. It is perhaps ironic that men should be given the credit for having made motherhood into the sanctified role it has assumed in Western society. But the key point to be aware of in such a conversion is that a woman can bear a dozen children without ever having had an orgasm.

But Millett's focus is on the sado-sexual aspects of patriarchy, not its paternal. She writes:

> The history of patriarchy presents a variety of cruelties and barbarities: the suttee execution in India, the crippling deformity of footbinding in China, the lifelong ignominy of the veil in Islam, or the widespread persecution of sequestration, the gynacium, and purdah. Phenomena such as clitoridectomy, clitoral incision, the sale and enslavement of women under one guise or another, involuntary and child marriages, concubinage and prostitution, still take place—the first in Africa, the latter in the Near and Far East, the last generally. The rationale which accompanies that imposition of male authority euphemistically referred to as "the battle of the sexes" bears a certain resemblance to the formulas of nations at war, when any heinousness is justified on the grounds that the enemy is either an inferior species or really not human at all.[46]

In any case, the thesis that the subjugation of women was the political extension of the male's aggressive, sadistic sexual impulses is not very tenable since most men are neither sexually aggressive nor sadistic. The key to patriarchy is probably to be found in Millett's own observation about it. She writes:

> Perhaps patriarchy's greatest psychological weapon is simply its universality and longevity. . . . While the same might be said of class, patriarchy still has a more tenacious or powerful hold through its successful habit of passing itself off as nature.[47]

All of which brings us to another theory about the origins of patriarchy: that it was the male's response to biological necessity. Because of the human infant's long period of dependency, requiring the close attention and devotion of its mother, the male was required to provide sustenance for both mother and child. In addition, once the male acquired an interest in paternity, it was in his own interest to protect both mother and child and provide them with sustenance. That women had to be forced to accept this arrangement would indicate that women are not naturally good mothers. Yet no mammal on earth requires the kind of mothering that does the human infant, for the newborn human baby is the most helpless of newborn mammals. He has few specific responses to external stimuli when he is born. The only essential responses that the newborn baby possesses are sucking movements of the lips and mouth, movements he acquires during his early life as a fetus, and crying, a faculty acquired at birth after taking his first breath, which allows him to signal danger.

Thus the human baby is really born too soon. Other mammals are able at birth to move to their mothers' bodies and seek and hold a nipple. But the human baby is completely passive and helpless. He needs affectionate stroking to recreate the warmth of the fetal situation, to make up for the loss of the womb, and, above all, to stimulate growth. The only way his state of equilibrium can be maintained is through the ministrations of an attentive mother.

Thus it was recognized by men, who were now concerned with their role in creating the child, that mother and newborn infant required special care and sustenance so that the child could survive and grow. Infant mortality was undoubtedly very high in precivilized times; and, since there were no contraceptives, women of all ages and conditions had children. Unless the males shared in the responsibility of protecting and rearing the young, the chances of infant survival were substantially reduced.

Possibly female sexuality created so much instability that men had to impose their control over it. It should be noted that to master women men first had to master themselves. Self-discipline was a prerequisite to the creation of a patriarchal society. But since it took about 5,000 years to establish patriarchy, the process of male self-disciplining probably took as long. One does not develop capacities of mastery beyond what it is that needs to be mastered. Dr. Sherfey writes: "The strength of the drive determines the force required to suppress it."[48] In other words, we can measure the strength of female erotism by observing the elaborate patriarchal structure that had to be created to suppress it.

But the truth of the matter is that the patriarchal system has never been 100-percent effective. It is a human institution, particularly susceptible to the strongest and most urgent pressures of human sexuality —male as well as female. But now, if women are to rise as the equals of men, then they will have to develop the self-discipline to master their own sexuality.

It becomes obvious after a good deal of study that the subjugation of women involved more than the suppression of female erotism. It involved also the creation of social institutions that favored procreation and family stability. In other words, the needs of children were much better provided for under patriarchy than prior to its institution. Thus, in a sense, both men and children were allies in the long struggle to subjugate women. In fact some of the women's libbers are as resentful toward the demands of children as they are toward the demands of men. In fact the idea of the mother-as-slave is as old as motherhood itself, and the idea of the infant tyrant is as old as childbirth itself. Freud has told us about the imperial sense of omnipotence each infant has on entering the world, and how difficult it is for the child to adjust to the growing awareness of his helpless dependence, and how important the nature of this adjustment is to the development of a healthy, strong ego.

Thus patriarchy required a double enslavement: the enslavement of women to children as well as to men. In all of this, what had to be sacrificed was the development of female sexuality, for a mother who was overly preoccupied with her sexual pleasure would be unable to accept the discipline of motherhood.

Here we come to one of the most interesting questions of all regarding women: Is there such a thing as a maternal instinct? Many mothers will swear that they have it and feel it. Others, notably women's libbers, will claim that there is no such instinct and that whatever it is those women feel, it has been put there by the programming of a patriarchal culture.

In reading much of feminist literature one gets the impression that, in the process of childbearing, a woman feels as if her body is being used by nature for an alien purpose. She has been chosen by an accident of biology to be the host of a developing new individual. She undergoes involuntary risks in carrying out this role, but she has no natural feeling for it. As Simone de Beauvoir says in *The Second Sex*: "Woman, like man, is her body, but her body is something other than herself."[49] In other words her desire to have children may have nothing to do with the fact that she can bear them. That is why adoption is just as satisfactory a way for some women to "have a baby" as actually conceiving one.

In other words there is no such thing as a maternal "instinct." Women bear children and raise them because their men expect them to do so. In fact it is even possible that the paternal "instinct" is stronger than the maternal one, if we take into consideration the number of secret abortions women undergo to terminate pregnancies their husbands may want.

Desmond Morris, author of *The Naked Ape*, a study of man from the zoological point of view, tells us a few things about human sexuality that may help us understand the motives behind men's subjugation

70

of women. First he points out that the male of our species has the larg-est erect penis of any living primate. Then he tells us that there is much more intense sexual activity in our own species than in any other primates, including our closest relations. Also, he writes:

It is interesting that, if one measures sexual responsiveness in terms of frequency of orgasm, the male is much quicker to reach his peak of per-formance than the female. Although males begin their sexual matura-tion process a year or so behind the girls, they nevertheless attain their orgasmic peak while they are still in their teens, whereas the girls do not reach theirs until their mid-twenties or even thirties. In fact, the fe-male of our species has to reach the age of twenty-nine before she can match the orgasm rate of the fifteen-year-old male.[50]

Perhaps the subjugation of women was carried out by the older, more mature males, who required less sex, to curb the increasing ero-tism of the maturing females, most of whom by then had become mothers. The older male, sexually well-tempered, less easily aroused, desirous of stability and comfort, more self-disciplined in his appe-tites, had to contend with the increasing sexuality of the older woman, who might desert the older male for the more easily excit-able younger male. Thus the sexual security of the older male was largely dependent on his ability to control the sexuality of women. Also the obvious inconvenience of this sexual pattern as far as the fam-ily is concerned meant that it had to be changed by force.

With the growing sexual freedom of women in our present culture, we see emerging the very sexual instability that caused primitive man to impose controls.

In an article on the "Battle of the Sexes," *Newsweek* of July 24, 1967, quoted Los Angeles psychiatrist Ralph A. Greenson, who made these observations concerning the sexual revolution's influence on marital relations:

Before World War II most psychiatric patients were women who com-plained that their husbands were sexually demanding. Today, the men complain that their wives are sexually demanding and the wives com-plain that their husbands work hard all day and play golf on weekends but are too tired when it comes to sex.

The sexually demanding woman is a frightening image for the Amer-ican male. The typical 45-year-old male is more concerned with preserv-ing his health than satisfying his wife. His fear of death supersedes all his other anxieties. The only hope for a happy future is for men to recognize their basic repressed awe of woman and for women to recognize that they have always been the stronger sex and have some compassion for men.

This, of course, tells us a lot about the average male. But there are also a minority of sexually active older males who then seek out younger sexually submissive females for their wives. We have Sena-

71

tors, Supreme Court Justices, actors, professors, and other elders showing the way. In other words the natural pattern of compatibility as far as the sex drive goes seems to be: older men for younger girls, and older women for younger men. Obviously this does not make for stable family relationships. Ergo, the patriarchal system.

It would be wrong to say that patriarchy merely suppressed female sexuality. It suppressed all sexuality. It created the "masculine" image of the self-disciplined male who held female virginity and fidelity as the highest romantic values. It created the "feminine" image of the passive, submissive female who became the sole sexual property of one man who assumed total mastery over her but rarely aroused her to orgasm. The end purpose of it all was to create social and family stability. It also permitted men to enjoy the heightened intensity of disciplined sex, the "forbidden fruit" as it were. One of the noticeable results of our sexual revolution is that more people are having more sex with less real enjoyment. A certain amount of frustration and self-discipline does contribute to heightened sexual hunger and intensity. The strictures placed on sexual expression by the disciplines of patriarchy tended to intensify sexual desire, making it necessary to reinforce the discipline required to control it. Many neuroses have resulted from such sexual repression.

Kate Millett accuses patriarchy of having successfully passed itself off as nature. Yet who could deny that the values upheld by patriarchy were in the interests of human survival and human advancement? Desmond Morris, in an oblique way, makes the whole process seem utterly natural. He states:

> Clearly, the naked ape is the sexiest primate alive. To find the reason for this we have to look back again at his origins. What happened? First, he had to hunt if he was to survive. Second, he had to have a better brain to make up for his poor hunting body. Third, he had to have a longer childhood to grow the bigger brain and to educate it. Fourth, the females had to stay put and mind the babies while the males went hunting. Fifth, the males had to cooperate with one another on the hunt. Sixth, they had to stand up straight and use weapons for the hunt to succeed.[51]

All of these requirements for survival, writes Morris, were also the necessary ingredients for our present monogamous system. He elaborates:

> To begin with, the males had to be sure that their females were going to be faithful to them when they left them alone to go hunting. So the females had to develop a pairing tendency. Also, if the weaker males were going to be expected to cooperate on the hunt, they had to be given more sexual rights. The females would have to be more shared out, the sexual organization more democratic, less tyrannical. Each male, too, would need a strong pairing tendency. Furthermore, the males were now armed with deadly weapons and sexual rivalries would be much more dangerous: again, a good reason for each male being satisfied with

one female. On top of that there were the much heavier parental demands being made by the slow-growing infants. Paternal behavior would have to be developed and the parental duties shared between the mother and the father: another good reason for a strong pair-bond.

It becomes more and more obvious that the genesis of patriarchy can be found in the meaning of the word patriarchy itself: fatherhood. When men developed the sense of fatherhood, they then insisted that women develop the sense of motherhood. To accomplish this, women's erotism had to be sharply curbed, and the concept of women as mothers had to be elevated above the concept of women as mere sexual objects. Female virginity before marriage and fidelity after marriage became the moral cornerstones of the patriarchal system. The responsibility to his wife and children became the moral end of a man's education, reinforced by religious belief. The father taught his sons to respect women because the latter became the mothers of their children, and he taught his daughters modesty and obedience to prepare them for their lives of sacrifice to their husbands and children. All of this was quite convenient for male sexuality. A male could not impregnate a female without having an orgasm, but a female could conceive a child without one. That is why the female orgasm was ignored if not discouraged. It had no function in procreation. Its only function was pleasure, which opened the door to all sorts of evil and instability. Thus virtue became equated with frigidity.

Patriarchy represented man's highest striving for self-restraint and self-discipline in the interest of bettering his lot in the long term. It set men's sights forward to future generations. Female sexuality tended to keep women bound to the short-term satisfactions: pleasure for pleasure's sake. Male self-restraint and self-discipline permitted him to project human effort beyond his own lifetime. He could not permit uncontrollable female sexuality to jeopardize the future. And thus the subjugation of women was not only justifiable but also a necessity. That men have always feared the consequences of unrestrained female sexuality is obvious if we observe how religion has treated women and their sexuality. In Western religion female sexuality is regarded as the source of all evil, chaos, and anarchy. And therefore the family unit, sanctified by religion, is every individual's chief source of order and morality.

The women's libbers, of course, are well aware of this. We have already quoted Germaine Greer, who advocates doing away with the traditional family in favor of what she calls an "organic" family. Her argument is that the traditional family is coming apart at the seams anyway and that something else will have to replace it. "The institution of self-regulating organic families," she writes, "may appear to be a return to chaos. Genuine chaos is more fruitful than the chaos of conflicting systems which are mutually destructive."

Is patriarchy on the verge of collapse? As a legal system in the United States it is quickly losing its force. The possible adoption of the women's Equal Rights Amendment, and the recent court decision in Massachusetts permitting a wife to abort her three-month-old unborn child against her husband's strong objections indicate clearly that patriarchy, or male domination over the female, will no longer have the sanction and support of the legal system. It will be each man for himself in creating his own private patriarchy, or creating none at all. There are a lot of men who are not at all interested in creating families, becoming fathers, or even husbands. Most men, in fact, do not want to control women; which is why *Cosmopolitan* is so frantically telling women how to pursue and control men.

The population explosion, the growing rejection of children among adults, the pursuit of pleasure for its own sake have made the institution of patriarchy, with its required self-discipline and self-denial, seem somewhat obsolete, something of a drag. We have civilization; we have technology; we have affluence. Where do we go from here? Not even the women have the answer for that one.

5

The Decline and Fall of Patriarchy

Every man must wonder what the overthrow of the patriarchal system is going to mean to the future of male-female relations. For male self-esteem has been very much dependent on man's role as father, husband, provider—the strong, solid, masculine image—an image that is being rejected by more and more American men. The heart of patriarchy is, after all, the paternal imperative, and without it patriarchy, that is male dominance, cannot be sustained.

But the truth is that American men can no longer stand the strain and tension of trying to control women. They no longer have the legal structure, the force of law that maintained this control with a minimum of personal effort, and they do not want—or lack the motivation —to acquire the self-discipline, the self-restraint, the repressed sexuality necessary to maintain that control, particularly if the values derived from it are no longer desirable. In our society, men can now enjoy being boys indefinitely. There is no urgent societal need for them to grow up, nor are there any penalties for failing to make the responsible fatherhood grade. Today most boys become responsible fathers because they want to, for personal reasons, not because anyone expects them to.

Curiously, but perhaps not so curiously, a lot of girls don't want boys to grow up, because they have the illusion that they can control them more easily as boys than as men. Now that males no longer want to control the females, the females are busily learning ways to control the males. For example, there are all kinds of guides for the single girl advising her how to get a guy by pleasing him sexually. On a more elementary level is Ellen Peck's *How To Get A Teen-Age Boy and What To Do With Him When You Get Him*, a sort of teenage girl's strategic guide to controlling boys. The name of the dating game, these days, is control, and the chief weapon is sex. *Seventeen* is full of letters from girls frustrated in their efforts to control boys. Some use the old trick of pregnancy to make the boys into premature fathers. Some boys marry the girls, other boys force the girls to get abortions.

But what is lacking in all of this is paternal guidance, paternal advice, paternal discipline. The fact is that American fathers are no longer supervising the moral education of their daughters. Read the questions young girls ask in *Seventeen*. These are questions that would never be asked if father had provided the moral standards and guidance for his family. But the American father has largely abdicated that role. The "new morality" now requires girls to set their own moral standards.

For the past twenty years the *Playboy* mentality—the mentality of the boy perennially at play—has gradually undermined the patriarchal value system. The *Playboy* philosophy holds that men are more interested in sexual pleasure than paternal necessity, more interested in freedom for themselves than in the control of women. The playboy is a rabbit, with the sex habits of a rabbit. No patriarchy was ever run by rabbits.

Patriarchy depends on male self-discipline for its maintenance. Its ideals are passed on from father to son, through the disciplining of sons by fathers, through the inculcating of patriarchal values. The two highest moral values of patriarchy, which have permitted men to dominate women for so long, are those of female virginity before marriage and female fidelity after marriage. The sexual revolution has destroyed this value system. Although few American males would insist that the girls they marry be virgins, marital fidelity is still an important emotional need for most men, although it is not as strongly held as an ideal as before the revolution. Women are no longer stoned to death for adultery.

But even some of the most liberated women are having profound second thoughts about their sexual freedom. In fact one of the most interesting articles I've come across on female disillusionment with the sexual revolution is one by a talented feminist poet, Karen Lindsey, in the *Boston Phoenix* of March 13, 1973. It is worth perusing in detail. Ms. Lindsey begins by setting the stage for her story:

76

One of the most interesting responses I got from my article on sterilization in the *Boston Phoenix* several weeks ago was from a 15-year-old girl who, among other things, spoke bitterly about the "sexual revolution." Here was someone who has grown up entirely in the era of Drugs and Sex, whose childhood had been framed by Walter Cronkite reporting on the freedom of the young and who sounded as bitter, confused and as hurt by the sexual revolution as I was ten years ago, as I still am, as I probably will always be.

Imagine a 15-year-old girl *already* disillusioned with her sexual freedom. Ms. Lindsey then recounts her own sexual history, and you wonder how many young women in America have been through the same. It all started in the early sixties when Ms. Lindsey was in college. "I was in love," she writes. "I wanted to sleep with the guy and I did." And so she got a taste of the "new and wonderful world" of sex. The affair didn't last very long, but she liked the sex and wanted more. "I was pretty and there were lots of nice guys around. So I slept with them and I dug it and they dug it and the Pill made it all okay. And it seemed to me that sex was a really lovely part of friendship."

But then she began to discover that it wasn't. Her girlfriend Tina had come crying to her one day because a guy she was hung-up on, one of the local SDS leaders, had asked her to sleep with him because—and get this—his girlfriend didn't want to put out until they got married. Would Tina be willing to satisfy him in the meantime? Naturally Tina didn't take this too well. In fact she almost had a breakdown over it. And who could blame her? This wasn't even a matter of a double standard. It was simply the new freedom of no standards at all. If some silly girl was willing to be of service to some horny boy, why should the girl then complain if the boy took advantage of her offer? However what probably jolted Tina was not so much the boy's proposal, but the knowledge that some other girl who was not putting out for him was going to get him. The boy did not have the sexual self-discipline to wait until marriage, but his girlfriend did. What a lesson for Tina. It would be interesting to know why the boy wanted to marry his virgin girlfriend instead of free, accommodating Tina. Could it be that his girlfriend had a sense of patriarchal values that the boy knew would be needed in the long haul when he was finished playing his SDS games? In any case, while this episode put the first seeds of doubt about the glories of sexual freedom in Ms. Lindsey's mind, it did not deter her from having more affairs. She writes:

> Shortly after the Tina incident, while I was a member of SDS and going with another member (which gave me a sort of one-of-the-fellows status with the other male members—I was hip and not hung up about sex so they could talk freely around me, but I was someone else's girl so I was off limits), I listened to the putdowns of one of the other woman members who wasn't sleeping with anybody. "The girl with the cast-iron clit,"

77

they called her, and I refused to acknowledge the queasy feeling in my stomach as I joined in their laughter.

Imagine Students for a Democratic Society rebelling against their middle-class upbringing, enjoying full sexual freedom with no patri-archal values, restraints, or hang-ups in sight, becoming the crucible that created the most forceful antipatriarchal faction of the Wom-en's Liberation movement. There they were, enjoying free sex in a kind of campus Eden, yet the one thing the girls were beginning to learn about was male sexuality in the raw, with no discipline, no re-straints placed on it except those imposed by normal jungle ethics. Clearly missing was the paternal imperative of patriarchy that would have given the guys a sense of responsibility. Yet it would be male chauvinism, i.e., patriarchy, that would be attacked when the wom-en's libbers had had enough of free sex. Would they attack patriarchy because of its strength or its weakness? Because it had failed to protect them or failed to free them? There was certainly no man on the hori-zon in SDS who wanted to control them. Maybe that was the trouble.

Ms. Lindsey drifted out of politics but continued to sleep with whomever she wanted. "The men were my friends and sex was part of our friendship they assured me and I assured myself." But then she began to realize that there was something lacking in sex without emotional involvement. Her sexual partners had little interest in her apart from the sex. When she needed emotional comfort they weren't there. "I began to realize that, far from being an integrated part of a relationship, my sexuality existed for these men solely as a function of their pleasure or fantasy. Some of them were simply out-and-out, old-fashioned, fuck-'em-and-forget-'em bastards. In a sense, they were the easiest to deal with. Harder to take were the ones who thought they really cared about me, because I'd lived up to some image they'd created."

Obviously Ms. Lindsey had hoped that somewhere in all this sexual activity some sorry jerk would either fall in love with her or start caring enough to want to marry her. But what was there to fall in love with? What was there to hold him? Would she be able to remain loyal sex-ually to one guy? She relates that she projected either of two images to her different lovers, depending on which one turned them on: the very dignified but sensual Lady Poet and the casual Swinging Chick. But if even she didn't know who she was—and there was a big differ-ence between a Lady Poet and a Swinging Chick—how could she have expected any one of her lovers to have fallen in love with her? Whom would he have fallen in love with? Where was the real Ms. Lindsey? Who was she? Obviously she would be whatever she had to be in order to get sex. Otherwise why put up a phony front? Nevertheless Ms. Lindsey was growing more and more bitter about men and their sexuality. Somehow it didn't occur to her that her own vagrant sexuality might be at the heart of her problem.

Her experiences, however, did not discourage her. She continued to be a true explorer in the realm of sexual freedom, but less and less impervious to disillusionment and disappointment. For example, even though she wanted to pursue her sexual partners aggressively, she found out that "real aggressiveness in a woman was a bad breach of etiquette." She elaborates:

> You had to give out signals, but you had to wait for the man to make the "first move," and you had to be a little coy so he could have the fun of breaking down your resistance by the power of his masculine charm.

Again it all seems like a terrible male plot to deprive women of instant pleasure. Some women seem to forget that in order for a man to be able to perform sexually, he has to be aroused. Ms. Lindsey obviously thought that all a woman had to do was make herself available. But male sexual arousal is a little more complicated than that. Nevertheless Ms. Lindsey was taken aback by it all.

"At first I couldn't believe this was happening. Sex was beautiful and free, and there were no more rules, I kept telling myself." Yes, Ms. Lindsey, the rules are gone, but not plain old human biology. "And the more I protested," she continues, "the more I saw what I had been doing for the past four years—working constantly and obviously to tread the line between the two cardinal sins of frigidity and nymphomania." So Ms. Lindsey was having a tough time controlling her sexuality. It's a very old female problem that primitive man successfully solved for the ladies by imposing patriarchy. Ms. Lindsey was living the life of prepatriarchal woman. That was a time of sexual freedom also, and you can bet your life that some of those precivilized women learned faster than others how to arouse the male. But the real meaning of sexual freedom, as Ms. Lindsey was discovering through her experiences, was quite disheartening. She writes:

> No one admitted the existence of rules; to admit that would have negated the myth of freedom we were clinging to. And the rules varied from man to man; it was necessary to try to sense each man's rules, and often the way the rule was discovered was by its violation—a sudden turnoff, a censorious attitude was the tipoff (never, of course, a direct confrontation, he could hardly accuse you of breaking a rule that wasn't there).

It's interesting that Ms. Lindsey should think in terms of "rules" when what she was really up against was the mystery of male arousal. Naturally, since each man is different, it takes different circumstances to arouse different men. Indeed there are some men who cannot be aroused by women at all. I suppose she expected to be able to arouse anyone she wanted instantly. And since it was sex she was looking for, with her experience she should have become a much better sexologist than she did. What does a woman who sleeps around want? What was the cause of her lack of satisfaction? What did she want from a guy? Obviously what she really wanted was for some guy to care enough about her to take control, straighten her out, cool off her sexual fires, and sock her in the teeth if she so much as looked at another guy. And Ms. Lindsey makes that quite clear when she writes:

> I began to feel nostalgic for the bad old days, when rules, if oppressive, were open and standardized, and there was a clearcut system of rewards and punishments. Purity and marriage might be a drag, but they did offer certain protection for the woman who toed the line.

Well, well, so patriarchy wasn't so bad, after all. If only the men wanted to control women again like they used to. But you can't turn back the clock. Since men no longer want to control women, women will just have to learn to control themselves. But it takes a lot before that happens, and Ms. Lindsey explains how it happened in her case:

> Finally, I saw something happening to my own sexuality. I had been pushing myself into being "free"—into sleeping with men I didn't give a damn about and sometimes wasn't even attracted to, because I'd gotten dependent on the notion of sex as fulfillment (and status). This realization had a dramatically immediate result. One night I lay there, suddenly aware that my body was having a great time while my mind was sitting back waiting for the whole thing to be over. The next morning we woke up, and my friend-for-the-night reached a sleepy arm out to me. I jumped up, chirruped "Well, how about some coffee?," kept up a merry stream of chatter all through breakfast, kissed him goodbye, and didn't fuck for a year.

That is what one woman had to go through before enough revulsion and protest arose from within her to call a halt to her own sexual vagrancy. "Where had the great dream of beautiful, healthy unfettered sex gone wrong?" she asks. What went wrong, she replies, was male sexuality.

> What I had seen in men was less earthy animal appetite than very human power tripping. The necessity for conquest, for challenge, strikes me as the major force in male sexual behavior, and if female "romanticism" has been ridiculed, it is at least a less ugly detour from simple sexual gratification than male power hunger is.

Of course all of her experience had been with men out on the prowl, not interested in paternal responsibility or sexual fidelity or romance, just out for sexual pleasure. What did she expect? You cannot isolate sex from the rest of the human being, and you cannot expect to find enchantment, bells ringing, a sense of constancy and concern, or even good old healthy "animal lust" in someone just out for a lay. And obviously some of the censorious guys who rejected her did so because they were looking for something more than just an easy lay. But you live and learn, and Ms. Lindsey finally learned, as we can tell when she writes:

> Human beings have other than physical needs, and I wonder if the most desolating trip that male culture has laid on all of us isn't its attempt to rigidly divide the areas of human need. I think we have denied ourselves something vital in the effort to divorce the most intimately shared physical experience from our emotional intimacies. I think our natures demand that there be at least some aspect of love in our sex, some aspect of sexuality in our love.

Bravo, Ms. Lindsey. You finally learned what primitive man learned when he decided that the only way to join the emotional with the sexual was to force women to curb their sexual vagrancy in the interests of fidelity, maternity, and family. For if a man is not interested in a family or at least in an enduring monogamous relationship, he rarely has a strong interest in fidelity, and there can be no love that endures without it. But like so many women's libbers, Ms. Lindsey learned only bitterness from her experience. The words fidelity or loyalty appear nowhere in her article, as if you can talk of love or sexual intimacy without them. So she ends her sexual saga on the bitter note of her own prejudice:

> Male mythology has demanded of men that their sexuality be a function of their control over women, and they have to struggle out of that component of their sexuality. God help them. And God help those of us who still have some need for them. It's going to be a hard struggle. But until men change, the sexual revolution is just another ugly, dirty joke, and the women aren't laughing.

So men have to change. It's bad for them to want to control women. But are the women now prepared to control themselves? Or must we watch every woman go through ten years of sexual freedom before she's capable of restraining herself, as in Ms. Lindsey's case? So men are damned if they do and damned if they don't. If they want to control women it's because they're on a patriarchal power trip. If they don't it's because they're indifferent and don't love them. Women want love and loyalty but they don't realize that you can't have loyalty without control, preferably self-control. But no one is born with self-control. It has to be learned. It can be learned in two ways: the easy way or the hard way. The patriarchal system taught it the easy way—by simple instruction; Ms. Lindsey learned it the hard way, and at that she only half-learned it. But all is not lost if fifteen-year-old girls are already disgusted with the sexual revolution. Apparently some girls learn very fast.

It's curious that the Women's Libbers direct so much of their fury against men who allegedly want to control women at a time when men no longer want to do so, and ignore entirely the frantic efforts of

81

women who now want to control men. Do not the women give themselves away? Aren't they saying "If you won't control us, we'll control you"? But Ms. Lindsey doesn't want to control any man, nor does she want any man to control her, or so she says. She has simply left the field of battle. "Celibacy may be uncomfortable," she comments, "but its mortality rate is pretty low." That's one solution to the problem. Another would be to try to establish an emotional bridge to a man first, and then the sexual bridge. But that takes sexual self-restraint and Ms. Lindsey may not be up to it.

It is significant that the most militant, anti-male faction of the Women's Liberation movement should have been born among those women who had been exercising the greatest sexual freedom with those young men who were most free of the restraints of patriarchy. Needless to say they were disappointed when their sexual anarchy did not produce the deep emotional satisfactions they thought that "freedom" would bring them. They had simply not been taught or had never learned that love is a manifestation of responsibility, and that responsibility is impossible without self-discipline.

Thus there is a certain unreality in the women's libbers' approach to male sexuality. They want the promiscuous, undisciplined male to exhibit all of the qualities of consideration, tenderness, and loyalty found in the male who accepts responsibility. And so, as far as Ms. Lindsey is concerned, "until men change, the sexual revolution is just another ugly, dirty joke." That is Ms. Lindsey's judgment after ten years of sleeping around, ten years of sexual freedom during which not one man ever tried to clamp a chastity belt around her or socked her in the jaw if she betrayed him. Undoubtedly her secret desire was for one of them to do exactly that. Yet she had the gall to write that "male mythology has demanded of men that their sexuality be a function of their control over women, and they have to struggle out of that component of their sexuality." But unfortunately—or fortunately, if that's your point of view—that is exactly what men have done and are doing, and the sexual anarchy all around us is proof of it.

I venture to say that the anti-feminist counterrevolution of the post-World War II period was more an attempt on the part of the women to bolster up a crumbling patriarchy than the conscious work of men seeking to reestablish control over women. And I venture to say that at this point in history there are more men than women who want to get rid of the patriarchal system, and that a resurgence of patriarchal values will come from the women before it ever comes from the men. Men are simply having too much fun to go back to the old self-restraints and discipline. And all one has to do is look at the climbing circulations of *Playboy, Penthouse,* and other such crusaders for sexual freedom to know that men are in no mood for the puritan patriarchal moral standards of yesterday. For the truth of the matter is that the decline of patriarchy started long before the Kate Milletts and Germaine Greers started ranting and railing about it. Philip Wylie saw the seeds of the sexual revolution sprouting back in 1943 when he described American sexual habits in *Generation of Vipers*:

We present ourselves to each other as the inhabitants of a highly continent society, monogamous, virginal to the altar, each bride and groom sworn to forsake all others, and one and all so delicately sensitive to the manifestations of sex that we arrest persons for going nude and teach our children about storks and flowers rather than people. . . .

But America's sex repressions have little to do with what is real. Our very pretense of "virtue" is denied by the facts—for we are not continent, chaste, or faithful at all.

A recent survey of drafted men showed, for example, that more than three quarters of the unmarried men from time to time had sexual relations with females. That statistic, all alone, means that every human being in the United States who talks or thinks about the chastity of the nation is uttering or pondering the veriest bilge. . . .

In another survey, designed to show the relative chastity of American women, and conducted by a leading woman's magazine, the results were so "appalling" to the editors that they omitted from the publication of the study all figures relative to female unchastity and marital fidelity—privately justifying the omission, I might add, by the fantastic statement that publication of it would have a demoralizing effect upon the young women employed in their own offices! Still—so many boys fornicate that the girls must.[52]

And so the *Playboy* philosophy took root in fertile ground. The degeneration of patriarchal sexual morals had already taken place, and Hugh Hefner merely formulated a new hedonist philosophy to make acceptable, if not respectable, behavior that was already common. Men were no longer interested in maintaining the patriarchal taboo on premarital sex. What with automobiles, wild weekends, smoking, drinking, necking in the movies, virginity was a drag. By the end of World War II America was ready to loosen the restraints on its ever-pressing sexual impulses. For years our popular culture had done little more than titillate the libido with bathing beauties, vamps, love songs, spicy stories, and torrid romances. Besides, Freud had made us all sex conscious, and the once-immoral notion of "free love" that, in the thirties and forties, had become associated with noble revolutionary causes. had taken on a daring and progressive coloring. By the time Hugh Hefner got the first issue of *Playboy* on the newsstands in 1953, with those famous nude calendar pictures of Marilyn Monroe, the Kinsey Report on male sexuality had already been out five years. In *Playboy*, however, the American anti-patriarchal male finally surfaced—from the back seat of his car.

The *Playboy* philosophy was astonishingly simple: the swinging, hedonistic life of unmarried sex was good for your mental health. Freud had taught us what terrible neuroses repressed sexuality could cause. So there was nothing wrong with good clean unmarried sex as long as both parties wanted it. Of course what the playboy really wanted was sex without the price that patriarchy had previously forced him to pay for it: a lifetime of responsibility to a wife and kids. As Hefner put it: "Variety, vitality and adventure of experience are more meaningful to me than the security of marriage. . . . The essence of our code is that life is an end in itself, and pleasure is preferable to pain. *Playboy* is something of a handbook describing the life you can enjoy." And for those who intended to marry: "If you spend your bachelor years doing what *Playboy* suggests, you wind up with a happier, more stable marriage."[53]

In a way Hefner is quite representative of the American anti-patriarchal male. He is not an intellectual or an artist, and he is the son of very devout midwestern Methodists. In his early years he married his college girl friend, whom he divorced in 1959 after a long separation. He has two children. If he is married to anything today, it is his magazine. But of course he continues to enjoy romantic interests in the manner prescribed by his philosophy. His affairs seem to last about two to three years. "My own romantic and sentimental nature draws me into relationships of considerable duration," he says.

What kind of women is he attracted to? "I pick good-looking, young girls because I get something very good out of the innocence and sweetness that exists at that level."

In the good old patriarchal days such innocent, sweet meat was generally unavailable unless you were willing to marry it. No father of the old school would have permitted his daughter to become the plaything of a playboy. After all, her innocence and sweetness were daddy's pride and joy as well as the girl's prize possessions. They were certainly worth a hand in marriage. Even today, according to Hefner, girls can become frantic about getting married, and he has had a tough time convincing his "special" girls that marriage is out of the question. "I guess some of them just give up on me," he says. "The most difficult thing for them to face is their inability to possess me."

What kind of girls have gotten involved with Hugh Hefner? First, they don't choose him. He chooses them. According to one of his staff, "Hugh Hefner can theoretically have any girl he wants, and he is supposed to be an expert on beauty and the epitome of all sophistication. So when he singles out a young girl to pay attention to, she's got to feel flattered."

One of the girls Hefner singled out for special attention was nineteen-year-old Mary Warren, a *Playboy* receptionist. He was attracted to her sweet selflessness—attracted involuntarily, he says. "I am not that much a master of my emotions." Mary found Hefner friendly and personal. He even knew people in her own Chicago neighborhood. An article by Diana Lurie in *Life* (October 29, 1965) described what happened after Hefner made her his "special girl":

> Deciding that her parents' fears for her were groundless, she lived in his mansion in the quarters overseen by a house-mother and rented to a dozen girls working in Hefner's empire. Mary began spending most of her time with Hefner. She organized the stacks of color transparencies for him to edit, fetched endless bottles of soda pop, answered the telephone, just waited. "I wouldn't think of interrupting Hefner," says Mary. "I would never have anything that important to say."
>
> But sometimes, during the picture editing, she might rub his back, and even try to talk to him, though he smilingly ignores her. Then again he might listen with real solicitude in an outpouring of her troubles. Talking about life with Hefner, Mary said, "I regard it as an honor, a pleasure and a wonderful experience."

And so Hefner let her make him the center of her life. That's what a girl does when she falls in love with a man. "You can," reflected Hefner, "go out and fight dragons a lot better every day if you have that kind of relationship going." But it only lasted about two years. Mary wanted him all to herself, which is a no-no in the Hefner philosophy of variety. He dated others, which caused her pain. And so she moved out of the mansion.

Her predecessor, Cynthia Maddox, a four-time *Playboy* cover girl, had fared no better. Ms. Lurie described this affair also:

> Cynthia was hired by *Playboy* right out of high school as a typist in 1959. She started dating Hefner about 18 months later—she was 20, he was 34. It lasted two and a half years. "When I first started to date Hef," Cynthia says, "it was so great. There was an excitement—just like being a movie star." The first few months she found it hard to relax with Hefner—he was so successful, popular, independent, famous. "I thought I was so much the opposite," Cynthia remembers. "Who am I? What do I have to offer him? I soon found out."
>
> Hefner says, "I care for women a great deal. I'm a very romantic, sentimental, human guy." He does not think women are attracted to him for his millions—and he is probably correct. All they get from him are their *Playboy* salaries. He does admit that a woman may be attracted to him because of his position. But he is capable of great charm, even gentleness, and he has a boyish, almost lyrical laugh. "Hef is really a very sweet and simple person," says Cynthia. "God, he's so nice. When he worked at the office, it was like having your father around." Hefner is well aware of this effect. "I give my special girl a feeling of depending on me," he says, "of being loved, cared for, needed and important."

In short it's a kind of father-daughter affair (house-mother and all), a Midwestern father deflowering his sweet, innocent Midwestern daughters, each one in her turn, as daddy's "special girl" reaches that special ripeness. And it's all very Midwestern, including the food, if we can take Ms. Lurie at her word:

At his meals with Cynthia, Hefner ate pork chops, chicken or pot roast often saturated with heavy gravy. Instead of swinging around the town every night, *Playboy*-style, they spent most of their time in Hefner's rooms. They watched Charlie Chaplin movies and listened to Jeanette MacDonald records. "I don't know how real it was," she says, "but it was beautiful just sitting there sighing."

But in time Cynthia began to act possessive, and the daughterlike sweetness and innocence began to fade. She was even jealous of his work. Sometimes she'd run around his office, stepping on layouts, copy, pictures and cartoons spread out on the floor. "Trampling his work was a great outlet for me," she says. "It seemed like I could destroy it. He became furious." And things went from bad to worse:

In public, Cynthia refused to show Hefner any affection. She realized he sometimes went out with other women and was ashamed that people thought she knew about it but still put up with it. At parties, "I just sort of kept away from everybody," she says, "with an air of independence like, 'Oh, yes, I know' and 'So what?' Inside it was killing me.

"Of course, I was always theoretically free to do as I pleased," says Cynthia, "but I abided by Hef's rules. If I was on a date with another boy, heaven help me if he even kissed me. At first I said to myself, 'I am not going to get involved with Hef—it is not going to happen.' But, oh so slowly, it did—and it was too late."

Hefner insists on his freedom, without any rules. . . . "The most difficult thing for them to face is their inability to possess me."

It never fails to come up, the issue of possession, freedom, and control. The anti-patriarchal male wants to enjoy sex without marriage, and he may insist that his girlfriend be faithful as long as the affair lasts, but when he's tired of her for any reason whatever, he simply lets her go. The girl, of course, goes into the affair with the hope that she will get him for good. She'll go along with "free love" if it will get her what she wants: marriage. And when she doesn't, the letdown is very, very painful. It's enough to turn any girl into a women's libber. Which is why there are so many of them these days. But the plain unadulterated truth is that the playboys of America are engaged in a gigantic sexual rip-off, and some of the girls are beginning to wise up. But the girls need not reject men in toto. They simply have to learn to control their own libidos. There are still plenty of men who appreciate such outdated virtues as constancy, consideration, and premarital chastity. They are usually not the sexually aggressive men. Yet one of the bitterest complaints of the girls these days is that the boys aren't hot enough.

Basically the *Playboy* philosophy is that of "free love" reformulated and smartly packaged with hi-fi stereos and sports cars for the middle-class market. Previously you had to be a noble soul, a poet, an artist, a revolutionary in order to enjoy the transcendent physical pleasures and dramatic emotional tortures of "free love." *Playboy* has now made it available at popular prices—emotionally and financially—for the vast American middle class. But it really doesn't work with our middle class because the latter folk don't like love with too much suffering. They like their love like their pot roast, a little on the dull side. Dull but constant, predictable, and comforting, like a bottle of Geritol.

Yet the symbol of the rabbit now symbolizes America's sexual morality. What can be less representative or evocative of the mysteries of human sexuality than this ridiculous bunny? It originated, of course, in Hefner's mind, and Richard Todd, who attended a *Playboy* International Writers' Convention in 1971, described Hefner explaining the bunny's genesis:

> He couldn't recall what inspired the rabbit, which was there in the first issue and turned into one of the most recognizable trademarks in the world. "I'll tell you something interesting, though," he said, shifting his voice to a note that suggested intimacy but implied also that it was time to go. "I suppose the Freudians could make something out of this. When I was a little boy I had a blanket, a sort of security thing, and I called it my bunny blanket."

For all practical purposes the weak Hefner bunny symbolizes the end of patriarchy as we have known it for the last 10,000 years. The women's libbers are a delayed but furious reaction against patriarchy's demise. True, men still dominate in the professional and commercial world. But only because there are not many women who are willing to put into their careers the kind of effort that is required to reach eminence in any field. Those women who have have achieved notable success.

As for sex, we are living in a period of sexual anarchy in which everyone seems to want the impossible. Women want sexual freedom and they also want the deep satisfactions that can only come with loyalty and constancy. Men want to enjoy deflowering a succession of sweet, innocent girls without feeling any guilt and without causing the girls emotional pain. Boys want girls with sexual experience who will then be faithful. Girls want boys to seduce them and then respect them. Everybody wants to be loved, but nobody wants to love. And in the mad rush for sex, parenthood is pushed aside and babies become a nuisance. Nature created sexual pleasure as a strong aid to reproduction. The pleasure was the bait; raising children was its real end. But with our brilliant technology we have succeeded in isolating the sexual pleasure from its fuller context of human responsibility, and we have thought that we could build a human value system based on its enjoyment alone. Apparently, however, the only human being who can live by such a system looks more like a rabbit than a human.

6

The Sexualization of Women

No man can contemplate the widespread sexualization of women, understanding fully what that sexualization will mean, without feeling a cold chill running down his back. For such sexualization can only lead ultimately to the massive defection of women from their roles as loyal wives attached to men who do not necessarily satisfy them sexually. And yet why should men worry, since the sexualization of women cannot take place without their full cooperation, unless women turn en masse to Lesbianism or vibrators? Yet men are becoming concerned as women learn more and more about their orgasmic potential, become more sexually aggressive, more sexually demanding. For 10,000 years the patriarchal system relegated the female orgasm to limbo. The reason for this was quite simple: women could conceive without an orgasm. So why arouse pleasures and desires that many men did not feel comfortable with or competent enough to satisfy?

Prior to the development of modern science and psychology man had a rather negative attitude toward female sexuality, perhaps as a dim residual memory of what it was like in prepatriarchal times when female sexuality expressed itself without patriarchal restraints. To many men in those days female sexuality was a source of evil and unhappiness in the form of bloody jealous rivalries, emotional instability, and social anarchy. Accordingly female sexuality was so completely suppressed by patriarchal society that for centuries we scarcely knew what it was. We believed that it did not exist at all in virtuous women, and obviously the Virgin Mary was an institutionalization of that belief.

But the last forty years have seen a steady erosion of the restraints on male sexuality and, as a result of this growing freedom for men, women have learned that there is no one to stop them from discovering their own sexual potential. In fact they have been encouraged to do so by psychologists, marriage counselors, sexual investigators, and the anti-patriarchal males who have had their own ulterior motives in encouraging female sexual freedom. And so we have seen the appearance of such new magazines as *Playgirl* and *Viva*, featuring center foldouts of nude males and catering to the sexual appetites of women. And the women are slowly and cautiously making us all aware of how sexual a woman can be. In the spring of 1974 I saw an attractive woman on a TV panel show with several men admit that she was a "crotch watcher." For a woman to make such an admission, in public, to a group of men on television is nothing short of revolutionary. Yet this is only the beginning of female sexual liberation.

The subjugation of women some 10,000 years ago required the brutal suppression of female sexuality in the short range and the continued repression of female sexuality in the long range. Thus women were educated to be as sexually passive and submissive as possible, feeling as little pleasure as possible. If any sexuality were manifested, it was the male's. After all, the male had to have an orgasm to impregnate his wife, but his wife did not need an orgasm to conceive. And from this unequal situation arose the myth that men were sexual and women were not, that the male sex drive was strong and that the female drive was weak. But, as we are learning today, the opposite is true. Not only is female sexuality stronger, but it demands of men far more than many men can or want to give. The man who cannot satisfy his wife will have a difficult time retaining her fidelity, particcularly if she is economically independent.

At this point in human history men still have a very vague understanding of female sexuality, if they have any understanding of it at all. Nor do men fully understand their own sexuality, since human sexuality is so governed by individual variables and manifests itself on so many levels—the emotional, the physiological, the cultural—that at best we can only observe, theorize, and speculate. The most basic and observable differences between male and female sexuality have served to govern our prevalent attitudes. But now we are discovering a whole new dimension to female sexuality in what has not been observed for at least 10,000 years, in what has been repressed.

Sometimes in reading the works of female liberationists one almost feels as if women are not merely another sex but another species. They seem to lack a certain dimension that is present in the male sex, a transcendent dimension that perhaps men have acquired because of their lack of child-bearing ability. It is the metaphysical dimension, the spiritual dimension that permeates the works of male philosophers, scientists, poets, but is often lacking in the writings of women, notably the women's libbers. For men, religion is another dimension in human yearning, an attempt to achieve spiritual union with the all-powerful forces that govern our lives, an attempt to mitigate the pain of physical isolation in a hostile universe. For women, however, religion has been more an obstacle to female freedom than an opening to the spiritual world. Religion places some moral restraints on male sexual behavior, but it does not condemn male sexuality. To some extent it even looks benignly on male homosexuality, if we consider the Biblical story of Jonathan and David. When it comes to female sexuality, however, religion, and particularly Western religion, has taken a much more restrictive attitude. Religion has always emphasized the child-bearing functions of women and condemned the female's pursuit of sexual pleasure. Adultery has been considered the very worst of sins, punishable by death.

Women's libbers insist, of course, that religion was created by men for men. But was religion created because men needed a moral code for sexual behavior or an unlimited dimension for spiritual growth, a dimension they needed to make up for their physical lack? Perhaps it is because woman's reproductive function binds her to earth more securely that she does not have to look to heaven. When a woman bears children she becomes a "mother" with all that the term implies, experiencing that maternal dimension with its deep closeness and intimacy with another life from which men are largely excluded. Men basically envy the relationships women can have with their children. Serving as a stud hardly compensates for that lack, and all men spend their lives finding ways to dispel the terrifying fears of isolation. That is why men invented patriarchy, to minimize the appalling predicament of male isolation. Sexuality brings people together. However its unrestrained, uncontrolled exercise can also tear them apart. And that is why men fear female sexual freedom.

What is a sexualized woman? Is she Helen Gurley Brown's single girl in pursuit of a man? Is she a nymphomaniac? Is she a wife having an adulterous affair? Perhaps we can best describe her as a woman who is keenly aware of her sexual pleasure; that is, she knows what arouses her and can bring her to orgasm, and considers male sexual competence of central importance in her relationship with a man, or at least of considerable importance. She judges a man, as far as a love relationship is concerned, on how well he can satisfy her sexually.

91

Obviously a definition of this kind has to be broad enough to include the variable tastes and dispositions of many different women—from those who become sexual addicts to those who may be highly sexualized but exercise great self-control. How does a woman become sexualized? It may start early in life through self-exploration and masturbation, or she may become sexualized through the skilled hands of her boyfriends. In any case she becomes keenly aware of her own physical responses and actively seeks the kind of sexual experiences that satisfy her. Unless she is fortunate enough to find a husband who can truly satisfy her, the sexualized woman must have the freedom to pursue her sexual partners or at least be open to their advances. She is usually economically independent of a man and she must know a great deal about contraception. She may or may not be monogamous in her sexual liaisons. She may or may not have room for motherhood in her life. Rearing children is bound to interfere with her sexual freedom. However children may also serve to attract some men to her. But to the sexualized woman the sexual experience she has with a man is of crucial importance in determining whether the relationship will last or whether she will be faithful. Naturally the emotional element will be of importance and may mitigate against sexual pleasure, although many sexualized women find it quite easy to separate the emotional from the sexual.

The sexualized woman of course prefers to be satisfied by a man she can also love. But it is questionable whether she can love a man who cannot satisfy her. She is not the self-sacrificial girl who marries a paraplegic. She may remain married to a man whose physical condition no longer permits him to satisfy her, but she will probably, but not inevitably, be tempted into extramarital affairs. And that is the reason why many men tend to feel emotionally insecure with a sexualized woman, since they can never be sure of her constancy, particularly should they no longer be able to satisfy her. Thus the sexualized woman creates a climate of instability, insecurity, and impermanence about her relationships. She clearly cannot sincerely espouse the "till death do us part" vow in marriage, unless she intends to carry on side affairs with or without the knowledge of her husband. Her marriage, therefore, if it does endure, is marred by disloyalty and betrayal, causing torment to all involved. An example of what can happen when a married woman becomes sexualized through an adulterous affair was rather clinically given by a letter writer to Dear Abby (*Boston Herald Advertiser*, May 12, 1974). She wrote:

> I was faithfully married for 18 years to a man I can only describe as a kind and considerate husband. He doesn't chase and is a good provider and a good father. Bed hasn't been very exciting for me for many years, but I put on an act for the benefit of his ego. He had no idea he wasn't the greatest lover, but I didn't know how bad he was until I ran into Jimmy, which is why I have this problem.

Jimmy was my high school boyfriend who just happened to be in town (he travels) on business. It's a long story, but let me just say Jimmy and I have been meeting at a motel a few afternoons a month for the last five months. We're not "in love" (he's married, too) and nobody is going to leave anybody over this. We're just filling a need in the lives of one another. (His wife is a prude). I never knew a forty-year-old woman, married for 18 years, could come to life the way I did.

The problem is that the "act" has become harder and harder to keep up at home. Comparisons in techniques and results leave me a wreck! Now I'm in a trap of my own making. It was all right as long as I didn't know what I was missing.

There is no way to approach this with my husband. I'd be apt to get one rap for complaining, and another for knowing the difference. At 40, I'm not ready to give up sex and at 50, my husband isn't going to get any better in bed. Where do I go from here?

Abby suggested that the woman take her husband to a Masters-and-Johnson-type sex clinic at a local university for private counseling and a course in human sexuality. "Quit trying to kid your husband and suggest that the two of you take (the course) together. When enlightenment replaces ignorance and inhibitions are broken down, miracles occur. But this is possible only when both parties sincerely want improvement. So if you want a more satisfactory love life with your husband, spend the energy."

It is hardly likely, however, that Abby's reply will be enough to dispel this woman's problems. Her marriage, she writes, was "all right as long as I didn't know what I was missing." The real problem is that her adulterous affair has merely increased her dissatisfaction with her marriage and she must now choose between exciting sex and marital stability, between sexual freedom and fidelity. Yet she writes that "nobody is going to leave anybody over this." But her husband might conceivably leave her if he found out. Abby suggests that the woman take her husband to a sex clinic so that he too can be sexualized. But perhaps after he's sexualized he may go after a younger woman, especially should he find out that his wife has betrayed him. He does not chase now. But there's no guarantee that a course in human sexuality won't awaken desires that may send him out looking for younger, more attractive women.

Had this woman simply obeyed her marriage vows, or the Ten Commandments, or resisted temptation, she would not have opened this can of worms. The restraints placed on sexual behavior by our ancient moral codes were conceived out of bitter human experience. Lucky are the marriage partners who are equally sexualized and equally in love with one another. But since we now know the extent of human sexual incompatibility, particularly between men and women, it is obvious why the restraints were conceived. Sexual and emotional compatibility are the exception rather than the rule. Once we accept this reality, then we realize that every marriage requires a high degree of self-sacrifice.

93

It is true that good sex is marvelous therapy. "I never knew a 40-year-old woman, married for 18 years, could come to life the way I did." But there must be something wrong with a woman who requires an adulterous affair to bring her to life. "Comparisons in techniques and results leave me a wreck!" she writes. So why stop with Jimmy, we might ask. The next man might even be better than both her husband and her lover. One gets the impression that this woman is quite aware of what she has started. Nevertheless, she writes, "At 40, I'm not ready to give up sex and at 50, my husband isn't going to get any better in bed."

So it all comes down to choices, difficult choices few of us like to make. Suppose this woman's husband refuses to go to a sex clinic. What then? Does she leave him for a life of sexual freedom in the metropolis of her choice? Where will she find her lovers to give her the kind of sex she wants? Will she start enticing other married men? Younger men? Does she care what her children will think of her?

I suppose there are ways for this woman to activate her husband sexually without risking disclosure of her adultery, and perhaps she will find them. But it is easy to see, by this simple story, why men distrust sexualized women, and why most marriages become desexualized after a few years. One look at the grotesque shapes so many married people permit themselves to grow into is a good barometer of the decline in sexuality in most marriages. If the couple are of low sexual appetite to begin with, the decline is probably very rapid. There are those, however, with strong sexual appetites who maintain healthy sexual relations well into what we call old age. The variables, from individual to individual, are obviously very great.

But perhaps what is most revealing in the Dear Abby letter is the lack of conscience in the woman and her ability to separate the sexual from the emotional. This is not to say that men are not capable of having the same attitude when they are unfaithful to their wives. But a woman's immorality is much harder to take, perhaps because we have invested women so heavily with the motherhood image. Of course the women's libbers object to this double standard, and they have every right to do so. But most men will expect a woman's maternal responsibilities to infuse her with a higher sense of morality. There is growing evidence that increasing female immorality, particularly on the part of mothers, is having a very demoralizing effect on children. Maternal immorality can have a much more shattering emotional impact on a child than paternal immorality.

Despite all the attempts of the women's libbers to prove how equal the sexes are, the more men learn about women the more they realize how different they are. In fact, reading all of the new literature written by feminists only makes one more keenly aware of the great emotional and physical incompatibility between the sexes that has been largely hidden by the patriarchal system, which merely forced women to conform to the emotional and sexual needs of men. That men had to resort to force is an indication of the underlying incompatibility and conflict between the sexes. For only the greatest frustration and emotional torment—and not organized sadism as some women's libbers insist—could have forced men to resort to the repressive measures that had to be taken in order to bring women firmly under their control.

The women's libbers object to the moral codes that the patriarchal system evolved as aids in the subjugation of women. But we must marvel at man's intellectual genius in creating such effective cultural and social devices to maintain the integrity of the family, as well as his control over women with a minimum of physical force. However, with the moral codes crumbling all around us, men will in time be faced with the dilemma of deciding how far they can permit female liberation to go, how far they can permit the sexualization of women to progress without a physical counterreaction. The women, who have been advancing their freedom slowly and cautiously, have not yet reached the point where men have been sufficiently provoked to strike back. There are still plenty of women who like the patriarchal scheme of things, and most young girls are still pursuing the traditional patriarchal values of marriage and family. They still want church weddings and they still take the traditional marriage vows and they still want faithful husbands. But the divorce rates indicate that the vows are a mere archaic formality for a very large number of people who find that "love" does not endure very long after the honeymoon's afterglow. Yet love and romance are still what the girls are looking for.

Helen Gurley Brown's single girl is not a women's libber's idea of a sexualized woman. She is a girl who wants to find a husband and is doing all in her power to attract and hold the man she wants. She is often a career girl, economically independent by necessity rather than by choice. She enjoys working for men and with men. Her goal is to find *the* man, and to this end she will make her apartment "sexy," learn to cook meals *he* will like, wear clothes that will make her look attractive to *him*, keep her figure in good shape, etc. In a world of crumbling patriarchal values, she loves men and wants to find the one man she can love and respect. She has a sex life, but it is subordinate to her goal of finding the right man, which may take years. Writes Ms. Brown:

I married for the first time at thirty-seven. I got the man I wanted. It *could* be construed as something of a miracle considering how old *I* was and eligible *he* was. . . . But *I* don't think it's a miracle that I married my husband. I think I deserved him! For seventeen years I worked hard to become the kind of woman who might interest him.[54]

No women's libber is going to work seventeen years to become

95

the kind of woman who might interest any man. Not on your life. And that's why the women's libbers hate *Cosmopolitan* and everything it stands for. Sure, *Cosmo* is for women getting equal pay for equal work, and it's for all sorts of women's rights, including the right to a sex life even though a girl is single, but its main message is to teach women how to please men. Which merely means that for most women the pursuit of a man is still the most important purpose of their lives.

Nevertheless high school girls are being encouraged to enjoy premarital "recreational sex," with the result that venereal disease has reached epidemic proportions among teen-agers and there are increasing numbers of teen-age pregnancies, abortions, and illegitimate births. The sexualization of these young girls is having a disastrous effect on thousands of them. Whoever sold teen-agers on the idea that there is such a thing as premarital "recreational sex" ought to be shot. Unless one understands that sexual pleasure was created by nature as bait for the more painful responsibilities of existence, one cannot understand sex, one cannot understand love, one cannot understand life. Unless sexual pleasure leads to human responsibility, it then becomes the shallowest and most depressing of pursuits. That is why the promiscuous search for the perfect orgasm is so futile. In the search one is merely seeking the perfection of one's own pleasure. And indeed you may find someone who enables you to attain that special perfection. But then what? Unless you then devote yourself to loving that person, you've achieved nothing but a momentary physical excitation.

If we understand that nature created sexual pleasure as bait, then we may also be able to understand why male and female sexuality differ from one another. Barbara Seaman, in her book *Free and Female*, writes:

> Women *are* different from men. Our sexuality is both less and more: less in that it is easily suppressed and more in that the limits of our potential almost defy measurement.[55]

Yes, it is true. Women are capable of experiencing far more intense and prolonged sexual pleasures than men. And perhaps this was nature's way of compensating women for the responsibilities and pains they had to bear as mothers. The more pleasure a woman wanted, the more likely she'd pay the price in pregnancy; and in the noncontraceptive world of prehistory pregnancy was unavoidable. Yet nature is not so cruel as to exact a price for every bit of pleasure. Women are only able to conceive during a small number of days of their menstrual cycle. Thus nature provided women with their own contraceptive roulette in which those women who got to like sex most were also the ones most likely to get pregnant. And pregnancy and childbirth forced a woman to accept a discipline and responsibility that precluded her becoming addicted to sexual pleasure.

Today, however, with modern contraception, the woman who enjoys sexual pleasure the most no longer has the discipline of child-bearing imposed on her. She can become a compulsive sex machine, never satisfied, never fulfilled. In this regard nature seems to have been an accomplice in the imposition of patriarchy. For women are capable of conceiving without experiencing any sexual pleasure at all, let alone an orgasm. That man should have elevated the unsexual-ized virgin mother to the status of the mother of God indicates to what extent he was revolted by female sexuality. Perhaps it had reached the point in human society where female addiction to sexual plea-sure became so strong that it actually interfered with the rearing of children and created untold emotional and social difficulties for the males. The sexualized woman simply refused to pay the price of her pleasure. In so doing she upset the delicate balance of responsibilities required to maintain the species. Thus female sexuality, because its pleasures were not required in the reproductive process, was curtailed and ruthlessly suppressed. That physical force was used goes without saying. Strong sensual drives do not respond to verbal argument. They do respond to a corporal counterpoint, or what the behaviorists now call "aversion therapy."

Patriarchy was an attempt to create a more stable balance of sex-ual economics. Women were deprived of sexual pleasure but were compensated by economic security and the lifelong devotion of hus-band and children. As mothers, women achieved positions of high moral standing. Men achieved greater sexual pleasure for themselves but at the price of tremendous economic effort, self-discipline, and self-restraint.

Today the balance of sexual economics has been totally destroyed. We have been told that the planet is too crowded and that we are to produce fewer and fewer children. Women are told that their repro-ductive functions are no longer needed. Men are trying to gain sex-ual pleasures without paying the price in responsibilities. It's the *Playboy* rip-off. Teenagers are encouraged to indulge in so-called rec-reational sex. And women are becoming sexualized in preparation for wholesale sexual addiction. All of it is leading to a kind of sexual inflation, in which each sexual act is worth less and less in terms of ecstasy, fulfillment, and satisfaction. Without love, without loyalty, without commitment, without responsibility sex becomes an almost meaningless pastime. Unless sex is used as a means to a more re-sponsible end, its pleasures become minimal. It is almost a law of nature: the deeper the pleasure, the higher the cost in human respon-sibility and commitment. In the days of prehistory, when men were satisfied to insert their phalluses in free-roaming females, their plea-sure was limited and so was their responsibility. When they created the patriarchal system and took responsibility for the care and feeding of wife and children, their sexual and emotional pleasures were increased but so was the price in human effort.

It is this inexorable law of nature that makes "recreational sex" an untenable concept. The more recreational it becomes, the less pleasurable. That is not to say that every sexual act must lead to painful responsibility or love or commitment. It merely means that sexual pleasure can provide a greater degree of fulfillment if it is enjoyed in a context of responsibility, deeper intimacy, or commitment—if it is commingled with the sacrifices of love.

Today, however, the emphasis is on the enjoyment of sex without emotional involvement, with much stress put on variety and experimentation. But in order to practice such recreational sex one must forget about loyalty and love, the two primary values that elevate human relationships above those of the lower species.

Now that we have indicated why most men have a negative or at least ambivalent attitude toward the sexualized woman, the question becomes: can a virtuous woman be sexual? Must a woman, in order to be virtuous, become a sexual nonentity? Obviously not. She can be sexual without being sexualized. In a virtuous woman, the values that contribute to her virtue are stronger than her sexuality, which can be quite strong. In a sexualized woman, the sexual need or addiction is stronger than her ability to maintain love and loyalty.

Thus, with growing female liberation, women are in a greater dilemma than ever over how to conduct their sex lives. The patriarchal moral code was incredibly simple: you remained a virgin until marriage, and you remained faithful to your husband no matter what kind of a sex life he provided. There was something fatalistically poetic in the way such a lifelong commitment was made, because it was understood that no one could foresee the inevitable troubles and difficulties ahead. The basic incompatibility of the sexes must have been recognized far back in prehistory, and regardless of the difficulties, the pain, and the sacrifices, the one constant that remained throughout in a world of war and upheaval was the union of two people.

The prehistoric human experience that led to that simple moral code—that solved so many problems caused by the vagrant weaknesses of the species—may be too remote from today's conditions to justify its being the basis of a new moral code. Yet I wonder how really different are the sexual conditions today from those of prehistory. I read recently of a well-known pair of researchers in animal behavior, a husband-and-wife team studying primates in Tanzania, who were raising their children the way chimpanzees raise them. Apparently the chimpanzees are doing a better job than modern mothers. The wife, Dr. Jane Goodall—whose book, *The Shadow of Man*, was published in 1971—was quoted as saying:

98

Watching chimps and baboons makes you know 100 percent how important it is for the mother to be with the child. When I read about women wanting to put their children in kibbutzim or day-care centers I get hopping mad. In captivity when you see them take baby chimps from the mothers they turn out unstable. In the wild, a rough or rejecting mother has unstable youngsters. . . . No book on child raising has ever been based on the needs of the baby primate, which is what a child is. They're all based on the convenience of the mother.[56]

Have civilization, technology, affluence, and new concepts of individual freedom buried our instincts so that we can no longer recognize them? How different are the human needs for love, intimacy, and loyalty today than they were in prehistory? Nothing has really changed in what must transpire between a mother and infant to insure that infant's survival and healthy growth. Nothing has changed in what must take place between sexual partners. Nothing has changed in what lovers seek from one another. The imperatives of love are the same as ever: loyalty precludes promiscuity because any extramarital sex may open the door to betrayal and alienation. And this goes for both men and women.

If we decide that in order to enjoy freedom we must dispense with loyalty, then we ought not to expect to enjoy the emotional security that loyalty provides. Freedom merely means having a choice. One can either choose loyalty or promiscuity. Society no longer forces people to remain loyal to one marriage partner, for better or for worse, till death do us part. It is now a matter of personal choice and personal conduct. Nor is an adulteress any longer stoned to death by her neighbors. She may merely lose her husband, the respect of her children, and whatever security the marriage provided. And of course an unfaithful husband courts similar risks. Divorce has become our accepted way out of an unhappy marriage, but it does nothing to prevent the suffering of children who learn through their parents that love and loyalty are too fragile to survive. Of course it is no longer fashionable to sacrifice oneself for one's children. I don't say this to condemn parents who get divorced. Today a marriage is no longer regarded as a permanent unconditional commitment. It is now a contract that can be terminated quite easily through mutual consent. Most divorces, statistics show, are obtained by young people who marry too soon for the wrong reasons. There is a tendency these days for young people to go after the facade rather than the substance. So they marry because the bridal magazines make it all look like a huge vanilla fudge sundae, and they come apart because they find that the substance behind the facade is too difficult to cope with. Another human being may be your greatest source of happiness, but he may also be your greatest source of torment. The good provider may be a lousy sex partner. The good sex partner may be a lousy provider. It is rare that we find all good things in

one person. Human beings are just not built that way. But our affluence and technology have spoiled us. Like children we want everything. We refuse to make difficult choices, choices that in previous
societies were made for us. The trouble with today's smorgasbord
approach to life is that everything looks good and it is becoming increasingly difficult to make some of the simplest choices. Like the
woman in the Dear Abby letter who did some comparative sexual
shopping. She found out that other men could do it better than her husband. "It was all right," she writes, "as long as I didn't know what I
was missing." The key to this woman's dilemma is in the word "missing," and it is also the key to our modern dilemma. Nobody wants to
miss anything. The modern fear is that if you've missed something,
you just haven't lived.

The big thing that a lot of women do not want to miss these days is
an orgasm: the biggest, longest, bestest orgasm they can have. Having
orgasms regularly and profusely has now become something of a status symbol for women. Along with the mink coat and the Cadillac
must now come the orgasm. And not just any old orgasm. It's got to be
that textbook orgasm brought forth with the loving help of a sensitive
husband who through a course in human sexuality can now play the
female sexual organ like a skilled musician.

It is almost unavoidable, and perhaps too easy, for a man to make
light of the female orgasm. His own orgasm is a pretty well defined
experience, quite visible, and quite functional. On the other hand the
female's orgasm is neither visible nor functional. The muscular contractions take place within the recesses of the vagina and nothing
similar to an ejaculation accompanies it. The egg can be fertilized
with or without an orgasm, and chances are that most human beings
were conceived without their mothers having orgasms. So the female
orgasm has no reproductive function. It is purely a pleasure trip. Nor
does it provide the release and relief of the male orgasm. Barbara
Seaman writes:

> Recent sex research suggests that the female orgasm may increase
> pelvic vaso-congestion, which sparks a taste for further orgasm. *The more
> a woman does, the more she can, and the more she can, the more she
> wants to.*[57]

So the female orgasm is rather open-ended. An example of how
puzzled some girls can be about the whole matter was given by an
eighteen-year-old reader of *Playgirl* magazine (June 1974). She
wrote: "I hear a lot about orgasm and climaxing, and I hate to sound
naive, but what is orgasm, and what is climaxing? Is it all physical or
partly mental? How can you really tell you're climaxing? Can the guy
you're with tell?"

While some girls don't even know what an orgasm is, others are greatly concerned about their inability to have one. An article in *Cosmopolitan* of May 1974 dealt with that problem. Entitled "Why Girls Can't Have Orgasms," the article concluded that "genital shyness is the *biggest* problem in not achieving orgasm." The author wrote:

> The sex revolution has given us the information, technical know-how and "approval" for our basic sexy natures, but still we suffer from, incredibly, sexual shyness! . . . Many of us still feel our sexual parts are *ugly*!

In the end, however, it all comes down to male cooperation and competence. If many women know little about female sexual physiology, most men know even less. *Cosmopolitan* pins the problem down:

> Unfortunately, a number of us *still* think that if a man is truly loving he'll *know* instinctively what to do. We feel it's an insult to *him* and to the great love between us to take his hand and put it where we want it, to tell him to stop—or not to stop! The clitoris, of course, is the critical area to orgasm and some men need to be reminded and re-reminded it's the push-button of arousal.

Thus we get back to the essential cooperative role men will have to play if women are to be sexualized. Considering the fears and anxieties the sexualized woman arouses in men and the genital shyness of most women, the sexualization of women may indeed have to rely on other means for its realization. The *Cosmopolitan* article points that possible way:

> If you *cannot* talk to the man, feel you've faked too long already to suddenly *now* confess you've never had orgasm with him, there's something you can do by *yourself*: Use a vibrator, that clever little pleasure-bringer which stimulates in ways even the most deft lover can't always match. Vibrators have brought orgasms to many girls who never in their *lives* had one before.

Which brings us to the great question concerning the female orgasm: which is the more authentic orgasm, the clitoral or vaginal? Most women agree that clitoral stimulation is essential to female orgasm, while others concede that they can achieve orgasm by deep vaginal penetration. Vibrators, incidentally, are used to stimulate the clitoris and do not produce the supposedly superior vaginal orgasm. However perhaps the most original and definitive statement made on the female orgasm was one by Linda Lovelace, star of *Deep Throat*, in a *Playboy* symposium (September 1973), who voted, of all things, in favor of the anal orgasm. She said:

> If I were choosing which was the most fantastic orgasm—clitoral, vaginal or anal—I'd say anal is the biggest. And it's not at all uncomfortable, as most people psych themselves out to believe. . ... . My anal opening doesn't expand as much as my vagina, though. The first inch of your ass is really the hard part. Once it penetrates beyond that, it's a whole heat

trip. My whole body just starts bubbling—it's like a hot rush starting at my feet and running on up through my body to my head.

There is little that one can add to Miss Lovelace's vivid description. She has broken virtually all of the sexual barriers, including the barrier of bisexuality. Miss Lovelace states:

A man and two women is the ideal sexual relationship as far as I'm concerned. . . . A guy can be with one girl; he can be with the other girl; he can be with *both* girls. I mean, every man would like to be with two women—it's kind of double your pleasure, double your fun. And there's more for me to enjoy as a woman, too. A woman can satisfy a woman better than a man can. She knows how it feels to another woman, that's why. A man can be told, and he can try all his lifetime, but he doesn't know what it feels like. A woman shares more with you than a man does.

Will the sexualization of women lead to more Lesbianism? Says Madeline Davis, a Lesbian who made an impassioned plea for gay equality at the 1972 Democratic National Convention:

There are not only more Lesbians coming out; in sheer numbers, there are really more Lesbians. Maybe the women's movement has created this situation. Through commitment to women's causes, probably a number of women have realized that commitment must be total.[58]

It is still far too early to tell what all of this will lead to. Women's magazines have been publishing more and more articles about bisexuality, describing the experiences of heterosexual men and women engaging in side affairs with members of their own sex. What all of the articles have in common is a kind of titillating shallowness, for bisexuality is an enormously difficult subject to deal with seriously on the superficial level required by the popular magazines. It's difficult enough for heterosexual and homosexual couples to achieve ideal relationships. But bisexuality implies carrying on more than one affair at a time, or alternating between one sex and the other and trying to maintain a measure of equilibrium in one's life. It implies carrying on a double life without full fidelity to either partner, with the anxiety and tension that such psychic indecision must arouse. Yet Jane Margold, author of an article on bisexuality in the June 1974 issue of *Cosmopolitan*, could end her piece with these irresponsible lemon-meringue thoughts:

Whether or not we're all predestined to be *bi*sexual remains in question. Still, whatever happens in the future, I've concluded that, right now, for the many who've tried it, bisexuality offers a satisfying—and often loving—way of life.

The above is in the same class with the irresponsible malarky about "recreational sex" and all the glorious fun it can be if you can avoid getting pregnant, a venereal disease, or emotionally mutilated.

Of all the trends in our society, the sexualization of women is bound to have the most devastating effects in terms of family stability, responsible child rearing, and marital fidelity. Since there is no longer patriarchal authority to impose control over female sexuality, or for that matter male sexuality, women will have to learn to impose that control over themselves. There are signs that some women are already recognizing the need to do this. Dr. Natalie Shainess, writing in the July 1971 issue of *Mademoiselle*, expressed her concern in these strong terms:

> We live in times when to be a sex object and have a properly shaped breast is so important that many women sacrifice their maternalism on the altar of their eroticism. . . . All the sex books today are leading women to be whores, urging women to service men in any way that men want, but not helping them to respond to their own feelings and impulses. . . . A woman who is really authentic and responsible is fierce about how she uses her sex. . . . Sexual anarchy leads to sexual nihilism.

Another strong opinion on what the new sexual freedom is doing to women was given by Carole Klein in *The Single Parent Experience*:

> If rigid codes once inhibited sensual pleasure, sexual freedom brings its own problems. Overindulgence in the shiny new sexual candy stores can bring attacks of confusion, frightening lack of commitment and can cause quite serious depression. Studies of the "swinging singles" in various large cities indicate that much psychic pain is coming of misusing the same freedoms that ostensibly were going to bring happiness. One New York psychiatrist commented angrily that "the pill is the worst thing that's happened to this town." His theory was that because girls no longer had to consider whether a bedmate would be a potentially good husband or father, they drifted into liaisons that were transitory and meaningless and were often also emotionally destructive.

Even *Seventeen* magazine, which has been preaching the New Morality for the past five years, is beginning to put the brakes on its overly permissive attitude toward premarital sex for teenagers, although ever so lightly. Its June 1974 issue had an article entitled "The Right to Say No," written for the benefit of those girls who, for some strange old-fashioned reason, may want to remain virgins before marrying. The article ended on this hopeful note:

> Adults who counsel teenagers now feel that perhaps too much attention has been devoted to those who are sexually active and too much benign neglect to those who don't want to be rushed. "I am not urging a moralistic approach to sex," wrote Dr. Lee of Yale in his *New York Times* article, "but I believe that young people who want to remain virgins need as much reassurance that their choice is healthy and correct as those who choose to enter sexual relationships."

But notice the subtle inference in Dr. Lee's statement: Yes, it's healthy and correct to say no to a boy. But perhaps it's just a little more healthy and correct to say yes.

103

7

The Maternal Instinct

Do women have a maternal instinct? Do they have a need to bear children? If they do, then how can we reconcile this instinct with the growing insistence on the part of so many women, including mothers, that abortion—that is, the killing of the unborn—be made legal and readily available on demand? According to feminist Barbara Seaman: "There is not (insofar as modern science has been able to determine) any special maternal instinct which is exclusively connected with hormones or pregnancy or reserved unto females."[59] But many women will tell you that they have it and they feel it, that the urge to have children is very strong, very insistent, that without children they would feel unfulfilled, wasted, and even suicidal. Even some Lesbians admit to such strong feelings. Are they simply culturally programmed to have such feelings and desires? Or is there something more basic to the nature of the female and her biological capabilities?

We know that nature gave women a strong sex drive, perhaps to make up for the weaker male sex drive. We also know that when men developed a "paternal instinct," they instituted the patriarchal system and proceeded to suppress the female sex drive so thoroughly and so completely that for centuries we have scarcely known this strong drive existed. And today, as this drive is finally being unshackled, and women are free to engage in sex to their heart's content, the clamor for legalized abortion grows stronger. But sex, as everyone knows, was invented by nature to facilitate the reproduction of the species. And if nature made the female sexual drive stronger than the male's, the reason for it is obvious: to get as many women pregnant as often as possible.

But this still doesn't tell us if there is such a thing as a maternal instinct apart from the sex drive. Lucinda Cisler, an active feminist and secretary of the National Association for Repeal of Abortion Laws, writes:

> There is a profound fear of women's sexual potential behind the continuing insistence that (for women) sexuality and reproduction are inseparable. The physical fact is that in women these functions are potentially *more* distinct than they are in men: as Masters and Johnson pointed out quite explicitly—in a passage that seems to have been printed in invisible ink judging from the attention paid it—the clitoris is unique in that it is the only organ in human anatomy whose purpose is exclusively that of erotic excitation and release.[60]

So we know that nature provided women with a sex organ whose only function is to provide erotic excitation. We also know that nature provided women with the biological capacity to play host to a fertilized egg and nurture its growth until birth. If we look at women in this limited biological way, we may gain an understanding of the various body organs in isolation. But it is obvious that the human being must be considered in the larger context of its interaction with other human beings. No animal is as social as the human animal. No animal in its infancy is as dependent on its mother as the human animal. No species has developed its interpersonal intimacy to the level we have with our use of language as a powerful socializing agent. In short, humans by nature are intensely social and their social need is evident from the time of conception, when the fetus, for survival, depends on its mother's consent to stay alive. After birth the infant is totally dependent on its mother for survival, not only for food, but for human warmth and love, or stroking, as psychiatrist Eric Berne characterized it. Referring to René Spitz's study of infants confined to hospitals, Eric Berne wrote in *Games People Play*:

> Spitz has found that infants deprived of handling over a long period will tend at length to sink into an irreversible decline and are prone to succumb eventually to intercurrent disease. In effect, this means that what he calls emotional deprivation can have a fatal outcome. These observations give rise to the idea of *stimulus-hunger*, and indicate that the most favored forms of stimuli are those provided by physical intimacy, a conclusion not hard to accept on the basis of everyday experience.[61]

Thus the human infant begins life with an intense need to be loved in addition to being fed. The need to be loved is an emotional need that can only be satisfied through intimate human contact. This need obviously remains with human beings throughout life. Thus, to examine human sexual organs out of the context of human social interaction can be misleading as well as harmful, depending on what you do with the information. If the information about the clitoris leads a woman into an intimate relationship with her vibrator instead of another human being, then her life has hardly been enriched. But I am sure that some women would disagree.

The point is that our sexual and reproductive organs developed or evolved in a social context, with the survival of the species their primary determinant. Therefore to separate human reproduction from human sexuality can be a very hazardous game, with unpredictable consequences for the human race. Yet the entire thrust of the sexual revolution is to do exactly that: separate human sexuality from human reproduction. I would say that if the human race determined that it should produce fewer children, then it should, as a concomitant, engage in less sex—but not less love. Not because there is anything intrinsically immoral about having more sex with less human reproductive responsibility, but because sex has less and less value the more it is divorced from human responsibility. Sex was never meant by nature to be enjoyed independently of the price humans were expected to pay for it. Unless sex leads to intimacy and commitment, either to the children who result from it or the adults with whom one engages in it, or both, it becomes of diminishing value because its pleasures decrease.

Yet because women are being told that they are to produce fewer children, they have been encouraged to have more sex, with liberalized abortion laws, oral contraceptives, and other methods being used to separate sex from reproduction. The result may be sexual addiction on a large scale, with a constant preoccupation with sex, a constant unsatisfied sexual hunger. Homosexuals, whose sexuality is completely divorced from any reproductive function, are notoriously susceptible to sexual addiction. The pursuit of sexual pleasure results in more sex with less pleasure. Happy homosexuals will tell you that the primary function of sex in their lives is to open the door to intimacy, to permit the creation of conditions in which love can grow. To use sex merely as an end in itself is to slam the door on one's own human potential. That is why the very fact of the clitoris' unique erotic function should not make a woman jump for joy but should make her aware of the dangers inherent in separating the erotic from the emotional. Undoubtedly there are pleasures in masturbation, but invariably their intensity depends a great deal on fantasies involving other human beings.

All of which tells us very little about the maternal instinct. Perhaps the word "instinct" is misleading because it suggests something one

107

is born with rather than something one acquires as a result of human interaction. But when we speak of a maternal instinct we are speaking of a woman's conscious desire to have children, an emotional need to produce and rear a child. We are not speaking of something that happens mindlessly and automatically. So there is not necessarily a contradiction between a woman's maternal instinct and her use of contraception. Flann Campbell, in his essay *Birth Control and the Christian Churches*, quotes a Catholic wife who seems to confirm this thesis. She writes:

> I submit both from my experience with rhythm and my experience with the birth control pills that the latter represent an enormous psychological gain over the former. With rhythm you helplessly assume that you can't keep from having children, and all your energies are expended on keeping from having a dozen. The negative dominates. In the second case you know that you are the master of the situation, that you can choose to have a child as a free act of maternal desire. Psychologically there is an enormous gain when a child is not an accident, but is wanted.[62]

I doubt that a mother's love for a child is determined by whether the child is conceived consciously or accidentally. Love is not a planned emotion. Many of life's deepest pleasures are based on the accidental. A child does not choose his parents, or his race, or his country of birth. A mother may be able to choose when she wants to have a child, but there are many women who work very hard to conceive and simply can't. Thus there is an air of middle-class phoniness about "planned parenthood." The idea that you can space your children the way you space your vacations is so lacking in spontaneity that it is possible that the most planned family is the one with the least spontaneous love. This is not to say that contraception is completely unjustified and that married women should breed constantly. The realities of life in modern industrial society make some sort of control over pregnancy mandatory. But it ought to be the same kind of control that we exercise in every other aspect of our lives: control that enhances life, permits love to flourish, deepens commitment, heightens pleasure. The price for having many children may be high in responsibility. But the price for having few or none must be equally as high, if not higher, if life is to provide a sense of fulfillment. A sense of fulfillment ultimately adds up to a sense of self-worth. People who have brought up a houseful of children can feel a sense of self-worth in that achievement alone. People who have few or no children must achieve their sense of self-worth in other ways, far more difficult ways.

Thus I would tend to equate the maternal instinct more with spontaneity and less with planning. You often hear couples saying "We don't want to have children until we are ready for them." But is anyone ever *ready* to have children? Is there a moment when the couple says "Now" and it happens? Or does the little stranger arrive when *he* is ready? The woman with the strong maternal instinct is bound to have an element of fatalism in her personality, and to feel a sense of anticipation for the infant that begins to grow within her. She may be anxious about her economic ability to raise the child, but her anxiety is a result of concern not regret. The unplanned child asserts his presence. To the parents he emerges with a certain kind of insistent strength. "I'm here," he seems to say, "whether you like it or not." They may love him or beat him down because of it. But the mother must confront her child. The planned child enters with permission. "You may enter our lives," the parents seem to say. "But you must be everything we expect you to be. After all, we want you for our satisfaction and convenience, not yours."

But regardless of whether a child enters the world with or without permission, one can imagine the feeling a mother must have when a newborn infant is placed in her arms and she is told "Here is your child. This is what *you* conceived, of *your* body. You are now no longer alone. You have an infant completely dependent on you for life." Many women, unwed or in conflict with themselves, react adversely at first with postpartum depression. But the woman with the maternal instinct soon accepts the new infant with true joy. She looks forward to that marvelous, painful, pleasurable, frustrating, fulfilling task of raising her child, loving her child and being loved in return, watching growth, watching another life so close to her own take form. Each of us retains so much of our mother throughout our lives. And mothers pour so much of themselves into their children.

Perhaps all of the above sounds idyllic. There are plenty of inadequate mothers and plenty of unwanted children, unwanted in every sense of the word. But life would not be life if it did not abound in the idyllic, if love and pleasure and joy were not equally real, if mother and child were not the tremendously beautiful pair they are.

But we speak of mother and child when perhaps we should speak of mother and children, for most mothers have more than one child, and each new child represents a new relationship. What determines family size? Does the maternal instinct determine it? Some interesting light was shed on that question in *Too Many Americans*, by Lincoln and Alice Day:

> A study based on data collected in a large survey in Indianapolis some 22 years ago highlights the somewhat ambiguous effect liking for children has on the determination of family size. In this study it was found, first, that, whatever their relative social and economic positions, couples with an interest in and liking for children had not larger families but more effectively planned ones. The greater the liking a couple expressed for children, the greater the care they exercised in achieving the family size they desired. . . .
>
> The other major finding of this study we have already alluded to: though there was among husbands in all socio-economic groups a tendency for

more interest in children to be accompanied by larger families, a similar tendency was not found among wives. In fact, among those couples who planned the number or spacing of their children the largest families were found among couples where the husband indicated a strong interest in children and the wife only moderate or little interest. But among those couples where it was the wife's interest that was strong, family size tended to be low. Thus, the authors conclude: "The wife's liking for children does not appear to be expressed in terms of large family size."[63]

Thus it would appear that the paternal instinct is a greater factor in determining family size than the maternal instinct. The father may be interested in creating a family dynasty. The mother may be interested in developing an intense relationship with one or two children. The experience of bringing up a houseful of children may bring a couple closer together. It may drive another couple apart. We hear of couples getting divorced after raising their children. We know of others settling down to graceful old age.

The greatest assault on the maternal instinct, however, has come, as expected, from the women's libbers. Many of them seem to resent the fact that their bodies were given the capacity to bear children. To them it is all one big inconvenience. They particularly resent the discomforts of the menstrual cycle. And simply because they have the capacity to bear children is no reason why they should then have to raise them. Lucinda Cisler writes:

> The implicit linking of bearing the young with *rearing* the young raises all the basic questions about who should best care for children. These cannot be dealt with here, but a single comment may be appropriate: if women—in the present state of medicine—must carry pregnancies for nine months and then bear the children, one might ask why should men not then care for the infants during the next nine months, as their fair contribution?[64]

No doubt there are plenty of men who would enjoy rearing the infants themselves if they didn't have to worry about earning a living at the same time. There are men who can be as gentle and attentive with an infant as any woman. But most women *want* to rear their own children. They feel an affinity with the infant they carried. In their memories are feelings about their own relationships with their mothers. To be a mother is to be a human being with a special dimension—a greater emotional dimension, a greater dimension in purpose, for if children represent anything they represent the future. In addition there are women who want to bear and raise their husband's children, as an extension of their love for their husbands, as a tribute to the man they married. There is a tendency among women's libbers to underestimate the capacity of some women to love their husbands very deeply.

Yet feminist Frances Beal describes the loyal wife, devoted to home and children, in these unflattering terms:

110

A woman who stays at home, caring for children and the house, leads an extremely sterile existence. . . . This kind of woman leads a parasitic existence that can aptly be described as "legalized prostitution."[65]

The Marxist feminists also assume that there is no such thing as a maternal instinct. Roxanne Dunbar writes:

Our demand for collective public child care is throwing into question the private family (or individual) ownership of children. . . . In reality, the family has fallen apart. Nearly half of all marriages end in divorce, and the family unit is a decadent energy-absorbing, destructive, wasteful institution for everyone except the ruling class. . . .

How will the family unit be destroyed? . . . The alleviation of the duty of full-time child care in private situations will free many women to make decisions they could not before. . . . Women will feel free to leave their husbands and become economically independent, either through a job or welfare. . . .

Most women have been programmed from early childhood for a role, maternity, which develops a certain consciousness of care for others, self-reliance, flexibility, noncompetitiveness, cooperation, and materialism. . . . If these "maternal" traits, conditioned into women, are desirable traits, they are desirable for everyone, not just women. . . .

We can demand the development of maternal skills and consciousness in men.[66]

Lisa Hobbs is another feminist who believes that the "maternal instinct" is programmed into women by male culture and that now it must be programmed out. She writes in *Love and Liberation*:

If we choose to ignore the present realities of population growth and so close our eyes to the possibilities of the future, we will go on programming little girls into the belief that only by running a house and bearing babies can they vindicate their existence and find fulfillment. . . .

The time has not only come, it is past due, when marriage and motherhood as a life's goal should be cut out of the training of the female child. . . . The giving of dolls should be abandoned just as many women have refused to give their young sons guns, for one is proving just as destructive as the other. . . . It has become imperative that we speak before woman, kept in ignorance by man for so long, destroys the world. The day has come when motherhood should be the lot and privilege of a select minority.[67]

Obviously there are a lot of women in and out of the women's movement who don't think much of the maternal instinct, and perhaps this is the very reason why patriarchy inculcated maternal values in its females starting at a very early age. Yet it is hard to believe that a woman's experience as her mother's daughter, desiring to emulate her mother and relive that special relationship between mother and child, does not work on the psyches of many women. It is hard to believe that the desire to project one's life into the future beyond death through one's children is not present within the emotions of many women.

111

Since many women as well as men exhibit what we call the "maternal instinct," perhaps we ought to rename it the "nurturing instinct"—which can be found in both sexes. It would include all of those emotions and motives in men and women that bring heightened joy at the birth of a child and make us care for the new infant with all the love and concern possible.

Perhaps the maternal instinct is simply a sense of maternal responsibility coupled with an implicit recognition that the human infant requires particularly intense maternal care. All of us have been infants and all of us have known what it is to need a mother, and perhaps it is this haunting sense of maternal responsibility that many of the women's liberationists reject when they speak callously about turning over their infants to child-care centers so that the women can enjoy equal freedom with men. Of course, with the population explosion, women have been given the permission to dispense with their motherhood role and to seek other nonmaternal life styles. However women will still continue to be the source of the next generation; and there will be a next generation, no matter how small or large it will be.

Jane Beckman Lancaster, writing in *The Female Experience*, explains why the maternal role, of necessity, will continue to impose restrictions on women:

> So far as the future of the female role goes, there is little evidence to suggest that women who choose to forgo motherhood or who become too old to reproduce cannot take the same roles as men. . . . However, the demands of the maternal role itself, imposed by the biologically based needs of children, will continue to affect the lives of many women.
>
> Human infants need stable caretakers during their early years if they are to develop healthy personalities. Day-care centers generally are not adequate substitutes for mothers. . . . A small child needs some stable figure, male or female, who is willing to play a nurturing, protective role for the first four to six years of its life. This person, whether biological parent, grandparent or foster parent, must be willing to give the same commitment to the child that the child gives in return. . . .
>
> Persons who elect to play the maternal role must accept some restrictions on their activities. . . . Biology does place role restrictions on women. But it is not the biology of women themselves; it is the biologically based emotional needs of children that are demanding and undeniable.[68]

Thus we can see why to many women's libbers children are the real enemies of female liberation. They do make slaves of their mothers. A woman with a maternal instinct understands this and is willing to make the sacrifices that maternity demands.

There is also evidence that a loving, protective, loyal husband enhances a woman's maternal feelings and that his presence in her life makes child rearing more fulfilling. Women, for example, whose husbands are present at a natural childbirth delivery experience far more positive and elated feelings about themselves and the infant than women who go through the normal kind of delivery.[69] The latter experience, in fact, may provoke negative feelings in the new mother.

Related to the maternal instinct are also the sexual aspects of the mother-infant relationship, particularly in respect to breastfeeding. According to psychologist Niles Newton, in an article entitled "Trebly Sensuous Woman":

> A mother-infant relationship without enjoyable breastfeeding is in some ways similar to marriage without enjoyable sex. . . . The survival of the human race has long depended on the satisfaction gained from the two voluntary acts of reproduction—intercourse and breastfeeding. . . . Direct breast stimulation and breastfeeding both can trigger orgasm in some women, although less marked reactions are more usual. . . . The sensuous nature of breastfeeding is seldom recognized in our society for the same reason that orgasm during delivery occurs so rarely: our culture makes a strenuous effort to keep sexual pleasure out of the nursing experience.[70]

Obviously nature intended to leave as little to chance as possible in making breastfeeding pleasurable. The infant needed the nourishment *and* the body warmth too badly.

Perhaps the most extreme denial of the maternal instinct is to be found in Shulamith Firestone's *The Dialectic of Sex*, one of the more important and radical of the feminist books, dedicated to Simone de Beauvoir and strongly pro-Marxist. Ms. Firestone writes:

> *Pregnancy is barbaric.* I do not believe, as many women are now saying, that the reason pregnancy is viewed as not beautiful is due strictly to cultural perversion. . . . Pregnancy is the temporary deformation of the body of the individual for the sake of the species.
>
> Moreover, childbirth *hurts.* And it isn't good for you. Three thousand years ago, women giving birth "naturally" had no need to pretend that pregnancy was a real trip, some mystical orgasm (that far-away look). The Bible said it: pain and travail. The glamor was unnecessary: women had no choice. They didn't dare squawk. But at least they could scream as loudly as they wanted during their labor pains. . . .
>
> Today all this has been confused. The cult of natural childbirth itself tells us how far we've come from true oneness with nature. Natural childbirth is only one more part of the reactionary hippie-Rousseauean Return-to-Nature, and just as self-conscious. Perhaps a mystification of childbirth, true faith, makes it easier for the woman involved. Pseudoyoga exercises, twenty pregnant women breathing deeply on the floor, may even help some women develop "proper" attitudes (as in "I didn't scream once"). The squirming husband at the bedside, like the empathy pains of certain tribesmen ("Just look what I go through with you, dear"), may make a woman feel less alone during her ordeal. But the fact remains: childbirth is at best necessary and tolerable. It is not fun.
>
> (Like shitting a pumpkin, a friend of mine told me when I inquired about the Great-Experience-You're-Missing. What's-wrong-with-shitting-shitting-can-be-fun says the School of the Great Experience. It hurts, she says. What's-wrong-with-a-little-pain-as-long-as-it-doesn't-kill-you? answers

the School. It is boring, she says. Pain-can-be-interesting-as-an-experi-
ence says the School. Isn't that a rather high price to pay for interesting
experience? she says. But-look-you-get-a-reward, says the School: a-baby-
all-your-own-to-fuck-up-as-you-please. Well, that's something she says.
But how do I know it will be male like you?)[71]

With an attitude like that toward childbearing, it is not surprising
that Ms. Firestone advocates the development of artificial reproduction techniques to spare women the trauma of pregnancy and childbirth. She elaborates:

> Artificial reproduction is not inherently dehumanizing. At very least,
> development of an option should make possible an honest reexamina-
> tion of the ancient value of motherhood. At the present time, for a
> woman to come out openly against motherhood on principle is physically
> dangerous. She can get away with it only if she adds that she is neurotic,
> abnormal, childhating and therefore "unfit." ("Perhaps later . . . when
> I'm better prepared.") This is hardly a free atmosphere of inquiry. Until
> the taboo is lifted, until the decision not to have children or not to have
> them "naturally" is at least as legitimate as traditional childbearing,
> women are as good as forced into their female roles.[72]

I have quoted Ms. Firestone at length to demonstrate how extremely anti-maternal some women can be, thus indicating that
the "maternal instinct" is by no means an innate female drive. Nor
is Ms. Firestone's anti-maternalism limited to the experiences of
pregnancy and childbirth. In a chapter entitled "Down With Childhood," she writes: "The heart of woman's oppression is her childbearing and childrearing roles."[73] And the prison in which all of this oppression takes place, she tells us, is the "patriarchal nuclear family." She
then goes on to develop a fascinating thesis that childhood is a myth
created by civilization, that the differentiation of childhood from
adulthood is a rather recent cultural development. She writes:

> Before the advent of the nuclear family and modern schooling, child-
> hood was as little as possible distinct from adult life. The child learned
> directly from the adults around him, emerging as soon as he was able
> into adult society.[74]

However, she contends, modern society has changed all of that, particularly with the development of schooling:

> . . . The school was the institution that structured childhood by effectively
> segregating children from the rest of society, thus retarding their growth
> into adulthood and their development of specialized skills for which the
> society had use. As a result they remained economically dependent for
> longer and longer periods of time; thus family ties remained unbroken.[75]

Ms. Firestone basically sees women *and* children as equal victims
of patriarchy and argues that women have been forced to rear children far more than children need rearing. On that last point she has

some valuable insights, but tends to get carried away beyond the point of no return. She states:

> And with the increase and exaggeration of children's dependence, woman's bondage to motherhood was also extended to its limits. Women and children are now in the same lousy boat. Their oppressions began to reinforce one another. To the mystique of the glories of childbirth, the grandeur of "natural" female creativity, was now added a new mystique about the glories of childhood itself and the "creativity" of child*rearing*. ("Why, my dear, what could be more creative than raising a child?") By now people have forgotten what history has proven: that "raising" a child is tantamount to retarding his development. The best way to raise a child is to LAY OFF.[76]

And so, she concludes, "The interrelated myths of femininity and childhood were the instruments of oppression." Ms. Firestone ends her chapter on childhood in this interesting, impassioned way:

> We must include the oppression of children in any program for feminist revolution or we will be subject to the same failing of which we have so often accused men: of not having gone deep enough in our analysis, of having missed an important substratum of oppression merely because it didn't directly concern *us*. I say this knowing full well that many women are sick and tired of being lumped together with children: that they are no more our charge and responsibility than anyone else's will be an assumption crucial to our revolutionary demands. It is only that we have developed, in our long period of related sufferings, a certain compassion and understanding for them that there is no reason to lose now; we know where they're at, what they're experiencing, because we, too, are still undergoing the same kind of oppressions. The mother who wants to kill her child for what she has had to sacrifice for it (a common desire) learns to love that same child only when she understands that it is as helpless, as oppressed as she is, and by the same oppressor: then her hatred is directed outward, and "motherlove" is born. But we will go further: our final step must be the elimination of the very conditions of femininity and childhood themselves that are now conducive to this alliance of the oppressed, clearing the way for a fully "human" condition. There are no children yet able to write their own books, tell their own story. We will have to, one last time, do it for them.[77]

Thus, Ms. Firestone paints a rather strange picture of a revolutionary alliance between anti-maternal women and suffering children, all victims of the same patriarchal oppression. Her arguments border on the unreal and arise from a frame of reference with which few people, including women, can identify. It would be a mistake to assume that feminists in general share her anti-maternalism. Feminist sociologist Alice S. Rossi, one of the founders of NOW and a mother of two children, reflected on such views in an interview published in *The Female Experience*:

> When it comes to views on men, marriage and motherhood, I certainly am not in total agreement with the radical feminists. Take a book like Shulamith Firestone's *Dialectic of Sex*, for example. What is the mes-

sage? It pooh-poohs maternity. In fact there is a curious irony here, which is that Firestone has bought a very masculine, technocratic concept of the future. . . . For example, Firestone argues that because there is discomfort in pregnancy and pain in childbirth, let's get rid of it. The sooner we can have artificial fertilization and gestation, have our kids without our bodies, the better. Because housework and raising children aren't always edifying, let's institutionalize them away, get rid of the whole business. This is presumably to use technology in the new world. One of the major problems with this philosophy, of course, is that it blunts the impact of legitimate feminist ideas on a lot of unawakened women. . . .

The point is that the radical feminists have not been through all that much yet. Most of them have not had children. Most of them are not married, and they are under 30. They simply have not been through it. They don't know the pleasures, and they are afraid to experience some of the bittersweet pains. . . .

They haven't experienced the positive side of parenthood so they don't know how to talk about it. They haven't experienced the pleasures of *giving* in marriage, not just *getting* in heterosexual and homosexual relationships.[78]

Another feminist mother, Letty Cottin Pogrebin, in an article entitled "Motherhood!" in the May 1973 issue of *Ms.*, wrote:

I have found myself, now and then, in fierce arguments with people who can see no merit whatsoever in having children. These are not the proponents of Zero Population Growth; they are arguing as if they believe in zero population. And no matter how I resolve never to proselytize parenthood, I find myself extolling the joys of a small child's smile in answer to their accusations that I produce offspring to guarantee my own immortality. . . .

If one has never known thunderous fear when a child is lost in a crowd, or shared the sweet intensity of a small boy's secret, or felt the blissful vertigo of a little girl's first bicycle solo, then explaining mother love—or father love, for that matter (though here I must speak only for myself)—will be rather like explaining the sea to a landlocked people.

Thus the feminists contain within their movement extremely divergent views and attitudes toward motherhood. The trouble with Ms. Firestone and her obsession with male oppression is that she seems to miss the whole point about life and its struggles. The "oppression" we must all face—men, women, and children alike—is the simple "oppression" of reality: the oppression of winter, hurricanes, earthquakes, drought, disease, human want, human hungers, aging, etc. Life battles against the elements on this planet. Life battles to survive. The entire effort of life is to survive in a basically benevolent universe that nevertheless has its many dangers and pains. That life requires effort, work, self-discipline, and the sacrifices made for children for the sake of survival goes without saying. That in the long run we *all* suffer, sometimes far more than we enjoy, is par for the course. We don't put up with life's pains because we are masochists. But if it were not for human masochism—the ability to make something positive of pain—life would be intolerable. Masochism, which is so important to the self-sacrificial aspects of love, is a tremendous aid to survival. It only becomes dangerous when we become so addicted to masochistic pleasure that we create more suffering than comes to us in the natural course of life.

Unfortunately life will always be "oppressive" because survival makes painful demands on us. Subsistence is the primary demand for survival and it is no small feat on the part of the males to have gone out into the world and reshaped it through science and commerce to create a world in which many more people can live. But men could never have done this if they had had to worry constantly about their wives' chastity and their children's safety. And so they created a system—albeit an imperfect one—in which they could achieve basic material security for many millions of people. But their technological success did not eliminate the potential oppressiveness of reality. Thus anyone who intends to find fulfillment and joy through technology alone is in for a rude awakening. The chief source of happiness for most human beings is still other human beings primarily through intimate relationships. Children achieve their primary happiness through a relationship with their mothers or some other close parental figures. Adults achieve intimacy primarily through sexual love with a nonrelative that leads to commitment and responsibility. But it is becoming apparent that an adult ability to achieve happiness depends a great deal on what one has experienced as a child in that primary relationship with one's mother. The mother-infant relationship is the crucible of emotional growth. A woman with a maternal instinct seems to understand that.

In summing up, how shall we characterize the "maternal instinct"? First, we must recognize the individual differences of women. The fact that nature has equipped them with the biological means to bear children is not enough to give them a maternal instinct. After all, the human race was divided into two sexes to facilitate the reproductive process. Thus to expect women to have an innate maternal instinct apart from the reproductive process that involves *both* sexes is perhaps expecting too much. Women, I believe, get their maternal instincts from their mothers. The mothers they had seem to pass on to them a positive feeling about child-mother intimacy, a positive feeling about mother-love. Men too can acquire the same maternal instinct from their mothers, and they translate it as adults into father-love. But because women, through their bodies, can experience the full added maternal dimension in physical terms, they can experience a stronger bond with their children than can most men. I believe that the maternal instinct is learned in much the same way that the ability to love is learned, from one's own early childhood emotional experiences. Child abusers, doctors have discovered, were abused themselves as children. The crucial emotional learning takes place in our earliest years, and that is why the emotional vibrations a mother transmits to her infant are so very important in that child's emotional development.

It is perhaps just as well that women who do not like children, who fear childbirth, who see children as oppressors and intruders, not have them. Perhaps too many women who should not have children have them, and that is why there is so much juvenile unhappiness today. In that respect we can see good in the feminist movement if it wins for those women with no desire to become mothers the right to adopt life-styles more in keeping with their personalities. No woman should be forced to become a mother if she does not want to become one. But this does not in turn justify the mass killing of the unborn merely because women who don't want children are careless about preventing conception.

I believe that the humane quality of a society—and the women's libbers talk grandly of humanizing society—can be judged by how its adults deal with children and childbirth. I was brought up in a family where the birth of each child was greeted as a tremendous blessing, where each child's special identity was recognized while it was still in its mother's womb, where the death of an infant or a young child was mourned intensely. There was always the sense of oneness, uniqueness, specialness about each new addition to the family. That particular infant became an important addition to the network of relationships that is the family, and even an adopted child was welcomed and given his special place; all the more so because it seemed that an adopted child needed a greater measure of love than a natural child because of its initial deprivation. Thus the idea of abortion has always been abhorrent to me.

But since I am not a woman it would be equally abhorrent to me to force any woman to carry to term a pregnancy that she did not want. If I were a doctor I would not perform an abortion unless the woman's life depended on it. A society that permits the routine mass killing of the unborn because men and women are careless and irresponsible simply encourages more carelessness and irresponsibility as well as a degradation of the sanctity of life. I believe in a woman having control over her own body. But I also believe in her having control over her sexuality. A society that encourages premarital recreational sex will have to deal with the consequences of legalized abortion and its demoralizing effect on all human relationships. The fetus is in the earliest process of becoming a full human being, with its own chromosomes having already determined its unique features and traits. It is not a worm or a glob.

To encourage recreational sex at a time when we are discouraging childbirth seems to be a contradiction. Yet we increase the need for abortion when we encourage recreational sex. Of course if women can't get abortions legally they will get them illegally, with the added dangers to health. That is one of the arguments for legalized abortion. There is no way to prevent a people from cheapening life if that is what they intend to do. Just as recreational sex ultimately diminishes the pleasure of sex, so the easy availability of abortion cheapens the concept of life. It cannot be otherwise. Just as promiscuity makes it impossible to enjoy the pleasures of loyalty, abortion makes it impossible to grant life greater sanctity.

It is all a matter of choice. A society must decide what values it is going to uphold. If indiscriminate sexual pleasure is to be elevated above the sanctity of human life, then the society that adopts such moral standards must live with its consequences.

8

The Family in Crisis

Everyone needs to belong to someone, and the worst fate that can befall anyone is to belong to no one. We all start out by belonging to our parents. That early sense of belonging is very important to our healthy emotional growth, and if it is missing or mutilated in our childhood we suffer its deficit for all of our lives. Everyone is related to someone and even adopted children yearn to know who their true blood relatives are. The curiosity is there, not so much to know parents who may be long dead or who may have abandoned them, but to know where one came from and whether one has brothers and sisters and other blood relations.

Go to any major airport on any Sunday afternoon and watch parents meeting children, or wives meeting husbands, or children meeting parents. Watch the intense embraces, the tears, the laughter, the hugs, the joy. Some families are emotional, some are reserved, some have a clean prosperous look, some look poor but buoyant, some are refined, some are crude. But what all of them have in common is the sense of belonging that comes from having nurtured and been nurtured, of having fed and been fed, from having loved and been loved. The family is where you were first fed milk, had your face washed, and were dressed in warm clothes. It's where someone first said "I love you"—or "I hate you"—and where you no doubt first said it back. It's where for as long as you live you are part of a special emotional fabric—positive or negative—but for most people positive. Your relatives look for you at birthdays and marriages and christenings and funerals, and when you die they are usually the ones who bury you. The family is where it all happens, creating emotional bonds and loyalties—weak or strong—that last a lifetime. As Robert Frost put it, but not quite in these words, "A family is where they have to let you in." And when children become adults they start new families of their own.

The curious thing about the family is that its nucleus is made up of two people who are not at all blood-related, or at least not closely blood-related. Some cousins do marry. But most people marry others who were at one time total strangers, people who may have been born and raised thousands of miles apart. They join together, sometimes after only a short courtship, and create children who are then blood-related to their parents and their siblings. A brother and sister will be brother and sister forever. A mother and daughter will be mother and daughter forever. But a husband and wife may not be husband and wife forever. In fact, the most vulnerable point in the family is its nucleus—and the cause of its vulnerability and instability is also the cause of its creation in the first place: sexual attraction.

What about love? Sexual attraction starts it all. It is what makes us choose one stranger over another to become involved with. There may or may not be premarital sex, and there may be a strong sexual attraction or a somewhat weak one, depending on experience, upbringing, appetite, and drive. But whatever the case, physical intimacy is necessary if children are to be created and if sexual tension and hunger are to be alleviated. There are marriages without sex, but there can't be any natural families without it.

It is generally acknowledged that the family was an outgrowth of the patriarchal system that came into being when men developed a paternal instinct, that is, an emotional and economic interest in paternity. The earliest family organization did not resemble our modern small nuclear family. It was what sociologists call a *stem family*: the head was the oldest male parent, who ruled a number of sons and their wives and children. The work of the household, which included many home-industry tasks that are no longer performed in families, was divided according to the status of the female involved, with the oldest wife supervising the smooth operation of the whole. The family in those preindustrial times was a sort of economic unit organized for survival in a world with few amenities and lots of hardship. You lived according to the rules of the patriarch, who represented final authority and governed your life, and there was very little room for the luxury of romantic love in such a setting. You had the security and protection of a large family, but you had no freedom to develop in ways detrimental to the family.

There was no place in such a social organization for detached persons. Everyone belonged to a household and was under the rule of a *pater familias*.

As society began to industrialize and people became more dependent on industry for survival, the authority and economic power of the patriarch was undermined. The stem family evolved into the *extended family*; that is, a nuclear family including grandparents and perhaps a few other close relatives. Related families tended to live close together, so that one knew one's aunts and uncles and cousins almost as well as one knew one's immediate family. But with the growth of industrial society, the tremendous migrations of families, and the increased freedom and mobility of individuals, the *nuclear family* has been reduced to its minimal economic and emotional functions. Now that the state has assumed more and more of the welfare functions of the family, the family has become whatever two people, brought together by romantic love, can or want to make it.

The nuclear family is really a product of modern industrial life, tailored to its economic realities. It has not been with us long enough to stand the test of time or to have undergone all the adjustments necessary to see it through the transition from the postindustrial era to the era of advanced technology. The Western world is simply changing too rapidly, and postindustrial technology has only been with us such a very short period of time—since World War II—for the nuclear family to have been fully tested. Therefore, while much of the criticism leveled at the nuclear family may be justified, it is unfair to attack an institution that has not really had time to become an institution. In a sense the nuclear family is one of those pseudoinstitutions created by modern advertising much in the same way that Christmas or the wedding have been commercialized and exploited to the point where their spiritual substance is assumed to exist but is rarely examined or experienced. The modern nuclear family, idealized in consumer magazines, beautifully packaged, is vigorously sold and eagerly bought by value-starved young marrieds, but without any real understanding of the human dynamics behind it. The consumer buys the package, not the substance.

Thus both the form of the family and its substance have changed. The patriarchal stem family was an organization for survival in a world that made harsh demands on everyone. There was little room in it for romantic love or other self-indulgences. There was little privacy. It was like living in a commune with an authoritarian patriarchal hierarchy. Life's pleasures and deprivations were taken in stride. You had virtually no opportunity for nonconformity because survival out of the family was almost impossible, but you had the security of knowing the limits of your life.

The extended family of the transitional industrial period provided more flexibility, more freedom to go one's way. But it still provided a good deal of needed emotional and economic security. Families tended to be large, lived close to other kinsmen, and included more than two generations.

The modern nuclear family, however, provides the least emotional security of all. In many cases it is held together by the weak mixture of sex and romance, and splits apart before the children are fully grown. If it remains intact, the children leave it as soon as they can achieve independence. The aging couple then retire to a mobile home in a warmer climate, or wind up in a special housing project for the elderly, visited by their children and grandchildren much in the way that people are visited in hospitals and prisons and mental institutions. If we live in an age of anxiety, much of the anxiety must be due to the increasing isolation of individuals in a society that makes it more and more difficult to establish satisfying and durable emotional attachments.

It is important to note that originally the family was created as a means of maintaining the survival and social values of patriarchal society, with its prevailing repressive attitude toward sex. Until only the present century, marriages were generally arranged by parents, with little or no consideration given to the sexual and romantic aspects of a husband-wife relationship. If the match made sense economically and practically, it was assumed it would make sense sexually. Besides, what was considered of much greater importance in marriage than sexual pleasure and romantic titillation was family cohesion, continuity, and stability. You didn't choose your parents, with whom you were intimately and emotionally involved all your life, so why should you choose your spouse? The permanence of the husband-wife relationship was not based on the romantic needs of the husband and wife, but on the survival needs of the children. Thus stability and continuity were to be the most important products of family life, and the disruptive potential of man's vagrant sexuality was unequivocally held in check. Sex was sacrificed on the altar of stability and continuity. Its only function was procreative.

Why were stability and continuity so important? Because it was probably recognized by human beings, long before psychoanalysts came on the scene, that the emotional health of both adults and children, as well as economic survival, depended a great deal on family stability and continuity, and that the stability of society in general depended on the social cohesion of families. We are relearning all of this today, as the disastrous results of divorce and family disintegration are reflected not only in a terrible toll of juvenile unhappiness but of adult unhappiness as well.

Why do we have the highest rate of marital failure today? Because too many families are created by couples whose bond is based on sexual pleasure and satisfaction, and when that pleasure and satisfaction are replaced by frustration and anger, the relationship deteriorates. When "love" is based on sexual satisfaction alone, it ends when sexual satisfaction is gone. Therefore an enduring relationship is always based on a more reliable bond than sex alone. Too many couples marry, however, on the basis of a strong sexual attraction and little else. They marry with the expectation that that strong sexual attraction will always be there. But then, as they live together, they discover that there is a difference between their sexual appetites. One partner begins to feel frustrated because the other doesn't want to engage in sex often enough. The conditions of married life begin to change the pattern of arousal. Frustration leads to anger, which leads to fights, which leads to estrangement and more frustration. Extreme frustration leads to bitterness and hatred, and thus a couple is led to the verge of a breakup. Unless the couple have enough residual love and appreciation for each other as human beings rather than sexual partners alone, they will be unable to break the cycle of frustration-anger-hatred and reverse the trend toward breakup.

Because people have come to believe that sexual desire and satisfaction must be the major ingredients in the cement of a husband-and-wife relationship, the modern nuclear family has become an extremely unstable institution. The statistics bear this out. In 1973 there were 16 million divorced citizens in the United States, representing at least 8 million broken marriages. The number of children traumatized by these family breakups amounts to at least 16 million. In 1973 alone 913,000 couples were divorced, or one for every four marriages. It is expected that the divorce rate will reach more than a million couples in 1974. The year 1973 also saw the lowest birthrate in American history, as well as the lowest first-marriage rate since the Depression. The Women's Liberation movement and the sexual revolution are no doubt partly responsible for the surge in divorce. The percentage of women initiating divorce proceedings has increased enormously, and the runaway wife is no longer a rarity. The fact that a woman can get a court to force her husband to leave makes it unnecessary for most women to run away. But she can't force her children to leave with him, and so some wives just disappear. The *Boston Herald American* of January 12, 1974, described one case where a man came home and found the apartment stripped of furniture, his wife gone and his small son asleep on a mattress on the floor. The man found his wife a year later but she had no interest in returning to her husband and child.

And it isn't only the younger couples who are breaking up. *Good Housekeeping* of February 1974 described the breakup of an old marriage. The wife—after twenty-five years of marital life and three grown children—decided that her husband was too dependent, too childlike, and threw him out. She rationalized her action in this way:

"If love is need and dependence, then S———did love me. If love is wanting to care for and protect, then I loved him. But dependence and care, a natural bond between mother and child, is no basis for a marriage. When one person does all the leaning, respect erodes—and with it, sexual feeling. S——— —I saw this at last—had become my fourth child."

And so it goes. Old families are breaking up because one partner becomes too dependent and sexual feeling has dried up in the other, and new families start disintegrating before the infants are out of the cribs. But why the sudden epidemic of divorce that started in 1969? After all, marital dissatisfaction is not a new phenomenon. Those of us who were brought up in the thirties and forties were certainly aware of parental discord. One Boston magistrate, Judge J. Fox, speaking from twenty years of experience on the bench, explained it:

> What used to pass for common irritants in marriage is now a cause for running to court. Marriages may be made in heaven but the maintenance work has to be done down here. The discipline, the love of family isn't there any longer. They won't take in stride the pain that comes with such an intimate relationship.[79]

One of the more disturbing reasons for the current increase in divorce is the desire to escape parental responsibility. In a major cover story on family breakups, *Newsweek* of March 12, 1973, reported this alarming trend:

> Many people seem to need relief from parenting. One of the more startling developments in recent years is the growing number of broken families in which *neither* parent wants custody. "It's a critical problem," says John R. Evans, chief judge of the juvenile court in Denver, "and it's definitely increasing. We are having a wholesale abdication of parental responsibility. We either have to find placement for the children or give them to welfare." The dread of getting stuck with the children may even be holding some marriages together. Chicago divorce lawyer Joseph N. DuCanto tells of one couple that has entered into a written agreement: the first one to ask for a divorce has to take the kids.

Another reason why divorces have increased so greatly is because they are so much easier to get. New "no fault" divorce laws are making divorces obtainable virtually on any grounds. According to *U. S. News and World Report* (April 22, 1974):

> California, which far outdistanced other states in 1973 with 117,000 divorces, pioneered the "no fault" divorce law in 1970. As one attorney describes it, a decree is granted on little more than a statement by either of the partners as follows:
> "In the course of our marriage, there arose irreconcilable differences which led to the irremediable breakdown of our marriage. There is no chance for reconciliation."

Some counselors and attorneys see these changes in divorce laws as causing many marriages to end unnecessarily.

Says Donald Schiller, Chicago lawyer and vice chairman of the American Bar Association's committee on divorce law:

"Individuals now take divorce as an easy solution to marital problems. Many people divorce before giving a potentially good marriage a chance, and many people divorce without looking at their personal problems that could be solved by counseling—so they are back in court for second and third divorces without learning anything."

Thus, if we expect nothing but sex and romantic titillation to hold the nucleus of a family together, families are going to disintegrate at an ever-increasing rate. But there are indications that the divorce wave of the early seventies will level off as more and more people become aware of the basic psychological reason for marriage and family: to give a person a sense of belonging, the same sense of belonging he had as a child and that he still needs as an adult. *U.S. News and World Report* quoted one divorced businesswoman as saying: "Sometimes the pain of marriage is better than the emptiness of divorce."

People marry because, as one divorcee put it, "People are just desperate to have someone know them. And marriage is the only way." The *Newsweek* report on broken families ended with these evocative observations:

The hunger to taste that intimacy fires the dream of marriage and the dream dies hard. "My daughter says she doesn't have a family, only a mother," divorcee Karol Hope wrote in a recent edition of *Momma*, the newspaper she edits for a group of single mothers in Los Angeles. "She wants a daddy and a baby and a crazy, raucous family dinner hour. My heart saddens. I want those good feelings for her. Something is missing. I am missing the satisfaction of a life unfolding according to plan, ordained by God, my mother and the president of the PTA. Rhythm is interrupted. Permanence is gone. So is security."

Routine, permanence, security—an unromantic set of virtues that will continue to lure most Americans into marriage for years to come. The trouble is that, in less exalted form, they will undoubtedly continue to become the very banalities, habit and humdrum that help drive us to the divorce courts.

It is obvious that what we want most from family life—the emotional security that comes from cohesion and continuity—cannot be obtained from vagrant sexuality or romantic emotionalism. It is obtained from commitment, self-sacrifice, and love in the deepest sense, the love that deemphasizes the sexual and emphasizes the spiritual. It may mean developing a higher tolerance for emotional pain and sexual frustration in order to gain the deeper satisfactions of loyalty and unequivocal belonging. Yet, if we take the statistics seriously, we find that for many people it is not easy to establish a sense of loyalty and belonging if the feelings are not fully reciprocated.

Of course there can be no nuclear family without marriage, yet

127

some people see marriage as an utterly hopeless institution. Writes Richard Boeth, general editor of *Newsweek*, twice married and twice divorced:

> It is novel and bizarre of us latter-day Westernoids to imagine that we can make something tolerable of marriage. It doesn't seem to have occurred to any earlier era that this was even possible. The Greeks railed against marriage, the Romans mocked and perverted it, the early Christian fathers loathed it with psychotic intensity, making a sacrament of marriage precisely in order to channel and dam up the sexual energies of the faithful. (By the seventh century the church was denying the eucharist to couples who had made love any time in the previous three days.) . . .
>
> At what time, in what place, did marriage have a happy name among its practitioners? Mankind has surely known its thousands of buoyant marriages—Albert and Queen Victoria, maybe, or John and Abigail Adams—but they stand for marriage in about the same degree that the Birdman of Alcatraz stands for the prison system. And history considers only the rich; among the poor, marriage was, on the whole, unspeakable.

Yet as unspeakable, intolerable, and painful as marriage is, it just happens to be less unspeakable, intolerable, and painful than loneliness. Perhaps people will have to learn to measure marriage not in terms of what gives them the greatest pleasure, but in terms of what gives them the least pain, for there is no continuing arrangement on earth among or between human beings, heterosexual or homosexual, that does not entail pain to some degree. Everyone who has been in love or has been a child or has been a parent knows this. And certainly everyone who has been married knows this.

Some marriages break up because one partner thinks he will find a little more happiness with another spouse. That he may at the same time cause misery to a houseful of children is not figured in the equation of pleasure versus pain. We are generally concerned with our own pleasure only and tend to minimize the pain we can cause others. This is not to say that no divorce is justified. It merely means that people should face the prospect of living with another person more realistically than they do. We have painted a conformist ideal of the middle-class nuclear family, with all the marvelous accouterments our technology has given us, only to find that happiness does not come in a can, cannot be bought with a charge account, and is not something tangible like a shiny automobile in a showroom. Happiness is the end product of countless actions and interactions. It is a state of mind that comes out of being and doing, and unless you can be and do what it is that creates happiness within you, you never really achieve it. Too many people feel that happiness is the result of something that is done to you, rather than the result of the many things you do.

Are there any viable alternatives to monogamous marriage? Are there any viable alternatives to the family? Perhaps some variations are suitable for some special people. But all of the recent experiments in group marriage and in communal living, for example, have only confirmed what many astute observers of human behavior have already suspected: that man is, in his intimate love relationships, basically a monogamous animal. Carl Rogers, in his study *Becoming Partners: Marriage and Its Alternatives,* writes:

It has been borne on me . . . that it is far more difficult to sustain a healthy and satisfying relationship in a triad or a group marriage of four or more than it is to sustain it in a two-person marriage. . . . Consequently, communes have fallen apart because of the inability to resolve the problems of highly complex relationships.

Dr. Deane William Ferm, in an article about marriage in *Parents* magazine (February 1974), comments:

Other recent studies indicate that monogamous coupling tends to become the standard in most communes, and that women members soon become the primary advocates of conventional family living with close contact between parents and their own children. Some relatively intimate structure seems required to bring order out of chaos.

When Dr. Wardell B. Pomeroy of Kinsey Report fame was asked in a *Playboy* discussion panel (September 1973) if traditional marriage was breaking down, he answered: "If you mean by traditional marriage a dyadic relationship between a man and a woman who are legally married, then no. I don't think there is a breaking down. There's more of it than ever, and it's here to stay. If you're thinking of traditional marriage as a male-dominated, chauvinistic institution, then yes, I think it's breaking down." On group marriage, one of the so-called alternatives to monogamy, he had this to say: "One of the things I'd say about group marriage is that it's tremendously complicated. To have a dyad is difficult enough. When you add a third and a fourth person, the complications are increased exponentially, not just arithmetically. The majority of them don't work, or they work for only a limited time—a year, two years, four years. They fall apart because of the tremendous complexities. It's said, and I believe it, that the sexual interaction is the least important confusion; they can usually handle that. It's the other interpersonal relationships—dominance, money, child care, for example—that aren't so simple to contend with."

Thus, we can be reasonably sure that the dyad relationship between men and women will continue to be the basis of the nuclear family. The family is not only essential for the emotional security of children, it is also essential for the emotional security of most adults. It is not without significance that the highest suicide rate is to be found among detached adult males who must live with emotional isolation and loneliness. Emotional separation is a terrifying predicament that leads to hopelessness and, in many cases, suicide. The skid-row alcoholic is probably the most visible and most extreme example of this predicament.

Because of our burgeoning divorce rate, however, we are now seeing an ever-increasing number of single-parent families, fathers bringing up children without mothers, mothers bringing up children without fathers. Today one of every six American children lives in a single-parent home. Stories of divorced career-women raising three or five children single-handedly can be found in the popular magazines. What they usually tell is a story of determination, strength, pride, resilience, and self-confidence—together with the financial problems, the nighttime loneliness, the searching for self. But they prove that the family can survive, even if the nucleus is truncated. They prove that a strong mother can keep things together in the face of great obstacles. Some women seem to thrive in such situations, and the children generally assume more responsibility when they see mother working so hard to keep home and hearth together. Great love and devotion between children and parent often develop in such situations.

If, however, as most psychologists and sociologists agree, the dyad nuclear family will continue to exist simply because there is no other viable substitute for it, then perhaps we ought to take a closer look at it and see what we can do to make it work better. First, we must be willing to admit that the basic differences between men and women, particularly their sexuality, are always a potential source of incompatibility. This is nothing new. As early as 131 B.C. one of the Roman Censors recommended the adoption of a law compelling everybody to marry, observing that "if it were possible to have no wives at all, everybody would gladly escape that annoyance, but since nature had so ordained that it was not possible to live agreeably with them, nor to live at all without them, regard must be had rather to permanent welfare than to transitory pleasure."[80]

Thus the sexual and emotional incompatibility between the sexes was recognized early in civilized life. That is why marriage had to be largely desexualized and made into a sacred trust, protected by strong restrictions, legal and religious, with divorce very difficult to obtain. Only in this way could such basic incompatibility be overcome for the sake of cohesion, order, stability, and security. But with the moral, legal, and religious restraints now falling apart, the family has nothing to hold it together except self-sacrificial love, something far more demanding than romantic love.

If modern marriages are disintegrating at an appalling rate, it is for two reasons: disappointment in the expectations that romantic love creates; and the growing restlessness of women who have come to believe that marriage and family are depriving them of some greater self-fulfillment as human beings. As expected, some of the most scathing criticisms of the nuclear family have come from women's libbers who, first of all, view marriage and the family as patriarchy's most effective instruments of oppression, developed primarily by men to control and subjugate women. That women do derive some important benefits from the arrangement is usually ignored.

But it would be unwise of us not to give the women's libbers' complaints and criticisms a fair hearing. While Germaine Greer has some good things to say about the extended family, she uses such adjectives as "isolated," "claustrophobic," and "neurotic" to describe the nuclear household. She writes in *The Female Eunuch* of the "intense introverted anguish of the single eye-to-eye confrontation of the isolated spouses."[81] She is particularly critical of the close intimate relationship of mother and child in the small nuclear family, where the Oedipal situation, she comments, "is now intensified to a degree which Freud would have found appalling." She elaborates:

> Father is very really a rival and a stranger. During the day the child may be bullied as often as petted: what is certain is that he has too much attention from the one person who is entirely at his disposal. The intimacy between mother and child is not sustaining and healthy. The child learns to exploit his mother's accessibility, badgering her with questions and demands which are not of any real consequence to him, embarrassing her in public, blackmailing her into buying sweets and carrying him. Dependence does not mean love.[82]

True, dependence may not mean love. But out of what does a child's love grow? Ms. Greer paints an equally dismal picture of the isolated wife who becomes increasingly antisocial:

> The home is her province, and she is lonely there. She wants her family to spend time with her for her only significance is in relation to that almost fictitious group. She struggles to hold her children to her, imposing restrictions, waiting up for them, prying into their affairs. They withdraw more and more into noncommunication and thinly veiled contempt. She begs her husband not to go out with the boys, marvels that he can stand in the pouring rain at the football and then be too tired to mend the roof or cut the grass on the finest day. She moans more and more that he doesn't care what the children are up to, that discipline is all left to her, that nobody talks to her, that she's ignorant, that she has given the best years of her life to a bunch of ungrateful hooligans.[83]

The complaints, of course, are complaints we have all heard to some degree in every family. We also complain about the weather, even though we know that there must be rain and snow and hurricanes and frosts and heat waves. But no one suggests that we do away with the weather. But Ms. Greer suggests that we do away with the nuclear family because modern man has not been able to do anything but make a mess of it. She is particularly bitter about the couple at the center of the family, who live in a kind of symbiotic cocoon. She writes:

The term *couples* itself implies the locked-off unit of male-female. . . . This is virtually what the nuclear family has become. Women's magazines sadly remark that children can have a disruptive effect on the conjugal relationship, that the young wife's involvement with her children and her exhaustion can interfere with her husband's claims on her. What a notion—a family that is threatened by its children! Contraception has increased the egotism of the couple: planned children have a pattern to fit into; at least unplanned children had some of the advantages of contingency. First and foremost, they *were* whether their parents liked it or not. In the limited nuclear family the parents are the principals and children are theirs to manipulate in a newly purposive way. . . . To be sure, I recognize that efficient contraception is necessary for sexual pleasure and that sexual pleasure is necessary, but contraception for economic reasons is another matter. "We can only afford two children" is a squalid argument, but more acceptable in our society than "we don't like children."[84]

What is Ms. Greer's solution to all of this? Since the small nuclear family is the breeding ground for neuroses of all sorts, and since we are threatened with overpopulation, she suggests that women ought not to be encouraged to create new families.

There is no reason why all women should consider themselves bound to breed. A woman who has a child is not then automatically committed to bringing it up. Most societies countenance the deputizing of nurses to bring up the children of women with state duties. The practice of putting children out to nurse did not result in a race of psychopaths. A child must have care and attention, but that care and attention need not emanate from a single, permanently present individual. . . . A group of children can be more successfully civilized by one or two women who have voluntarily undertaken the work than they can be when divided and tyrannized over by a single woman who finds herself bored and imposed upon.[85]

Ms. Greer therefore suggests the creation of self-regulating "organic families," much like the extended family, created for the purpose of raising children, with each organic family run by one or two dedicated women who enjoy mothering. The paternal role in all of this would be quite peripheral. Of course this will never come to pass on any large scale for the simple reason that too many mothers want to raise their own children. They do not feel bored or imposed upon. Granted that many mothers do feel that way, too many others, feminists and even Lesbians among them, want to have and raise their own children. The psychological and emotional need to do so is simply too great to be wished away.

It is perhaps ironic that the feminist movement should pay so little attention to the maternal imperative. This is probably due to the fact that the feminist movement is so greatly dominated by anti-maternal women. If Germaine Greer's alternative for the nuclear family seems radical, Shulamith Firestone's is even more so. Since she is aware that our sexual biology is the underpinning of the male-female relationship that forms the nucleus of the modern family, she suggests that we "free humanity from the tyranny of its biology." As a Marxist, she believes that "the failure of the Russian Revolution is directly traceable to the failure of its attempts to eliminate the family and sexual repression. . . . Any initial liberation under current socialism must always revert back to repression, because the family structure is the *source* of psychological, economic, and political oppression."[86]

So what's her alternative? A variety of life-styles: singles, some people "living together," and "households." She prefers to use the word household because "the word *family* implies biological reproduction and some degree of division of labor by sex, and thus the traditional dependencies and resulting power relations, extended over generations."[87] Eventually, children would be produced by artificial reproduction.

The radical feminists tend to become unreal when dealing with human nature. They continuously fail to understand that human institutions that have lasted as long as marriage and the family are based on human nature and that no amount of reform that does not take human nature into account is going to be of any use. Ms. Firestone might just as well have blamed the failure of the Russian Revolution on its failure to extract human nature out of human beings. Mass murder has been used over and over again to reform the human race, only to prove that the humans who are left insist on still behaving like human beings.

If few people take Germaine Greer or Shulamith Firestone seriously when it comes to the family, it is because it's impossible to take them seriously, even though they write with passion and have a lot to say that is interesting. But they seem to speak from such a limited emotional experience and with so little wisdom—but with much intellectual brilliance—that after you've read them you think you've just witnessed a spectacular display of fireworks; after which all that remains is some smoke and memories of brilliant crackling lights. And then when you return to the real world of real problems you discover how irrelevant so much of the feminist bombast is. Sometimes feminism takes on the character of a gigantic temper tantrum, with as much practical wisdom as you're likely to find in such unrelenting fury.

It is unfair to take institutions like marriage and the family at a time of great technological and social change and expect them not to reflect the stresses and strains of life in the second half of the twentieth century. What is amazing is not how inadequate these institutions are but how unimaginatively people use them. Too many people expect the institutions themselves automatically to provide happiness with little or no effort on the part of the people involved. There is the illusion that happiness comes ready-made with a wedding ceremony or a suburban home with kids as if by magic. People expect happiness to occur at the flick of a switch, like turning on the color TV or the stereo. The assumption is that an equation of things equals happiness.

Because the family is turning out to be so unstable and vulnerable in a world of uncertain moral values, some social scientists have suggested creating alternate models closer to reality than some of those suggested by the feminists. An interesting book edited by Herbert A. Otto in 1970 and entitled *The Family in Search of a Future* presented a number of such ideas. John F. Cuber, a professor of sociology at Ohio State University, suggested that in place of traditional marriage we have "pairings," that is, people pairing off for mutual convenience, with or without sex, with no suppositions regarding permanence. Responsibility for rearing and socializing children would be shared by parents and state. "More provisions for institutional and state participation would be needed in the socialization process," he concludes. Again the state is called upon to perform parental functions, as if the state has some magic formula for socialization that the parents don't. The assumption is that state functionaries, living off the parents' taxes, would be wiser and more adequate in dealing with children than the parents themselves.

Edward C. Hobbs, a professor of theology at the Church Divinity School of the Pacific, suggests a "dialogue-centered marriage" that would be a lifetime bond and difficult to break once children were present, but which would permit sexual freedom. His rationale is that since "we are in the process of abandoning the permanence of marriage while maintaining its sexual exclusiveness, we may seriously ask whether something approaching a reversal of these two attitudes toward marriage might not promote a healthier and happier model for American family structure." An interesting idea, but it is unlikely that institutionalizing infidelity will improve anything.

Sidney M. Jourard, a professor of psychology at the University of Florida, suggests serial polygamy to the same person. That is, as soon as your marriage starts going sour, you go to a family-invention consultant who helps you restructure your marriage or make the kind of radical accommodations that add up to a new marriage between the same two people.

Psychotherapist Harold Greenwald suggests other forms of marriage to be added to our socially acceptable repertory of relationships. He thinks that some couples would fare better in a nonlegal voluntary association. "If state registration were eliminated," he argues, "people would stay together for the only reason that makes marriage really viable—because they wanted to."

Ethel J. Alpenfels, professor of anthropology at New York University, suggests that since three out of four people who divorce remarry

134

within three years of their divorces, we extend social sanction to "progressive monogamy" or "serial marriage."

Margaret Mead recommends marriage in two steps, or two types of marriage: individual marriage and parental marriage. The first, individual marriage, would be between two people who wanted to know each other intimately before making a commitment for parenthood. This marriage would be easily dissolvable without complications because of its limited responsibilities. If the couple then decided they wanted to start a family, they would move into a parental marriage that would be based on a larger set of responsibilities and be more difficult to dissolve because children would be involved. This would tend to assure the kind of family continuity that children need.

And so our social scientists are busily tinkering with the contraption of matrimony to see if they can come up with a better mousetrap. But I have a feeling that it is going to take more than sociological tinkering to improve marriage. Human incompatibility will always be with us. Ultimately every marriage and every family is a variation on a theme. The institution of marriage is as flexible or inflexible as the two people involved. The sociologists assume that if we make the institution more flexible this will encourage people to be more flexible. It may and it may not. People seem to be taking matters into their own hands, choosing to live as they please. There is far greater tolerance for nonconformity these days than ever before, and it is more than likely that this tolerance will grow in depth and understanding.

But while people in general grow to accept nonconformity without feeling threatened, they will also, no doubt, prefer the traditional family to the other arrangements available. Since most people are heterosexual and monogamous and family-oriented we can expect the nuclear family, with all its faults, to be the prevalent social organization of our society. What people need to make marriage work better is a better understanding of human nature, particularly their own personal variation of it. I have no doubt that the family will survive the even more cataclysmic crises of the future. The need to belong, especially in a shattered world, will be too strong, and the beginning and end of all belonging is—whether we like it or not—in the family.

9
Maternal Politics: Prenatal

Maternity, as a biological fact, begins at the moment of conception, but maternal politics begins when the mother-to-be finds out that she is pregnant. At that moment she becomes aware that another life has started to grow within her, that another life will start impinging on her own. Some women greet this awareness with joy; others with dread and loathing; still others with ambivalence. The last group is usually torn by conflict. The woman may desire a child that her husband or boyfriend doesn't want, or she may be torn between wanting to accept the responsibility of a child and wanting the freedom to pursue a demanding career, or she may be a mother who feels that she has had enough children.

Whatever the pregnant woman decides, she must make a decision about another life whose future she controls. It is a political decision based on her power and control. She may decide to permit the new life to grow, or she may decide to kill it. Some people will object to the word "kill" when speaking of abortion. But you cannot abort an unborn child without killing it, and sometimes the killing can be quite gruesome. For example, the accepted manner for killing a fetus more than sixteen weeks old is to inject a saline solution into the amniotic sac. What excruciating torture this five-month-old, highly developed unborn human being must go through as its life processes are snuffed out has not been determined by medical science. If you object to the battering of a postnatal infant, you can hardly accept the salting out of a five-month-old prenatal one. After all, viability—that is, the ability to live outside the mother's womb—starts in the sixth month, only a month away for the infant about to be salted out of existence.

Most abortions, however, are performed in the earlier stages of pregnancy, when the developing child is sometimes no more than an inch in size, passing from the embryonic into the fetus stage. But no matter how young and small the developing human being may be, no matter how much it may look like a glob—but it never actually does look like a glob—the fact is that the mother knows that in a certain number of months a new individual will emerge, forcing upon her a long-term responsibility and a lifelong relationship. Having a child is far more than a biological process. It is a psychological and economic one, requiring a commitment that many women are not prepared to make. So it is academic whether the pregnant woman decides to kill the new human being in its earliest stages of development or in its later stages. The decision to kill the unborn child is based on its future impingement on her life. After all, it isn't pregnancy per se that bothers her, for she could live with a month-old symbiotic partner inside her if it remained that way indefinitely. But she knows that it is going to grow, and it is growth that she stops when she has it killed.

That it is a political decision based on a one-to-one relationship is obvious when you reflect on what is being decided: the life of a developing human being. And there are proabortionists who admit it. For example, Nicholas von Hoffman, in an article on abortion in *Playgirl* (August 1974), put it this way:

> Anyone who has sifted through the literature of abortion's pros and cons can't help but be struck by the thought that neither side is against killing human beings, it's *when* they disagree about. The anti-abortionists are generally inclined . . . to let 'em live till they're old enough to perish in the electric chair or on the field of battle. The liberals like to nip 'em in the bud, or, to be more precise, in the womb, although those of us who are partial to prenatal snuffings out seldom defend ourselves by claiming that abortion cuts down juvenile delinquency.

So it is conceded that killing an unborn infant is equivalent to killing a man in the electric chair or sending him to war to be killed. These are all political decisions having to do with the control of one individual over another, or a group of individuals over other individuals. The argument often given by women who want legalized abortion is that they want to have control over their bodies, that the decision to abort is one of control of self. Mr. von Hoffman writes:

> It is certain that for millions of women, abortion has come to mean that they get their bodies back from mothers, priests, brothers, and lovers

who have sought to control them for endless numbers of moral and social reasons. In the bad old days of ten years ago, this elemental right not to have unwanted strangers living in your womb was so rarely recognized that few women asserted it. . . .

I'm afraid that Mr. von Hoffman misses the point. It is not the unwanted stranger living in her womb that the mother-to-be is concerned about. Her concern is the unwanted stranger *after* he or she has emerged. It is that lifelong relationship between mother and child she is thinking about. The issue of control is not between the pregnant woman and society, but between the mother-to-be and the individual growing within her. The moral, psychological, emotional, and economic commitments of motherhood are the issues the pregnant woman grapples with. To control that situation, to pass a life or death sentence over that growing human being within her, is the political control the proabortion woman wants. Population control or church doctrines are side issues compared to the central issue of maternal responsibility and commitment to an unwanted child. Some women will let fate or "God's will" determine when they must accept the maternal commitment. Other women will insist that they retain full dictatorial control over the making of that commitment regardless of what takes place in their wombs. Of course they cannot exercise that control without the assistance of medical science, and that is where maternal politics extends beyond the control of mother over child in utero and extends itself over the legal system that previously prevented her from exercising that control. In a sense it is maternal politics in conflict with sexual politics. In our present climate, maternal politics seems to be winning the struggle.

But for most people the abortion issue is centered on the supposed issue of who is to control a woman's body: society or herself. Yet an abortion cannot be performed without the complicity of society. If women were able to perform self-abortions, the issue would be clearer than it is. But because the institutions of society must become accomplices to abortion, the issues involved become far more complex. For example, what about the legal rights of the unborn child? In legal circles there has been a trend to increase his rights as a person, or at least a potential person. Children whose mothers had taken thalidomide, even as early as two or three weeks after conception, have won cases in court for damages and have been awarded considerable sums of money for their support. Damages have likewise been awarded to unborn children harmed by automobile accidents while in their mothers' wombs.

How are we to reconcile these significant legal trends toward recognizing the rights of the unborn child with the new abortion laws that allow the life of that same unborn child to be taken for reasons that sometimes add up to no more than the mother's social convenience or psychological satisfaction? Unfortunately, women want it both ways. They want the protection of the legal system when an outside agent, such as a drug company, harms the child in utero, and they want its protection when they themselves become the agent of the child's death. Some day a woman will sue a doctor for salting out a fetus when she was too ambivalent to know what she was ordering him to do.

That society is at present blind to these complex issues was strikingly brought home to this writer by an article on abortion that appeared in the *New York Times* of August 10, 1974. The article quoted Dr. Karlia Adamsons, professor of obstetrics and gynecology at the Mount Sinai Medical School in New York as saying:

> During 1973, 177,000 abortions were performed without a single mortality. I don't know of any medical procedure of comparable complexity that can compete with that track record.

But what about the 177,000 infants who were killed in the process? For a professor of obstetrics, who is supposed to be concerned with the delivery of healthy babies, blandly to ignore the mortality of 177,000 developing human beings, borders on the insane. If anyone should know how much life there is in a prenatal infant, a professor of obstetrics should. But apparently some members of the medical profession are quite capable of participating in mass infanticide without so much as blinking an eyelash. It reminds one of the doctors in the Nazi concentration camps who were able to perform hideous experiments on adult prisoners with no qualms of conscience at all. They too were playing God.

Perhaps Dr. Robert E. Hall, author of *A Doctor's Guide to Having an Abortion*, best expressed the curiously unscientific attitude of the proabortionist members of the medical profession, with this statement:

> Few believe anymore that abortion represents the killing of a human being. It is now generally recognized that the rights of an actual human being take precedence over those of a potential human being.[88]

So it is a matter of what you *believe* abortion to be, not what it actually is. If enough people believe that abortion is not murder, then it isn't murder. If enough people believe that the earth is flat, then it's flat. Forget the facts. David R. Mace, in his book *Abortion, The Agonizing Decision*, writes:

> The fact must be faced that what abortion means is the killing of the embryo or fetus. The use of this unpleasant word is avoided in most discussions of the subject. Even in medical books the writers speak of "evacuating the contents of the uterus" or "removing the fetal tissue." But it is simply dishonest to evade the fact that the embryo or fetus is alive when the operation begins and dead when it is over. Just what has been killed is a perplexing question, which I am not competent to discuss.[89]

140

Yet it must be discussed, because it is a significant manifestation of maternal politics. If Kate Millett can mince no words in asserting the existence of sexual politics and condemning the male sex for instituting a virtual sadistic reign of terror over the female sex, then there is no reason for us not to examine maternal politics as candidly. I do this not in the interest of condemning women but in the interest of understanding them. Biology, or God, has spared men the agony or the ecstasy of having to face the maternal commitment. But it was an interest in paternity that brought about the male's need to control women, or, as Kate Millett might put it, to institutionalize sexual politics. Postnatal maternal politics existed long before male-instituted sexual politics. However prenatal maternal politics is a product of modern technology and must therefore involve the complicity of male scientists and doctors. But technology is a two-edged sword. While it has helped make abortion safer and more acceptable, it has also increased our knowledge about life before birth, and we know now that the unborn child is much more human at a surprisingly early stage in development than was ever thought possible previously.

So why don't we look at abortion from the unborn child's point of view and have a look at what goes on in the dark recesses of the mother's womb. David Mace sums up the process nicely:

> We now know that from the moment of conception a new and unique being exists with a life of its own and all the potentiality of growth into a fully developed person. Nothing will be added to this being from conception to the end of his human life, at perhaps seventy years of age, except oxygen to sustain his life and body-building chemicals to increase his size and develop the complex structures of his body that are already preplanned in the genetic package he receives when he is conceived. . . .
>
> The implantation of the zygote is simply the point at which he runs out of the original food supply the ovum provided and latches onto his mother's bloodstream. The birth of the baby is simply the point at which he switches his life support system from his mother's bloodstream to the resources of the world outside the womb. His life is an unbroken, continuous process of development, not from the cradle to the grave, but from conception to the grave. All of this is not the teaching of theology. It is the scientific teaching of biology.
>
> To destroy this life at any point is to kill a human being. If you decide that you are justified in doing this, you have crossed a very dangerous line.[90]

Thus, legalized abortion may open the door to other forms of legalized murder. All of these problems must be considered as we institutionalize prenatal maternal politics. But I am a firm believer that extensive knowledge can help us make decisions we can accept. Thus it is important to know what exactly goes on in the process of the creation of life.

The creation of life takes place after a wonderful, mysterious, and dramatic sequence of events. I am not talking about what two people

141

do in bed when they make love. That too is wonderful and often dramatic, but it does not necessarily lead to the creation of a human being. I am talking about the events that take place microscopically in the innards of human beings. None of this has anything to do with maternal politics, but the events that take place are so interesting that they are worth reviewing. The development of a human being begins with the union of two single cells, a sperm cell from the male and an egg cell from the female.

The female egg comes from the ovary of the mother. The mother has two ovaries and these contain more than a quarter-million immature egg cells. It is believed that the female has all of her eggs from the time of her birth. When a girl reaches sexual maturity, ovulation begins to take place. That is, each month one egg ripens in the alternate ovary about two weeks before an expected menstruation. The ripe egg literally bursts out of the ovary, as if irresistably compelled to break out of a prison, and falls into the trumpet-shaped opening of a hollow tube. This is the Fallopian tube, which has an internal diameter the size of a hair bristle and is about four inches long. One such tube leads from each ovary to the mother's womb, the uterus. The minute round egg has a peculiar destiny as it flows toward the uterus on a gentle current of fluids within the tube. If it is not fertilized by a male sperm cell within a very brief period of time—usually from three to twelve hours—it will disintegrate. Its bursting forth represents a peculiar gamble. If it is fertilized it will survive for the duration of a new human being's life and may be passed on to further human beings ad infinitum. If not, it dies.

If fertilization does not take place, the uterine lining, built up to receive a fertilized egg, disintegrates and results in the well-known menstrual flow. If fertilization does take place, menstruation does not occur. Thus when a woman misses her period it is a sign that she may be pregnant. The twenty-eight-day menstrual cycle is regulated by a woman's gland system that secretes the activating hormones. We call it a menstrual cycle because the most visible manifestation of it is the monthly discharge of tissue fragments, blood, and mucous secretions resulting from the disintegration of the engorged uterine lining. But the really important or central aspect of the cycle is ovulation, which is not at all visible. When menstruation is seen in the fuller context of ovulation, it becomes a fascinating biological process rather than a social trauma. That is why it is so important for young women, coming of age, to understand what is going on within them. It is the marvelous process of life, renewal and regeneration, that is taking place within them, not some shameful condition to be discussed in whispers.

The male sperm cell, which can prolong the life of the egg if it meets up with it in the dark warm confines of the Fallopian tube, is produced by the hundreds of millions in the testicles of the father. Like the female cells, the male cells have a very brief life span once they leave the testicles. They retain their fertile vigor for no more than one to two days after ejaculation. The short life of the sperm cells and of the egg cell limits the period during each menstrual cycle in which a new human being can be conceived. This period is usually confined to two days during any one month. Thus, nature has provided women with a built-in contraceptive system permitting them to enjoy much more sex than will ever result in conception. The rhythm method, of course, is based on this knowledge. The pill, on the other hand, was developed by researchers who were originally interested in getting childless women pregnant. The pill consisted of hormones that stimulated ovulation. But it was found that some hormones, when taken orally, did just the opposite. Thus was developed the contraceptive pill.

Once the male has ejaculated his semen in the female, the sperm cells start their way up toward the egg. For the great majority of sperm the way up through the uterus and the oviduct is the road to destruction. Millions succumb in the acid secretions of the vagina. Only a few dozen of the original millions reach the vicinity of the egg, which at this time is still drifting high up in the ovarian tube. In 1973 a Japanese gynecologist filmed this entire process by surgically inserting a microscopic electronic camera in the uterus of a woman. He was able to photograph a frenetic crown of sperm cells surrounding the egg, trying to find a weak spot on its surface in order to penetrate it. As soon as one sperm cell did, the ovum secreted a chemical barrier that killed the others. (These remarkable pictures were published in the July 20, 1974, issue of *Paris-Match*.)

Thus only one sperm cell among millions is permitted to mate with the egg. Once the sperm penetrates the egg, it heads straight for the nucleus. Here takes place the exchange of chromosomes that carry the genetic plan for the new individual. From this remarkable exchange between two microscopic uniting cells a new individual unlike any born before or to be born afterward is created.

Geraldine Flanagan, in her fascinating book *The First Nine Months of Life*, describes what happens immediately after fertilization:

> As the synthesis of the two different parent nuclei is completed within the single egg, two new nuclei arise. The genetic make-up of these two new nuclei differs from that of either parent: it is a blend of both. That moment, when the two new nuclei form and the now fertilized egg divides in two, is the beginning of the life of a new individual. This is zero hour of Day One.

The new life begins to develop rapidly. During the first week the first two cells increase two by two to more than one hundred cells. Meanwhile it has taken three or four days for the cluster of cells to drift down the Fallopian tube. On the fourth day it arrives in the uterus. By then the new life has depleted most of the food supply in the ovum, and by the end of the first week after fertilization the cluster becomes attached to the inner lining of the womb, drawing nourishment from the mother's body. Several weeks later, by the time the mother knows she's pregnant, the new life has developed into a substantial embryo.

It should be noted that although the embryo attaches itself to the uterus wall and draws nourishment from it, it is a separate entity from the mother, nesting in the womb for the purpose of survival. This nesting causes a change in the mother's hormone balance that prevents menstruation from taking place. (Scientists are working on a way to induce menstruation after nesting has taken place. Thus the possibility is very real that pill-induced early abortion will replace contraception as the chief means of birth control.)

It is important to know that by the time a woman suspects that she is pregnant, the growth processes of the new individual are well under way. The new life will be two weeks old before she realizes that she has missed her period. When her menstrual bleeding is four weeks overdue, the new life is already in its sixth week. As soon as pregnancy is confirmed, which is usually in the fourth or fifth week after conception at the earliest, maternal politics starts to operate. The mother must decide whether or not she is willing to accept the maternal commitment that nature is about to impose on her. The survival of a new individual is at stake.

During those first few weeks the new individual doesn't look like much; but it is very much alive and in the process of miraculous development. For example, during the third week of life the body begins to unfold. Although it is no more than one-tenth of an inch long, the brain already has two lobes and the early spinal cord is bordered by the future vertebrae and muscle segments. By the twenty-fifth day, the heart has already started to beat.

By the end of the fourth week the embryo is ten-thousand-times larger than the size of the original fertilized egg. In the sixth week the embryo has gained a complete skeleton. The skeleton is not yet made of bone. It is made of cartilage. The appearance of the first bone cells marks the end of the embryonic period. In its seventh week, even though it is less than an inch long and weighs about a thirtieth of an ounce, the new person has all of the internal organs of the future adult. It has a face with eyes, ears, nose, lips, tongue, and even milk-teeth buds in the gums. The body has become nicely rounded, padded with muscles and covered by a thin skin. The tiny arms have hands with fingers and thumbs. By the seventh week this tiny baby has developed sufficient muscles and nerves to permit movement. If the area of the lips, the first to become sensitive to touch, is gently stroked, the baby responds by bending the upper body to one side and making a quick backward motion with the arms.

Thus, during the period when a woman must confront herself with the prospects of becoming a mother, an individual is growing by leaps and bounds within her. To evict the little stranger forcibly is to kill it, and she can do this with reasonable safety to herself up until the twelfth week. There are two ways to perform an "early" abortion. The older method is known as the D & C, which stands for dilation and curettage. The cervical canal is dilated with a series of tapered metal rods of increasingly greater diameters and the unwanted stranger is scraped out of the uterus with a hollowed-out, spoon-shaped instrument. The process takes from ten to thirty minutes and the mother's loss of blood may amount to half a pint. For the little stranger death results quickly from a cutoff of oxygen. A newer method, called suction or aspiration, entails removing the fetus through a plastic tube attached to a suction pump. This process only takes a minute or two and the mother's loss of blood usually amounts to only a few ounces.

Most women have their abortions between the sixth and twelfth weeks. A six-week-old fetus is less than an inch in size and is on the threshold of making his first physical responses to stimulation. But a twelve-week-old fetus is almost three inches in length and very much resembles a little baby. The baby can now move his thumb in opposition to his fingers. He can also pull up his upper lip in what looks like a lopsided sneer but is actually the initial step in the development of the sucking reflex. He can kick his legs, turn his feet, curl and fan his toes, make a fist, bend his wrist, turn his head, squint, frown, open his mouth and press his lips tightly together. Growth is phenomenal and unabated during this period. The will to live expresses itself in this surge of development.

Between the twelfth and sixteenth weeks maternal politics are frustrated by mother nature. During this period the baby has grown so much that he has reached half the height he will have at birth. For this prodigious growth the baby must take in a good deal of sustenance: food, oxygen, and water. This comes to him from his mother through the placenta, which is a kind of complex filtering system that permits the child to maintain his separate integrity yet draw nourishment and oxygen from the mother. The baby's link to the placenta is the umbilical cord. It is capable of carrying about three hundred quarts of fluid a day and is so well engineered that the blood stream within travels at four miles an hour and makes the round trip through the cord and baby in only thirty seconds. There is an advantage in the blood traveling with such force. That force distends the cord and gives it the consistency of a water-filled garden hose. Through umbilical cord and placenta the new human being can be a self-contained unit while he is completely dependent on his mother. His whole body functions as a closed system. He has his own blood circulation, pumped by his heart, which at four months pumps the equivalent of about twenty-five quarts a day.

Thus, from the abortionist's point of view, the life-support system is now too complex and the fetus too big to be scraped or sucked out without causing the mother a severe hemorrhage. So if she has waited this long before making her decision, her local abortionist will tell her to wait until the seventeenth week, or the fifth month, when a saline abortion can be performed. A saline abortion is a pretty gruesome business. It involves inserting a needle through the abdominal wall into the uterine cavity and into the amniotic sac, removing some of the fluid surrounding the child and replacing it with a concentrated solution of salt water. The child dies a slow, tortured death and twenty-four to seventy-two hours later is ejected by labor contractions. This is really an artificially induced miscarriage. Sometimes the little stranger is stubborn and doesn't die on first injection. Then the whole process has to be repeated.

The interval between the injection and the abortion is handled in several ways. Some doctors allow their patients to go home, if they live nearby, and then return to the hospital when the labor cramps begin. Other doctors keep their patients in the hospital and try to hasten the miscarriage by injecting a drug that stimulates the uterus to contract. Others remain in the hospital after the injection until the abortion occurs. Dr. Robert E. Hall, in *A Doctor's Guide to Having an Abortion*, describes to his patients what then may happen:

> In most cases the abortion will occur in bed, often with no one in immediate attendance. If the fetus is expelled while you are alone, ring or send for the nurse, who will help remove the placenta, call the doctor if there are any difficulties, and clean up the small-to-moderate amount of blood and fluid that accompany the process. There is no denying that this is an unpleasant experience. You should be prepared for the fact that the fetus will look fully formed and it may weigh as much as a pound.[91]

Undoubtedly the trauma of seeing one's own infant, killed by oneself, can have a lasting effect on the emotions of some women. One girl who went through such an experience described it in a letter to the National Right to Life Committee:

> I am twenty-four, single, and was raised a strong Christian. But I went against my faith, acted out of selfish love, and now have ruined my life. Although I had spiritual, and more, guidance from friends, I chose an abortion rather than put my illegitimate child out for adoption. I selfishly decided to free myself from fear so I pushed my God and my beliefs aside. But I waited over five months.
> I rationalized that I would make it half-right by doing it my own way. I received a saline shot and ran away to a motel where I spent two days in painful labor. Then there was a tiny baby girl—dead. The shock of hold-

146

ing your own self-destroyed child is indescribable. . . . I baptized her, asked God to take her, and then it hit me. I had killed! I stayed with my baby several tearful days, and then I buried her, alone, at night.[92]

It is doubtful that this girl would have gone through with the abortion at that late stage had she known the physical details of a saline abortion. Another important point about the saline abortion is that it can only be performed during a four-week period, the seventeenth through twentieth weeks, for at the twenty-first week the infant is fast approaching viability, that is, he may be well developed enough to survive outside the womb. Thus, because the infant has grown too large and has a good chance of surviving outside the womb of the mother who doesn't want him, the medical profession is duty-bound to preserve its life as it would the life of a prematurely born infant.

Not all doctors, however, are so concerned about preserving the life of a possibly viable fetus or one nearing the stage of viability. This was dramatically demonstrated in the Edelin case in Boston, involving the abortion of a possibly viable fetus. The case is worth reviewing because it brought to light the moral conflict raging within the medical profession over the entire matter of abortion. It involved a seventeen-year-old unwed pregnant girl who was referred to the Boston City Hospital for an abortion by a neighborhood health center.

On examination at the hospital it was determined that the fetus was between twenty and twenty-four weeks of age, with a strong heartbeat, making this an obvious borderline case. Nevertheless, the doctors agreed to perform the abortion, possibly because they were more interested in using the patient in a research study on amniocentesis (a technique that taps the fluid in the womb to pick up cells from the fetus for diagnoses of inherited diseases) than in prolonging the life of the fetus. The patient was also used as part of another research project to determine the effect of a particular drug on hormone levels in pregnant women. Thus, as far as the doctors were concerned, the teenage patient was little more than a valuable guinea pig. Even one of the newspapers commented on how "surprisingly impersonal" was the hospital's handling of its abortion patient.

On October 2, 1973, Dr. Kenneth Edelin, 35-year-old chief resident in obstetrics at the hospital, made from three to five attempts to induce abortion by saline injections. Which of the injections were for research and which for abortion was not made clear. But each injection resulted in a "bloody tap," which meant that the needle was hitting something it was not supposed to hit. It was therefore decided, on the next day, to perform a hysterotomy, a kind of Caesarian section, in which the fetus and placenta are removed by hand through an incision in the abdominal wall. Dr. Edelin performed the operation.

The manslaughter charge brought against Dr. Edelin was based on the testimony of a fellow doctor, an eyewitness to the operation, who stated that after making the incision Dr. Edelin placed his hand in the uterus, detached the placenta and waited three minutes, observing the wall clock, before removing the infant from the womb where it was still encased in the amniotic sac, and where it died from lack of oxygen. The prosecution contended that the infant was viable and could have survived had Dr. Edelin removed it immediately from the womb and permitted it to begin breathing air *before* severing the oxygen lifeline to the mother. The defense argued that there was no clock on the wall at the time of the operation, and that the delay in removing the fetus was due to the rupturing of the amniotic sac. In any case, the defense argued, since the fetus had never left the womb alive, it had never been a person, and therefore no crime had been committed against anyone. There was also the possibility that the fetus had died from the saline injections. But no attempt had been made before the operation to determine if the fetus was still alive.

The fact that expert doctors were brought forth to testify both for and against Dr. Edelin illustrated how divided the medical profession is on the entire issue of abortion. There was disagreement on terminology, semantics, and medical judgment and practice. For example, Dr. William T. O'Connell, a distinguished professor of obstetrics, testified that it was "poor medical practice" and extremely dangerous to the mother to detach the placenta from the uterine wall before removing the fetus. On the other hand, Dr. Allan C. Barnes, head of medical services for the Rockefeller Foundation, thought the procedure was "perfectly acceptable, perfectly proper." The jury was left with the spectacle of medical doctors not only disagreeing on surgical procedures but also contradicting one another on simple factual information, such as the existence or nonexistence of a wall clock. It confirmed that each doctor practices medicine in his own way, because whatever training he has received is modified by his own intelligence, judgment, morality, and sensibilities.

Curiously enough the mother who had ordered the abortion was not called to testify. Her identity and privacy were carefully safeguarded by the court. Yet she had initiated the entire procedure, and Dr. Edelin had merely been the instrument of her will. In fact he was quoted as saying: "I've always felt that if I never had to do another abortion I would be very happy. But the whole idea is that this hospital should be serving the community." Thus Dr. Edelin gave the impression that he was as much a victim of maternal politics as the fetus. Although Dr. Edelin could have joined those doctors who refuse to perform abortions, he chose to be the willing instrument of women who want abortions. For this the feminists came to his support. Several days before the end of the trial, the National Organization for Women (NOW) issued a statement which said: "We believe that Dr. Edelin, charged with manslaughter of a 'baby boy' as the aftermath of a legal abortion . . . is a scapegoat for those who would like to subvert the Supreme Court decision of January 1973, allowing women the right to choose an abortion during the first six months of pregnancy."

The jury, however, composed of thirteen men and three women, found Dr. Edelin guilty. It obviously did not agree with NOW or the other support groups which had tried to make Dr. Edelin into a sort of hero. Perhaps the jurors, who included a janitor, a mechanic, a bartender, a meat cutter, a teller, a draftsman, a metal press operator, and two housewives, were serving notice on the medical profession that they did not approve of the freedom the Supreme Court had given doctors to perform abortions without the slightest regard or consideration for the fetus about to be killed, despite its possible viability, no matter how slight. If neither the court nor the medical profession offered any protection for the life of the fetus, then perhaps the jury felt obligated to do so. Somebody had to protect the unborn from the insensible doctors of America.

With the verdict under appeal, each doctor must now weigh the risk of serving maternal politics and abdicating his moral and ethical sensibilities in behalf of sexual freedom, which usually turns out to be sexual irresponsibility. Dr. Mildred Jefferson, an officer in the National Right-to-Life Committee who had testified for the prosecution, explained that she had joined the anti-abortion movement because she felt that abortion was a retreat from the physician's allegiance to the Hippocratic Oath. "I do not want the profession I became part of to become a social tool, a social exterminator or potential executioner," she said.

Doctors, of course, are acting within our present law when they perform abortions, but they have the responsibility of determining when an abortion is both technically feasible and morally appropriate. The Supreme Court ruling of January 22, 1973, was very broad. It prohibited states from passing any anti-abortion legislation except statutes preventing abortions after the stage of "viability" had been reached, at about the twenty-fourth week of pregnancy. The legal rationale which permitted doctors to kill nonviable fetuses with impunity was summed up by Justice Blackman, who wrote the majority opinion and said: "The unborn have never been recognized in the law as persons in the whole sense." Nevertheless, the unborn are recognized as persons in the religious sense. At the Edelin trial, the operating room technician who assisted at the hysterotomy and held the basin into which the surgeon placed the aborted fetus, testified that it was part of hospital "protocol" to baptize the dead fetus as soon as it was removed from the mother! You hardly baptize a nonperson.

Thus the legal issue hinges on the matter of viability, which is not very logical. In essence the court is saying that you may not kill a fetus more than twenty-four weeks old because it can survive outside its mother's womb. But in practical terms it merely means that after twenty-four weeks the mother must carry her pregnancy to term. The mother, of course, does not have to keep her child after it is born. But it seems silly to rule that you can't evict a fetus from the womb *because* it is capable of surviving outside it! What kind of logic is that? It would seem that such a prohibition should apply to those fetuses which couldn't survive outside the womb.

Besides, why choose viability as the cut-off point? The human fetus is not viable before the twenty-fourth week merely because its lungs are not sufficiently developed for outside respiration. Nature decided that lung development could wait because it had nine full months in which to do its work. It gave priority to brain, neural, sensory, skeletal, digestive, and circulatory development before it completed its work on the lungs. So why penalize an unborn infant because nature decided to complete its kidneys before its lungs?

If one is to deal with the matter of abortion logically, perhaps it ought to be considered from a medical or technical point of view instead of an arbitrary legalistic one. Clearly the difference between an early abortion and a late one is so great that one must consider the circumstances of both in relation to mother, child, and the medical profession. Many doctors who will perform a D & C will not perform a saline abortion because the latter comes too uncomfortably close to infanticide. The baby is too big, and viability is only a few weeks away. The mother may not want the child, but why not give the child a chance at life? Why not find adoptive parents willing to accept the child at birth?

A woman who has waited until the fifth month before deciding on an abortion is obviously one who is ambivalent about the whole thing. Why not give the child the benefit of her confusion and ambivalence? Why not outlaw the saline abortion? Why not make it illegal to perform an abortion on a fetus more than twelve weeks or three months old? In 1975 the French passed a law permitting abortion up to the tenth week of pregnancy, which makes much more sense than our present court ruling. The reader may assume from this that I am for abortion, as long as it is performed in the first twelve weeks of pregnancy. The reader is wrong. I am against abortion, but I do not believe that simply because of an accidental pregnancy a woman should be forced to accept the maternal commitment if she does not want to. In other words I believe that women should have the right to kill their own unborn children up to the twelfth week. Why? Because I also believe that men should have the right to exercise sexual politics in their relations with women.

I do not believe that a woman should have to be anyone's mother if she does not want to. But I believe that she should know her own mind well enough to be able to make her decision on abortion early and promptly. If she cannot make up her mind by the twelfth week, then society should intervene in the child's behalf and the woman should be required to carry the infant to term, at which time she can decide whether to keep it or give it up for adoption. I believe that when we give women the right to abort their fetuses, we are indeed giving them the right to kill their unborn infants. But I believe that women should have this special proprietary right during the first three months of their unborn infant's life. It will give them something to think about.

I am willing to concede this right, even though I abhor the thought of abortion, because too many women want it and will seek abortion whether it is legal or not. I prefer to let women know what they are doing and to give them the full responsibility for their actions. I do not believe, as Nicholas von Hoffman does, in "prenatal snuffings out." I simply believe that women should have the right to kill their own unborn children up to the twelfth week of prenatal life for two reasons: because the maternal commitment entails a difficult, burdensome, life-long relationship with another human being; and because the mother has a proprietary relationship with the human being growing within her. In short I believe in maternal politics, not because I like it, but because it exists and will always exist. Mothers make their children who they are. While I prefer the woman who permits God to determine when it is time for her to accept the maternal commitment—as my own mother did—one cannot ignore that modern science has simply extended maternal politics into the prenatal period and that women shall require a new education before they can understand the power over life and death technology has given them.

I have come to this conclusion after talking about abortion not to unwed mothers but to long-time married women with up to six children. I was particularly influenced by one woman I admire and love who had an abortion because she did not want more than the two children she already had and to whom she was completely devoted. When I suggested that she might have carried her pregnancy to term and placed the child for adoption, she replied that she could not live knowing that a child who belonged to her was somewhere in the world unknown to her. Yet she had admitted at one time that her maternal instinct was so strong that she probably would have committed suicide had she not had her first child. How does one answer a woman who argues thus? Of course when prehistoric men found it impossible to answer such arguments they imposed sexual politics, the paternal commitment. That solved the problem until the present era.

But, as the reader may have already suspected, there is method to my madness. I want women to have the right to kill their unborn children up to the twelfth week of prenatal life so that they will understand the nature of abortion and take special pains to avoid unwanted pregnancy. Nobody wants to be a murderer, and if young women are educated to understand the nature of abortion they will conduct their sex lives with greater responsibility. You don't understand that abortion is murder until you are so familiar with the details of fetal life that you cannot escape the fact that a deliberate termination of the prenatal infant's growth is murder. Therefore courses in high school should be given in our process of reproduction and the growth of the human being, from conception to birth.

Not all unmarried girls who get pregnant rush off to the abortionist. Carole Klein, in *The Single Parent Experience*, describes some of them:

> Many girls played back and forth with the idea of abortion for months. Like Ilse, now a happy mother of a two-year-old daughter, it seemed the easiest solution, yet something kept her from going ahead and making it her solution.
>
> "I had actually finally talked myself into it," she said, "when I felt life. And that was it. Abortion was from then on out of the question. It's one thing to terminate something abstract, but when you're made really conscious that there's a human life inside you, well, I'm not religious but that's another matter entirely."
>
> A lot of single mothers report similar experiences. "Once you feel that baby move, forget it. He's yours," is said in some way over and over again.
>
> This instinctual reluctance to tamper with life was at the heart of many decisions to discard abortion as a possible alternative, even when the pregnancy was really unwelcome.[93]

It is obvious that the more thoroughly girls are taught the interesting and often astonishing facts about prenatal life, the less likely they will be in favor of abortion. And if they have strong qualms about abortion, the more careful and responsible they will be in their sexual relations. It is important to encourage such education because abortion is the willful termination of another human being's life, and legalized murder has a demoralizing effect on society as a whole. It demoralizes the medical profession and perverts its purpose. It opens society to the ill effects of condoned killing. The reason why we can get away with killing hundreds of thousands of unborn children is because they are completely helpless to oppose what is being done to them. But at

152

their level of development, their will to survive is intrinsically as strong as that of an adult, and if they were able to answer the question: "Do you want to live?" the answer would be an unequivocal yes.

Thus I would permit women the freedom to abort their unwanted pregnancies, but only up to the twelfth week, and only after they have been given a thorough knowledge of prenatal life. Only such knowledge will encourage the sense of responsibility needed in the exercise of freedom and personal power. I am convinced that anyone who becomes thoroughly familiar with the facts of prenatal life will develop a strong antipathy to abortion. But we must not forget that there are many people who approve of taking adult life for one reason or another. Which only means that no matter how much life the prenatal child may exhibit, this will not deter some people from justifying its murder.

Abortion cannot be performed legally without the help of the medical profession. Medical men, who are supposed to have the greatest respect for life, have been found willing to terminate the lives of hundreds of thousands of unborn children. Therefore we cannot expect moral leadership from them. They are the ones who hem and haw over the matter of whether abortion means killing a prenatal human being or disposing of unwanted fetal tissue. They merely skirt the moral issue by means of a semantic shell game.

To give the reader an idea of how far this semantic dishonesty can go, here's a description of the saline abortion from a book entitled *Unwanted Pregnancy* authored by Robert Bluford, a doctor of theology, and Robert E. Petres, a doctor of medicine:

> The saline termination has the effect of inducing a miscarriage. The more lengthy the pregnancy, the more fetal material there is to be aborted. Under the best conditions, the patient is attended by a nurse who receives the aborted material immediately and removes it from the patient. It is not uncommon, however, for a patient to abort unattended by a nurse or other attendant and to do so in her bed. The nurse usually responds promptly to a call from the patient and removes the abortice.[94]

Who's trying to deceive whom? We can't imagine any of these square-shooting women's libbers accepting such blatant semantic trickery to cover up the fact of what takes place when you abort a prenatal infant. We can't imagine Gloria Steinem or Germaine Greer or Kate Millett swallowing such semantic garbage when their entire liberation movement is supposedly based on telling it like it is. But the authors of *Unwanted Pregnancy* are probably addressing their book less to the readers of Kate Millett than to the readers of *Seventeen* and *Mademoiselle* whose minds are more easily manipulated. And mind manipulation is exactly what they are after when they write:

153

It is probably true that the older the pregnancy, the more time a woman has to think in terms of a baby. . . . Quite naturally, the less a woman has thought of her pregnancy in terms of an individual human being, the less she is likely to suffer an unpleasant aftermath of abortion. Here again it is helpful if she can distinguish between fetal material as potential for life and human personality itself.[95]

This was the kind of mind manipulation the Nazis employed to make it easier for their gas-chamber operators to murder millions of men, women, and children without any pangs of conscience. If you can think of millions of human beings as inferior pollutants, you can murder them without suffering any "unpleasant aftermath." The authors continue:

What it adds up to in terms of a woman's feelings is that the less time she has to think "baby," the better she will adjust after abortion. Most feelings of guilt about an abortion are rooted in the thought that the pregnant woman has done something not to herself, but to someone else, that is, a baby. A woman needs to be aware of the possibility that her own mental attitude, and the extent to which she allows herself to dwell on attributing personhood to the content of her uterus, will have a bearing on her feelings about abortion. Quite obviously her natural sensitivity as a mature person makes her vulnerable to depression and remorse if she is led to feel she has destroyed another person.[96]

But whether she feels it or not, the point is that she has destroyed another person. Everyone alive has been, at the beginning of his life cycle, a prenatal infant, as much alive and unique as a postnatal infant. Even Beethoven was once an embryo. And it is for this reason that an unwanted pregnancy can be such an agonizing situation. It does no justice to any woman to convince her that the child growing within her is any less of a human being simply because she doesn't want to mother it. Merely because a prenatal infant is unwanted does not change any of the facts about its existence. We were all prenatal infants at one time in our lives. But even the authors of *Unwanted Pregnancy* finally have to admit that in abortion something is killed. Their out is to quibble over what it is that is being killed. They write:

The basic question is, are we killing a person, and it becomes a matter of definition: What is a person? A person is someone who possesses a personality. Personality implies that that person is unique, that he is one of a kind, that he answers to a specific name, reacts to a specific set of circumstances, and acts in a specific manner. The embryo and the fetus in the uterus have none of these characteristics. They are not unique. Laid side by side at four or five months' gestation, they are virtually indistinguishable. They are not unique in any way, shape or form.[97]

The authors are wrong. Every human being, from the moment of conception, is unique. The new human being has a set of genes that will never be duplicated again. He has his own set of finger prints. He does not yet have a name or social security number, not because he is not unique, but because he doesn't yet need them. If permitted to live long enough, he will. Yes, a four-month-old prenatal infant doesn't have a "personality" that any of us are aware of, but neither does a two-week-old postnatal infant, yet killing the latter would certainly be classified as killing a human being. The truth is we simply don't know how much of a personality is developed in utero. We suspect, for example, that the emotional dispositions of autistic children are determined in utero. In any case, why do the authors tilt their semantic pinball machine by asking "What is a person?" Why don't they ask "What is a human being?" and whether or not all or just some human beings must go through the prenatal stages of development? But they pursue their reasoning about the prenatal infant to even more ridiculous lengths. They continue:

> They cannot think. Contrary to popular opinion, they cannot feel; far more important, they cannot remember. What person walking the face of the earth can remember the pain of being squeezed through the vaginal canal when he was born?[98]

Again the authors betray their ignorance of prenatal life. A seven-week-old fetus will respond to stimuli. By the seventh week his musculature and nervous system have developed sufficiently to permit physical response to the touch of a hair on his mouth. By the thirteenth week there is no doubt that the baby can feel. Writes Geraldine Flanagan in *The First Nine Months of Life*:

> This is an important landmark, as the quality of response is altered. It is no longer marionette-like or mechanical. . . . The movements are now graceful and fluid, as they are in the newborn . . . the fetus is active and reflexes are becoming more vigorous.[99]

By the sixteenth week the mother will begin to feel the baby turning and kicking against her sensitive abdominal wall. Babies can even have hiccoughs in utero, and some are actually born with a callus on their thumb from sucking it in the womb. Obviously the prenatal infant must gain some pleasure from exercising its sucking reflex or else he would not suck his thumb. And if he can already experience pleasure, he can also experience pain. So the prenatal infant is very much alive, very much a person in his own right. True the prenatal infant probably has no memory, but only because it is not needed at that early stage of development. Most people remember nothing of their first three or four years of life. But that is no reason to consider them subhuman.

The point we wish to make is that the revolting, uncalled-for denigration of the prenatal infant is only necessary to soothe the consciences of the abortionist and his clients. But it does an immense injustice to the true nature of prenatal life. There is probably no stage in life when growth is more miraculous and life itself more teeming with the raw somatic instincts of survival. All of us take something of the quality of that prenatal life into the postnatal world. Life is a single continuum, from conception to death. Each stage, from the earliest to the last, is both inevitable and important, and none can be skipped. We don't see what the women's liberation movement has to gain by being dishonest and quite unscientific about the earliest and most awesome stage of human existence.

The psychiatric community seems to be a little more honest than the medical doctors about facing the issue, but even they seem unwilling to call a spade a spade. In a study published in 1969 by the Group for the Advancement of Psychiatry and entitled *The Right to Abortion: A Psychiatric View*, the moral issue was summed up thus:

> There remains the moral issue of abortion as murder. We submit that this is insoluble—a matter of religious philosophy and religious principle and not a matter of fact. We suggest that those who believe abortion is murder need not avail themselves of it. On the other hand, we do not believe that the existence of this belief should limit the freedom of those not bound by identical religious conviction. Although the moral issue hangs like a threatening cloud over any open discussion of abortion, the moral issues are not all one-sided. The psychoanalyst Erik H. Erikson stated the other side well when he suggested, "The most deadly of all possible sins is the mutilation of a child's spirit." There can be nothing more destructive to a child's spirit than being unwanted, and there are few things more disruptive to a woman's spirit than being forced into motherhood without love or need.[100]

Thus even the most sophisticated psychiatrists are unwilling to admit that by granting women legal abortion we are granting them the right to kill their prenatal infants. Why is it so difficult for so many members of the scientific and medical communities to admit it? Why should they pretend that killing is something else than killing, unless they are afraid to face the natural consequences of what it is they approve of? Perhaps we can help the medical community better distinguish between belief and fact by presenting the case in different but more dramatic terms: Two women become pregnant. One welcomes her pregnancy, the other does not. One goes to a gynecologist and obstetrician to start planning her baby's healthy and safe arrival. The other goes to a gynecologist and obstetrician to plan the baby's death while in the process of prenatal development. Both prenatal babies are equally healthy, equally desirous of life as far as the intrinsic activity of each soma is concerned. One has been given a passport to life, the other a death sentence. One may even be given medical treatment in utero to insure its safe arrival. The other will be scraped out or given a shot of salt solution. Two doctors are performing two different jobs on two different prenatal babies in identical

156

stages of growth with identical intrinsic desires to live. In one case the baby is helped to survive, in the other he is deliberately killed. Is this a matter of belief or fact? It hardly seems a matter of religious belief when the events are seen in these terms. It is a simple matter of facts.

Medical science can now go to considerable lengths to insure the health and safety of an unborn infant. For example, *Today's Health* of June 1974 described the dramatic case of an infant being saved in utero from its mother's Rh blood disease through the use of amniotic taps, the very tapping technique used in the saline abortion. The article explained:

> Only a little more than a decade ago, such an intrusion into the sanctity of the womb would have been almost unthinkable. Today, amniocentesis (a tap of the pale amniotic fluid that surrounds and protects the fetus in the womb) is used to diagnose an increasing variety of fetal conditions.

Thus a treatment technique developed to save the life of an unborn child has now been adapted to the use of killing him. These amniotic taps can also be used to detect defects in prenatal infants, such as mongolism. One could quite understand a woman not wanting to give birth to a mongoloid. But the salting-out process is used to destroy not defective prenatal infants but perfectly healthy ones. Thus the medical profession finds itself in a moral dilemma it refuses to face. Should a doctor kill a perfectly healthy prenatal infant simply because the mother asks him to do so? The article in *Today's Health* states:

> Obstetricians have developed methods of detecting and monitoring many potentially dangerous pregnancy conditions such as diabetes, hypertension, genetic problems, and Rh incompatibility. When the condition affects the fetus, the physician can often intervene in the birth schedule by inducing or staving off labor in order to plan—in consideration of the health of the mother and baby—the optimal time for delivery. Physicians now are even able, in some cases, to treat a sick baby before it is born. And pediatricians, if alerted that a high risk baby is on the way, can utilize sophisticated technical devices to help save its life.[101]

Note the language used in describing these scientific advances that now permit doctors to "treat a sick baby before it is born." No reference to treating sick "fetal material." The writer speaks of a "baby" and the sophisticated technical devices to help "save its life." The process of saving the baby's life is not referred to as "prolonging the mother's pregnancy," but "saving the baby's life." So why refer to killing a prenatal child as "terminating an unwanted pregnancy"? The facts are not changed by semantic acrobatics.

As much as I abhor the idea of abortion at any stage, I propose that we take the semantic deception out of prenatal maternal politics by giving women the right to kill their unborn children until the twelfth week of prenatal life; not because I approve of such killing but because I do not believe that it is any longer possible to force a woman to accept the maternal commitment if she doesn't want to. It is better to make the process legal, but to discourage women, through education, from getting into the situation where they may have to use it. If a woman knows that she is not ready to accept the maternal commitment, she should behave accordingly. That is why the more all of this is discussed openly and honestly, the more likely that women will begin to assume greater responsibility for their sexual behavior. But since accidents will happen and sexual behavior is so closely bound to the emotions, we must consider human weakness and human error and match them with some human understanding.

I tend to have more faith in women than many men have. When we consider how easy it is now to get an abortion, we can be encouraged by the fact that in 1973 an estimated 3,141,000 births took place in the United States. True it represented the lowest birthrate in our history, but it also represented over three million decisions for life as against the approximately 700,000 made against it during the same year—three million acceptances of the maternal commitment as against 700,000 against it. The truth is that only women can put the abortionists out of business. But to do so they must exercise self-restraint and self-control, something very difficult to do in a society that encourages sexual irresponsibility. In the circumstances it is hard to be optimistic. In addition, technology seems to be outstripping us. For example, scientists are already developing a new pill that may make the present birth-control pills obsolete. The new pill would be taken only when a woman missed her period and feared that she was pregnant. So now we are extending the concept of contraception into the postcontraceptive period. Early abortion by pill will become the new form of "contraception." But in fact it will no longer be contraception but abortion. The new confusion will encourage even more semantic deception than we have now.

We are entering a very dangerous phase in human history, where technology is permitting man to play God in ways that are bound to destroy him. His weapons have now made postnatal life questionable, and his drugs promise to make prenatal life impossible. Perhaps we are on the road to suicide—not sexual suicide but just plain old suicide. But not all human beings want to play God, and hopefully there will be many women among them.

Basically the rise in prenatal maternal politics is the result of the decline of patriarchy. And the decline in patriarchy is due to the ever-increasing number of men who no longer want to maintain the discipline, self-restraint, and self-control necessary for patriarchy.

Women have taken advantage of this male weakness to assert themselves in ways never before attempted. The result has been social changes that none of us can as yet fully evaluate. We shall have to wait and see.

Some day men may want to restore the patriarchal system, but for the moment—and who knows how long this moment in history will last—they don't seem to want to. Therefore a total ban on abortion is no longer possible, not because so many women are for abortion but because not enough men are against it. Those of us who oppose abortion on principle can only hope to influence the decisions of women by contributing to their education when they are girls. If they are taught to consider life sacred and to understand its processes from conception to birth, they will be less likely to take up with boys who do not share their values. Education is necessary because the Ten Commandments are no longer the deterrent they once were. The fear of punishment from on high has been removed. Basically we live in a secular world where God lives not so much in human institutions but in human individuals, many of whom belong to no church or organized religion. There are still institutions in which the God of the Ten Commandments strongly prevails, such as the Mormon church and other fundamentalist religions. But if women can be said to have retreated from motherhood, it can be said that too many religious institutions have retreated from God. It isn't that God is dead in these institutions, it is merely that He has been excluded. As long as human beings can be created, as long as the miracle of life exists, it can hardly be said that God is dead. After all, when all is said and done, God is merely the faith within us.

10

Mother Love and Modern Obstetrics

One does not have to be a psychologist to know that a mother, through the quality of her mothering, can make or break her child. Through her tender nurturing and ministrations she can give her child a sense of living in a benevolent, beautiful, fulfilling world. Through abuse, rejection and neglect she can create for her child a malevolent, frustrating universe in which nothing good or fulfilling is possible. So we know that a child's emotional and mental well-being depend greatly on what kind of a mother he or she has. It depends, writes Rita Kramer in the *New York Times Magazine* of October 7, 1973, to a great extent "on the establishment very early in life of a mutually gratifying, continuing relationship with a mothering figure who cares for and stimulates the infant. It is in this relationship that the child begins to develop security and trust—a good feeling about himself and a sense that the world is worth moving out into and exploring. Psychologists have come to believe that if you start with these feelings you don't need much of anything else, and that without them, it doesn't much matter what else you have."[102]

I think the most significant phrase in Ms. Kramer's statement is "mutually gratifying." It implies that the mother must get as much pleasure out of mothering as the infant gets out of being mothered.

Pleasure in mothering? Judging from the complaints of the women's libbers and the reports of child abusers, you would think that mothering was anything but pleasant. In our pleasure-oriented society, we seem to be obsessed with one pleasure only—sexual—as if other pleasures didn't exist or were nowhere equal to it. Yet if mothering were not as gratifying as it is, the human race would have never survived, for, of all mammalian infants, the human infant requires the most care, the most attention, the most love. And the infant would never have received them if the mother-child relationship were not mutually pleasurable. Mothering is not all self-sacrifice. There is in mothering a tremendous amount of self-gratification, enough to make all of the self-sacrifice worthwhile. If this were not the case, few of us would be around to discuss it.

The quality of mothering obviously begins with a woman's attitude toward motherhood. If the society she lives in emphasizes the pains of motherhood and denigrates or denies its pleasures, she will approach motherhood with a negative attitude. If she were raised by a mother who derived little or no pleasure from motherhood, her own attitude toward motherhood is apt to be negative or at best ambivalent. If the society she lives in makes her feel guilty about being a mother, because she is polluting the environment, she may deny the pleasure of mothering and deliberately make it as painful an experience as possible.

But mothering is so closely connected with the species' will to live, its survival instincts, that it must harness the species' most life-giving forces. It starts, of course, with our strong sexuality. Sexual desire brings men and women together so that conception may take place. It does not necessarily bring love with it. Until recently it was considered necessary first to fall in love and marry before engaging in sexual intercourse. Today the sequence is different. Men and women now get together, have sex, maybe fall in love, and maybe marry. Too often the result is that pregnancies occur before a lasting bond has been established between two people, and abortion is the usual way out. The pleasures of motherhood are not only avoided and rejected, but the thought of motherhood sends many of these unwed women into panic, depression, and sometimes suicide. The species' most life-giving forces are frustrated and thwarted. The pleasure of sex turns into depression and bitterness, and the potential pleasure of mothering is perverted into a death sentence for the unborn child. Obviously, if over thousands of years the species developed the sequence of marriage first and sex later, it was because that sequence was much more in harmony with the species' life-giving and life-preserving forces than the reverse.

There can be no survival without children, and survival is the essence of life, not pleasure. Pleasure serves survival. It is survival's most important tool. Therefore, to separate pleasure from survival is to separate life from its life-giving forces. It is because of this that marriage must precede sexual intercourse if one is to live in harmony with our life-giving forces. Despite all of the means of contraception now available, the number of unwanted pregnancies is still quite high, indicating that, even with our technology, sexual intercourse cannot be divorced so easily from its natural consequences.

Sex creates a child but mother-love permits it to live. Mother-love does not grow in a vacuum. It demands certain favorable conditions for its healthy development. Yet I would venture to say that mother-love is as personal and individual an expression as romantic love. Each of us loves differently, according to his own emotional needs, resources, and capabilities. Each individual is unique, and there is nothing quite so individual as how one loves.

A mother's love probably starts before she has children. It starts in the thought of having children, in the anticipation of having a family. That is why we give little girls dolls to play with, not out of sexism but out of realism, to cultivate a sense of mother love without which the species cannot survive. Women can bear children. Men cannot. That is why we give the girls dolls. Nature gave women a certain capability that she denied men. That some women reject this capability alters nothing about its existence and alters nothing about nature having conferred it on one sex and not the other. Men must compensate for that lack in ways that attempt to give their lives as much purpose and meaning as the bearing and rearing of children. If men created civilization, it was most likely to help make mother-love easier to develop and motherhood a more gratifying experience, so that survival would be assured for one's children. After all, we now know that good mothering can free an individual to move out into the world and master it. Good mothering engenders self-confidence in the growing child. The Western ego is the result of Western mothering. It is not a racial or cultural accident.

What aspect of mothering creates a strong, assertive, creative ego? Rita Kramer writes: "The key word here is 'continuity.' Where this kind of relationship never gets established (children who grow up in crowded institutions) or when it is interrupted (by the disappearance or replacement of the mothering adult for whatever reason—death, divorce, hospitalization) very young children withdraw, regress, become depressed, sometimes even retarded."[103]

Continuity of family is the backbone of Western civilization because it provides continuity of the mother-child relationship. It is the cradle in which the Western ego is developed and it explains why our present family instability is creating so many unhappy, disturbed children, alienated both from their parents and the society that makes such alienation inevitable. The attraction of ego-destroying Eastern religions is only one symptom of this alienation.

A strong ego is probably a human being's most valuable asset in trying to master his environment, and there is no doubt that strong mother-love is the major contributing factor. When asked what his mother meant to him, Telly Savalas, the actor, made this observation:

> Who is the ultimate woman to me? The myth, the archetype, the mold from whom all others in my life have been but careless copies? My mother . . . . In fact, I know why I love my mother so much, and it is terrible in its simplicity. "Of all my sons, Telly," she would say to me often, "you are the most beautiful." How could I not love the woman who told me that?[104]

In an article about the composer Henry Mancini (*Boston Globe,* November 24, 1974), we are told this about his mother:

> Mancini's lovable mother, Anna, had a deep impact on his attitude toward life which tends to the casual. She always smiled. Even if she was harassed by housework and pinching pennies to make ends meet, she'd consistently radiate contentment. Pressures didn't bother her.

In an interview published in the *Boston Globe* of September 8, 1974, Bette Davis, perhaps Hollywood's greatest actress, spoke of her mother as her strongest ally and a consistently faithful friend. "She was a gutty, positive, hardworking woman," said Bette. "My biggest inspiration—and incentive—was to repay her some day so she wouldn't have to be a slave all her life. She had no money but she wasn't downed by that. She wasn't downed by anything or anybody." The reporter observed: "The only time in this interview Bette's face bore a benign expression was when she talked of her mother. Bette Davis—married four times, divorced three, widowed once—refused to discuss why her marriages were flagrantly stormy and/or failed." Husbands may come and go, but in some women's lives mother love remains unbroken in its intensity and continuity from the cradle to the grave.

Mothers who deeply love their children are rewarded by lifelong love from their sons and daughters. This is the ultimate gratification of mother love that begins when the infant is a small embryo in a woman's body. Think of it. A woman's child grows *inside* her body. We forget what a miracle that is. We take for granted the potential for love inherent in that awesome physical relationship. Men underestimate it because they can never experience it. Some women's libbers denigrate it because they resent their bodies being used for what they consider to be an alien purpose. They are women divorced from their bodies, alienated from the most basic human connection.

"Anatomy is destiny," Freud is supposed to have said in summing up female psychological development. The women's libbers have protested that their reproductive functions make them not a wit different from men. Yet anyone who has studied a woman's reproductive and hormonal systems cannot help but be impressed by the degree that nature has prepared her for motherhood and its necessary concomitant, mother-love. That nature must be supported by society in this preparation is all too obvious when one considers the needs of a mother and her child. They can only be satisfied in the context of a society's preoccupation with survival and its understanding of what survival is.

Most people are not terribly concerned about life beyond their own existence. But most parents are concerned about the continued lives of their children and, if fortunate, their grandchildren. Much of their effort is devoted to insuring the existence of their children after they themselves are dead. And certainly they want to be remembered. The elaborate customs of many societies devoted to the remembrance of dead parents are an expression of this concern: to be remembered. So that love, in its state of separation from its physical object, is spiritualized and becomes a force that survives death. We do not forget the love of our parents after they are dead, and we remain true to their standards of conduct long after their voices are stilled. The spirit that lives after their bodies have disintegrated is simply the continued emanations of love coursing through the veins of their children.

Does American society today provide the psychological and emotional support that makes good mothering and strong mother-love possible? We can answer that question better if we follow the course of pregnancy in America. First, American women are now permitted to distinguish between wanted and unwanted pregnancies. If the pregnancy is unwanted, our technology and our laws now permit a woman to terminate it without much trouble. Before you can say the words "mother-love," her local gynecologist can have the unwanted embryo sucked out of her uterus and flushed down the drain. What does having this choice mean for women? It means that the child's life now depends on whether the mother wants it or not. Its life is no longer an unconditional gift, sanctioned by God and society. But since it is difficult for most women to feel love for an embryo, they can now reject a potential love on the basis that it will be an inconvenience to them. Rejecting love for an unborn child because it is inconvenient or uninvited makes love itself a highly conditional and unspontaneous commitment. Perhaps, therefore, it is just as well that women have the power to terminate the lives of unwanted embryos if they cannot make a commitment to love them. Yet none of us arranges to fall in love at our convenience. Love is never convenient. In fact it is the antithesis of convenience. Its very essence is to demand sacrifice, discomfort, and pain. Yes, there is pleasure in love; sometimes just enough to make tolerable all of the pain and inconvenience that must go with it.

Our society is still ambivalent about the choice it gives women, and the result is that some women carry unwanted pregnancies to term, at which time they make their decisions. The *Boston Globe* of November 4, 1974, carried the particularly gruesome story of one young mother who tried to flush her newborn infant down the toilet of an airplane in flight. According to the story, the six-pound infant was found by an airline station agent as he prepared to clean the washroom. The baby's head and an arm were visible. They had to saw the fiber-glass toilet apart to free the child, who was still very much alive. The infant was taken to a hospital and later adopted by a family. The mother, a 23-year-old college student, was arrested several days later and charged with attempted murder or manslaughter. Obviously the girl was deranged. She had previously been convicted of manslaughter and had been in prison. But one would have thought that a college girl would know enough about such matters to have avoided such a predicament. The story told nothing about what her own mother was like.

Let us assume, however, that a pregnancy is wanted, or at least accepted by the mother to be. What happens then? She goes to a gynecologist-obstetrician who confirms her condition, puts her on a diet, and makes preparations for the baby's delivery when the time comes. In the interim the doctor monitors the pregnancy to make sure that everything is normal. The moment a woman decides that her pregnancy is wanted, the status of the embryo changes. It graduates from "fetal tissue" to "prenatal child" or simply "baby." And with it changes the attitude of the gynecologist. Instead of arranging for the baby's death, the doctor begins to arrange for the baby's safe arrival. There are many gynecologists and obstetricians who both kill and deliver perfectly healthy prenatal babies according to the wishes of the mother. (He's a "gynecologist" when he performs an abortion, an "obstetrician" when he monitors a wanted pregnancy.) I imagine that there are a good number of obstetricians who will not kill a perfectly healthy prenatal child merely for the mother's social convenience. The medical profession is divided. Yet there are obstetricians who will go to great lengths to save the life of a wanted but endangered prenatal infant, but will kill a perfectly healthy but unwanted one.

Prior to the development of modern gynecology and obstetrics, midwives took care of deliveries and there was no quibbling over whether the unborn child was wanted or not. In the first place, contraceptive techniques were so primitive that conception was accepted as an act of God. A woman's convenience or desires were of no consequence. Babies were born at home with the help of midwives and were all breast-fed. But modern medicine has changed all of that. Now there are gynecologists, obstetricians, pediatricians, nurses, hospitals, labor rooms, delivery rooms, anesthesia (general, conduction, spinal, caudal, epidural, paracervical, pudendal), intensive care units, "preemie" care centers, formulas—all part and parcel of pregnancies, births, and infant care. Modern medicine is less than a hundred years old, yet it has made a massive and drastic intrusion in the mother-infant relationship. True, it has saved many mothers from dying during childbirth and it has, in general, lowered the infant mortality rate; yet it has also increased the efficiency of abortion—so much so that more healthy unborn children are being killed today in America than ever before. When modern medicine speaks of infant mortality, it conveniently ignores the aborted healthy infants. In addition, the American infant-mortality rate is higher than one would suspect. The United States is sixteenth from the top, with Sweden and Holland vying for first place in safe childbirth.

What modern medicine has done for mother-love in America has yet to be determined. It has helped some women bear children, who would have never been able to do so without the help of modern medicine. That's a plus for mother-love. It has also helped women survive high-risk pregnancies, saved the lives of countless premature babies, and can now treat prenatal infants in utero to assure their safe arrival. However, on the negative side it has created the machinery for the efficient mass murder of perfectly healthy but unwanted prenatal children. It was hoped that modern contraception would eliminate the need for such clinical barbarism. But apparently American women have not been able to assimilate all of this technology into their emotional lives and confused moral values. The result is that modern medicine has decided to do whatever it is bid, especially when it is lubricated by generous government grants. It has, in effect, become a two-headed monster going in the direction of "progress" without the faintest idea what the word means. Modern medicine has no moral code whatever. The same obstetrician can on one day exert massive efforts to save the life of an endangered, but wanted, unborn child and on the very next day kill a perfectly healthy, but unwanted, one. Has modern medicine simply become the amoral servant of modern women?

There are about 18,000 obstetrician-gynecologists in the United States, of whom only three percent are women. Generally, gynecology deals with the female reproductive organs in the nonpregnant state, while obstetrics deals with the pregnant state and its sequels. Pediatricians, of course, deal with postnatal child care. The fact that

167

in the last one hundred years men have replaced women in the handling of pregnancies and child delivery is in itself an important change that must have its effects on the mother-child relationship. It may be good medicine, but it seems to be poor psychology. Women seem to need the support and care of other sympathetic women when they are pregnant, giving birth, or nurturing a newborn infant. Such support seems to aid greatly in the spontaneous development of mother-love. Mothering a new mother helps the latter in mothering her newborn child. The infusion of mother-love from another woman helps stimulate mother-love in the new mother. It gives her the time and freedom from worry that new mothers need in caring for and getting to know their newborn infants.

Although the obstetrician-gynecologist has become the servant of modern woman, he has not escaped the wrath of the women's libbers. Barbara Seaman, in *Free and Female*, catalogs the complaints that women have against the gynecologist. She writes: "Gynecologists have been a significant force in keeping modern women infantile and immature, for their authoritarian attitudes deprive women of autonomy over their own natural functions."[105] So, why aren't there more female gynecologists? Probably because the medical profession in general has not attracted as many women as other professions because of its demands. But the male gynecologist has become an important figure in the modern American woman's life. He prescribes her birth-control pills, inserts her intrauterine devices, performs hysterectomies, diagnoses cancer of the vagina, etc. He pokes around down there where many women feel embarrassed to have anyone poking around. He knows all about her reproductive organs and her hormonal system. It is this knowledge that helped him develop all of the new birth-control pills, fertility pills, and labor-induction pills. He has also developed the techniques of abortion to their present state of high efficiency. Before abortion was legalized he performed many a "D & C" to see if a woman had an infection in her uterus. If, in the scraping process, he also happened to scrape out a tiny embryo, who was there to know?

A woman's reproductive organs can be big business to the gynecologist. If he does two "D & C's" or two suction abortions a day at $200 apiece, that's $400 a day for a few minutes work. He can earn $2,000 in a five-day week and spend his weekends on the golf course or driving around in his Mercedes. But contraception and abortion technology is advancing at such a pace that the new morning-after pill and new "menstrual regulation" techniques may make the old-style abortions unnecessary. Nevertheless there is every reason to believe that some of the bad side effects of these new pills and the inevitable ignorance of many women will keep the gynecologists busy with abortions.

Obviously the gynecologist's role in preventing conception and facilating abortion on demand makes no contribution to mother-love. It may help some married women regulate the size of their families, but its contribution to the motherly instincts is negative. On the positive side it may save a mother's health by performing a needed hysterectomy (removal of the uterus); or diagnosing and treating ovarian cysts, cancer of the vagina, cervix, or uterus, and other such disorders. I suppose that at this confusing stage of our social and moral development we must accept the bad with the good, hoping that as the effects of the bad make themselves known a gradual shift toward the good will take place.

Once a woman decides she wants her pregnancy, she can now choose how to be cared for by her obstetrician, how the child is to be delivered (natural childbirth or under anesthesia), and whether she will breast-feed or bottle-feed her baby. Most women rely on the obstetrician, a male, to make these intrinsically female decisions for them. Women, in general, are so poorly educated in female matters, that the obstetrician has no choice but to make the decisions, and there is plenty of controversy as to the correctness or wisdom of some of these decisions. For example, for years American obstetricians have routinely insisted that pregnant women adhere to low-salt diets, diuretics (drugs to increase the flow of urine), and low weight gain. The result has been doctor-induced malnutrition among many pregnant women with serious harm to the unborn child. The situation has become so bad that one crusading obstetrician, Dr. Tom Brewer of Richmond, California, founded the Society for the Protection of the Unborn Through Nutrition. Elliott McCleary, in his book *New Miracles of Childbirth*, describes Dr. Brewer thus:

> He is a Ralph Nader of obstetrics, a crusader "dashing about in all directions," as one detractor put it, "on a pregnant white horse." For nearly a decade Brewer has been noisily scolding his fellow obstetricians for their adherence to prenatal regimens he was convinced were dangerous: routine low-salt diets, diuretics, and low weight gain. He blames such practice for much of U.S. malnutrition during pregnancy among rich and poor, which he claims is annually responsible for the deaths of more than 30,000 infants and birth defects suffered by more than 200,000 children. Maternal malnutrition, he believes, is responsible for most mental retardation in this country.[106]

Thus, mother-love can get off to a bad start if the mother-to-be deliberately undernourishes her unborn child by blindly following her doctor's orders despite her intuitive knowledge that she is not only starving herself of essential nutrients but also the unborn child. It was believed until only recently that the fetus was a kind of superparasite that drew from the mother all the essential nutrients for its health. But now we know that the placenta is like a sieve and that the child is at the complete mercy of its mother's habits. Thus, mother-love is

169

best expressed by a woman caring for herself while she is pregnant. Caring for herself is a way of caring for the child growing within her. That is why pregnant women need to be mothered, in order to make it easier for them to mother the child within. However, obstetricians are not mothers, and their care is not motherly. Their care is generally perfunctory and clinical if not authoritarian. I recently watched a television talk show in which an obstetrician was interviewed. Two of his pregnant patients were with him. It was obvious that the women were nervous and concerned about the health and safety of their prenatal infants. Yet the doctor discussed abortion and the various problems of childbirth all in the same breath, creating heightened anxiety in the mothers-to-be, perhaps making them feel unsure of their motherliness. Certainly no mother would discuss with her pregnant daughter the subject of killing the unborn with such clinical detachment while her daughter was worried about the health of her unborn child.

There is also the controversial subject of drugs. What kind of drugs should a pregnant woman be permitted to take? After the thalidomide tragedy, obstetricians are more careful of what they prescribe to their patients. There is also the matter of drugs administered during childbirth, some of which affect the infant to the extent that he may enter the world almost as drugged as his mother. Here we come to a woman's choice in delivery methods: natural or under some form of anesthesia.

"Natural" childbirth is something of a misnomer, for there is nothing natural about it. It is not a method of childbirth practiced by primitive tribes before the advent of modern medicine. It is a method of childbirth based on a highly sophisticated scientific understanding of what goes on inside a woman's body during the entire process of giving birth. Since fear of the unknown is what causes tension and therefore increases pain, it was considered likely that if a woman knew exactly what was going on within her during labor she would not fear her contractions; there would be less tension and therefore less pain. Thus preparation for natural childbirth involves a course in pregnancy, prenatal life, and childbirth, together with breathing and physical exercises to enable the mother to cooperate consciously with her own body in bringing forth the child. It is significant that the practitioners of the La Maze method prefer to call natural childbirth "prepared childbirth," for that is what it actually is.

Although natural childbirth was first developed by a British obstetrician, Dr. Grantly Read, most American obstetricians prefer putting their patients to sleep and delivering the babies painlessly. Why, you might ask, should any woman want to undergo anything but a painless anesthetized delivery? Because some women want to be awake at the moment of their child's entry into the world and want to hold him or her immediately upon arrival so that the mother-child bond is firmly established at the moment of birth. A woman who has been drugged during the birth of her child only sees him several hours later, after she awakes. There is always the question: is this really my child? Was some other child given to me by mistake? Such anxieties are especially prevalent in large maternity wards where there are many infants. In the days when babies were born at home there was never any doubt. But in the impersonal setting of the modern hospital, the mother-child bond is subordinated to the hospital's convenience and routine. Therefore how a woman chooses to give birth these days reflects the urgency of her own maternal tendencies. If she is strong for the maternal commitment, she will want to see and hold her child the moment it is born.

The purpose of natural childbirth is to enable the mother to experience an unbroken continuity between the time of conception and the arrival of the baby. After carrying the child within her for nine months, after feeling its movements and being aware of its growth, she wants to see him the moment he arrives. She does not want a sudden traumatic break in that continuity at the most critical moment in the entire process: the emergence of the child from her womb. She does not want to be drugged and asleep when her child enters the world. She wants to be there to greet him before any strangers do. She wants to be sure that he is her issue.

Natural childbirth was developed to meet the emotional deficiencies created by modern medicine, its authoritarian doctors, and cold, clinical delivery rooms. Writes Elliott McCleary:

> The fact is that scientific studies are at last confirming something that many mothers have long felt—that the present traditional health-care system frequently is damaging to mothers, babies, and to the launching of new families. The damage begins before birth, in the form of increased nervous stress upon the mother; the stress causes a more difficult and potentially more dangerous birth. At birth and shortly thereafter, the system interferes with the crucial cementing of family ties—between mother and baby, mother and father, all three together. It interferes with breast-feeding, with resultant physical distress to both baby and mother. Finally, it may on some occasions cause lasting emotional damage that contributes to emotional instability, child abuse, and the breakup of the family, troubles endemic in America today.[107]

What the medical profession is beginning to discover is that the typical American hospital is a very abnormal place for a woman to give birth in. It interferes with the spontaneous surge of mother love that takes place the moment a woman handles her newborn baby. For years the modern hospital has been interfering with crucial instinctual behavior important to the instantaneous development of a strong mother-child bond at the time of birth. One of the enlightened obstetricians working in this area is Dr. Marshall Klaus, who has pio-

171

neered in the development of family-centered maternity care. He was interviewed by Elliott McCleary and said:

> You can see why the early mother-to-infant bond was so important thousands of years ago. There were wild animals about, perhaps attracted by the smell of blood from the birth and discarded membranes. The human infant cannot care for himself. He has to be picked up and held and put to the breast. There's no way he can approach his mother, as does the baby goat or lamb.
>
> He must be irresistible to his mother so she will pick him up and quickly form a tight bond with him; otherwise he'll be killed. He contributes to this attachment of bonds, this lovemaking, with his eyes.
>
> At birth, a normal baby who's had a normal delivery has brilliant eyes (before the silver nitrate ointment is put into them as a health measure). The baby's eyes easily follow you—despite the fact that after that first hour you cannot get him to follow easily for five to six weeks; perhaps because after that first hour he is overwhelmed by all other kinds of stimuli which seem equally important. . . .[108]

Concerning the mother's physical and emotional gratification, Dr. Klaus had this to say:

> Dr. Niles Newton has made a very important observation that there's a similarity between intercourse, the birth of a baby, and breastfeeding. For example, in all cases, the uterus contracts rythmically. One of the things you notice if you put a nude baby next to the mother is a specific "getting acquainted" sequence shown in motion pictures we have taken. First she begins to touch the infant's toes and fingers and within eight minutes proceeds to massaging his entire trunk, eventually exploring much of the body. This might also be compared with the nuzzling and licking of her newborn by an animal mother. It's an identification, examining process.
>
> However, in humans during this period there's increasing eye-to-eye contact. And if you cover the eyes, the mother is upset. If the baby's eyes are closed because he's asleep, it will often be a day or two before the mother fully believes that the baby is hers.
>
> Another part of this is that, during this episode, the mother is excited. A physician who recently became a mother told me that, after her baby was born, she got very unusual feelings that she would *kill* a person who would at all harm the baby. That she would *die* for the baby. That was so atypical of her, and it was inappropriate to the situation, for no one was going to hurt her baby. . . .
>
> I would guess that in humans the critical attachment time is also in the first week of life. Furthermore, the more contact the mother has with her baby, the sooner she touches it, holds it, fondles it, she may have less bleeding, she'll feel better, she'll be stronger. I believe there's a reciprocal action of the mother on the baby and the baby on the mother. This has not been scientifically demonstrated, but many people have written papers on it, and if a mother of a "preemie" or ill baby goes into the nursery with her baby, she tends to move about much more easily and quickly. It is as if contact with the baby causes the release of maternal hormones which help her body return to normal.

Thus, mother-love can be helped or hindered by the way a hospital handles childbirth. In most modern hospitals mother and baby are separated at birth just when they should be kept together. The baby is placed in a nursery where it cries because it is away from its mother, while the mother lies alone in her bed, experiencing postpartum depression. Perhaps nowhere is the interference of modern medicine in the mother-child relationship more dramatically illustrated than in the issue of infant feeding. Until only about seventy years ago, almost all infants were breast-fed, to the full satisfaction of both mothers and babies. But with the development of artificial feeding techniques, along with the idea of rigid scheduled feeding promoted by male pediatricians and busy nurses, the mother-child relationship has become tense, uncertain, and nervewracking. Mothers no longer rely on their instincts and reflexes as they did for a couple of million years. Now they rely on the written words of a male pediatrician, who has never experienced childbirth or breast-feeding. In addition, many doctors give new mothers hormones to suppress lactation. These injections, usually administered immediately after delivery, may at the same time suppress hormonal-based maternal feelings, since it has been established that lactation increases the release of the hormone prolactin which increases maternal behavior and accounts for some of the enjoyment women get from nursing.

There is increasing evidence today that psychologically, emotionally, and physically mothers benefit greatly when they breast-feed their babies. In fact the movement back to breast-feeding has been inspired by mothers, not pediatricians, although some of the latter favor breast-feeding. Drs. Niles and Michael Newton describe the reciprocal pleasures in breast-feeding in their book *Child and Family*:

> The baby is put to the breast immediately after delivery. His sucking instinct is already fully developed so that he catches hold of the nipple and begins sucking. This sucking sets off the milk ejection reflex in the mother with the resulting discharge of oxytocin. Thus, the uterus is stimulated to contract vigorously. . . .
>
> Mother and baby stay close together after birth. Skin contact with the mother stimulates the baby's desire to nurse. Proximity to the baby increases the mother's interest in him. The baby is put to the breast whenever he indicates discomfort. This feeding act helps to warm and soothe him. He may stay at the breast for a half hour or an hour at a time. The comfort he receives there encourages him to fuss for frequent repetition. . . .
>
> The mother in turn has an intense physical desire for her baby. She is under the influence of the hormone prolactin, which has been demonstrated to increase maternal behavior in other mammals. Furthermore, she needs the baby at regular intervals to empty her breasts, which otherwise become heavy and painful. Finally, each successful breastfeeding causes the uterus to contract, as it does at the time of female orgasm. The survival of the race for the millions of years before the concept of "conscience" and "duty" were invented depended on the intense satisfaction gained from the acts of reproduction. Breastfeeding, like coitus, had to be pleasurable and satisfying if the race were to continue.[109]

173

When a woman bottle-feeds her baby no hormones in her body are stimulated. Thus she is deprived of the physical pleasures nature has provided mothers when they breast-feed. These recurrent pleasures not only make nourishing the child a happy task, but they also reinforce mother-love with physical pleasure. The truth of the matter is that breast-feeding does more for mother-love than it does for nourishing the child. While mother's milk is superior to cow's milk as a source of nutrition for the infant, we have no hard evidence that breast-feeding produces healthier or happier children than bottle-feeding. Virginia Pomeranz writes in *The First Five Years*: "I defy the most zealous champion of breast feeding as a superior method to pick out, from one hundred six-month-old babies, those who have been breast-fed and those who have been bottle-fed."[110]

Perhaps the differences between the breast-fed and the bottle-fed babies are too subtle to be visible. There may be subtle emotional differences that can never be measured scientifically. Certainly a woman who breast-feeds her baby brings to the role of motherhood an affirmative and unequivocal attitude quite different from the one who bottle-feeds it. That doesn't mean that a mother who bottle-feeds her baby cannot be as loving and devoted as the mother who breast-feeds him. Yet it is obvious that the mother who is afraid of or rejects the physical pleasure and intimacy of breast-feeding for whatever reason is emotionally different from the woman who seeks it and cherishes it.

It is important to note, however, that it isn't the babies or the doctors who have clamored for a return to breast-feeding, but the mothers. One breast-feeding mother wrote in *The Womanly Art of Breastfeeding*:

After three bottle-fed babies I am finally a successful nursing mother. The striking difference is the tremendous feeling of satisfaction that this baby has given *me*. Up till now I have been always completely baffled by the phrase "enjoy your baby." Not so with my breastfed baby. She, at three months, and I are already great friends. I feel as though I have finally arrived at motherhood. It's such a lovely warm glow that nursing imparts. And the nicest part of all is that this warm glow seems to be endless. It spills over into my relationship with all the rest of my family; there's always some to spare.

A second mother wrote:

So much is written about nursing being best for baby; we know that. I think more should be written about what it does for the mother. Patti is our fifth child, the first to be breastfed. I am amazed at the difference in me. I had no idea what I was missing and I'm sure that if anyone even hinted at it I would have resented it. It is a feeling of growth and development—it is hard to describe, but I feel as if I have finally arrived [motherhood]. I have such a sense of completeness, of fulfillment.

A third mother wrote:

> After three babies who were not nursed and having a grandma readily available, I was free to come and go pretty much as I pleased. I was afraid that I might resent being tied down to my breastfed baby. On the contrary, however, being tied down is more than compensated for by this wonderful feeling of being needed. She needs me as no other person in the whole world ever has and no one else can take my place with her. On days when as many things have gone wrong and my own performance has not been creditable I get renewed and refreshed when I am nursing my baby and realize that with all my faults she loves me and needs me just the way I am. When I finally put her down I find I am calm again and kinder to the rest of the family.[111]

The only problem with breast-feeding is that our society is not organized to make it easy. Most hospitals in the United States are unsupportive and unsympathetic to nursing mothers, and the same can be said for most obstetricians and pediatricians. But as more and more women go about rediscovering the pleasures of breast-feeding, "consumer demand" is beginning to force changes in the way some hospitals handle infant care. But women had to take the initiative. The movement back to breast-feeding began in October 1956, in a private home in Franklin Park, Illinois. There, a small group of nursing mothers who had formed La Leche League held their first meeting. The purpose of the league was to help other women who wanted to breast-feed but did not know how. Prior to modern medicine, breast-feeding as an art was handed down from older mother to younger mother. But with several intervening generations of bottle-feeding mothers, the art of nursing had all but been lost.

In reviving the art of breast-feeding we are also reviving the art of mothering, and we are rediscovering all of the fascinating reflexes and instincts that infants exhibit in trying to elicit adult care. For example there is the startle reflex, in which the infant appears to be shocked. He throws open his arms during sleep and extends both hands with widespread fingers. This spasm is present for only a short time after birth and then disappears. Any adult present and involved with the baby will spontaneously respond by placing his or her index fingers in the palms of the tiny hands. The infant's immediate response is to clutch the fingers, "hooking" the adult literally and emotionally.

Then there is the "rooting" reflex, in which the infant automatically turns his head, purses his lips, and "roots" (searches) for the nipple. To this signal the mother responds by offering the breast. Usually this reflex initiates feeding, but it must be responded to or it will not be continued. If the mother is not near, or if she doesn't respond, the reflex disappears and the baby must then signal that he is hungry by crying.

Before the advent of bottle-feeding "rooting" was one way for an infant to "entice" his mother to respond. His survival depended on his ability to elicit a favorable response. Today the infant's survival depends on the sterile routine of a hospital. Yet some mothers may need instant recognition of their infants so that feelings of intimacy can be aroused before curiosity is lost and the relationship between them is changed. Today we assume that a sense of duty is enough to elicit motherly responses from women. Yet it is obvious that nature relied much more heavily on warm emotional responses for infant survival than on any cold concept of duty. In fact many a hospitalized infant has died, although he was dutifully fed and treated but not given the stimulation and warmth of maternal love.

Another important and appealing reflex is the early infant smile. Adults watch eagerly to see the first signs of this response, and their joyful reaction appears to go far beyond simple curiosity. Anticipation of a smile may be one of the factors that encourage women to respond to new babies.

Then there are also the delightful body smells of newborn babies. These odors attract adults and act as care-eliciting factors, but the parent must hold the infant close to experience them. Writes Dana Raphael in her book *The Tender Gift: Breastfeeding*:

> Before hospitals became the place for deliveries, the mother and baby were tucked into the same bed at home. The infant received a great deal of stimulation and cuddling. It was an excellent setting for each to learn to respond to the other. . . .
>
> We are more concerned about keeping things sterile than we are in allowing the expression of deep and natural feelings. Why can't the responses to these various reflex mechanisms be seen as "love lessons" for the new mother? Many need them, for mother love is by no means automatic. In fact, this strictly human emotion can be entirely absent. Letting mothers respond to the sights, sounds, smell and touch of their newborns can put some of the deeply natural reactions back and intensify the love relationship between the two. . . .
>
> Most of these reflexes are short-lived. They disappear even faster if the opportunity does not exist for the mother or others to respond to them.[112]

Thus, if the child-delivery systems in our modern hospitals make it impossible for new mothers to respond to the care-eliciting reflexes of their infants, are we not putting unnecessary obstacles in the way of the spontaneous arousal of mother-love? Do we not create tense mothers and tense infants, unable to adjust to one another, because we have disrupted the natural processes whereby a mutually gratifying physical and emotional relationship can be started? Has not modern medicine thrown monkey wrenches into the delicate and subtle relationship between mother and infant?

One of the most important discoveries that the women who prefer breast-feeding have made is that a new mother needs the care and support of other sympathetic women in order to be able successfully to nurse her own baby. She needs this care and support during pregnancy to give her the emotional security to go through childbirth. During pregnancy women become increasingly introverted and passive and, in our fragmented society, expectant mothers seldom get the kind of emotional support they need from an experienced companion—a mature adult, or their own mothers. The postpartum breakdown in the modern sterile hospital is often triggered by feelings of abandonment, loneliness, and insecurity. Happy childbearing and child rearing require a warm social context in which care and concern are expressed and practiced. It requires the kind of social atmosphere in which such emotional expression is permitted and encouraged. The fact that we live in a culture that still has not fully accepted breast-feeding as the normal way of infant care indicates that we are still a long way off from understanding what motherhood and maternal gratification are about.

Nevertheless it is encouraging to note that only three years after Simone de Beauvoir's *The Second Sex* appeared in America in 1953 some women had decided to affirm their maternal natures by forming La Leche League. Does this mean that the Women's Liberation movement is in direct conflict with the promaternalism of La Leche League and the various groups promoting natural childbirth? Hardly— since many women's libbers are for natural childbirth and breast-feeding. Yet they resent the patriarchal system that for centuries provided women with the kind of supportive social context that made maternal gratification possible. The simple truth is that patriarchal values favor maternal values, and therefore they favor all of the possible gratifications women can get out of motherhood. But the fact is that today most young women cannot even conceive of maternal gratification. They don't know how to experience it, let alone achieve it.

Much of the blame for this state of affairs must be placed on modern medicine, which has dehumanized pregnancy, childbirth, and infant care. Fortunately the medical profession itself is beginning to recognize this and changes are being made; but slowly, since the routinized practices of a protected, highly organized profession tend to resist change. Only the demands of women will hasten the change. But women have to become much more aware of what is needed. The medical profession tends to forget that before modern medicine came on the scene the human race survived on strong doses of mother love. Before there were antibiotics, vaccines, and penicillin—all of which have been with the human race less than one hundred years— infants survived and thrived on mother-love. There is no substitute for it and every human being instinctively knows this. Mother-love is the world's most potent force for life. But as women retreat from motherhood they retreat from mother-love, and the human race cannot survive without it.

For the first time in history women are in a position to evaluate the enormous capabilities they have been given by nature. Men cannot bear children and cannot experience what women experience in pregnancy, childbirth, breast-feeding, and child rearing—all of which involve a woman's entire body, emotions, and intelligence. Men must therefore find other means to achieve a sense of purpose and self-esteem. They do this by creating the supportive context, the civilization, in which mother love can thrive. It is the height of irony for women to abandon what men must unconsciously admire as a superior capability: that of producing a new human being in one's own body. If men created patriarchy it was because they wanted and needed to be part of the entire process of human reproduction and survival, to achieve a sense of continuity with, an unbroken attachment to, the original source of life and love: the mother.

Men are attracted to women because of their maternal capabilities. Every man sees every woman as a potential mother. He cannot help it, because this is what being a woman means most to him. His first love having been his mother, he is attracted to other women because they remind him of her, because of a desire to recreate the physical intimacy that was lost when he grew away from her. Women are not attracted to men for the same reasons. Women recapitulate mother love by becoming mothers themselves. And in order to do so they need the supportive economic context provided by loving husbands. That is why women work so hard to get men to marry them.

Yet today women seem to be going against their own grain, against their own instincts. With so much potential for deep human gratification within their own bodies, it is pitiful to see women aping men in the hope of capturing the momentarily intense, but inferior, sexual pleasures men enjoy. It is hard to say how much of this is due to the fact that modern obstetrics and pediatrics have substituted maternal duty for maternal pleasure. But we can measure its effects by realizing, for example, how little the average American woman knows about breast-feeding and how much prejudice there is against it in our society. And so the return to breast-feeding, which in my view symbolizes a return to the full biological gratifications of motherhood, is very much an underground movement. True, La Leche League now has over 1,200 groups throughout the country, but that's only a drop in a very big bucket. Nevertheless there are already enough signs to indicate that a women's revolt against modern medicine, with the help of some truly concerned and dedicated obstetricians, may bring with it a new affirmation of maternal values.

11

Love and Loyalty, Attachment and Separation

No country on earth seems to be more love conscious than the United States, and no people on earth seem to be as confused and ambivalent about love as are Americans. In the 1930s, '40s, and '50s romantic love was the theme of countless motion pictures, novels, and popular songs. Today, with the women's libbers denouncing romantic love as a sexist plot and the sexual revolutionaries advocating full sexual freedom and promiscuity, the concept of love itself seems to have gone into eclipse. No one seems to know what love is. The word is probably used more than ever before, but in a kind of loose, undefined way. It is used widely by the young in a diffuse, collective sense to denote general caring and sharing. But ask a young person what he or she really means by the word love and you get more bewilderment than enlightenment. This is understandable, for no human emotion is more complex, more difficult to analyze than love. Yet without it the human race could not exist.

José Ortega y Gasset defined love as "an intense affirmation of another being, irrespective of their attitude towards us."[113] That definition, when I first encountered it, struck me as being very apt and very close to target. Yet it is merely one sentence drawn from an entire book about love. It is probably impossible to define love in one

179

sentence, for the simple reasons that expressions of love take many different forms (erotic, parental, fraternal), that individuals love differently (passionately, quietly, physically, spiritually), and that love manifests itself differently at different stages in life (as a dependent child, as an independent adult).

I think, however, that the most common element in all love is the sense of attachment to the object of love. Love emanates from us toward an object, creating a bond with that object: an emotional, spiritual bond, sometimes reinforced by physical contact. Love is, above all, attachment to someone or something. It is the antithesis of being alone, separate, detached. Our first attachment is with our mothers, and it is the particular nature of that attachment that determines what kind of lovers we become in later life.

First we start life firmly attached to our mother in her womb. When we emerge we are nurtured by her, establishing a direct physical and emotional relationship. If we are breast-fed by a calm, secure mother, the sense of attachment grows with a minimum of disturbance. If we are bottle-fed on some arbitrary time schedule by a nervous, insecure mother, the sense of attachment develops, but a sense of disharmony and tension may become part of that sense of attachment. As immobile, passive, helpless infants, our dependence on mother is complete, and so is our sense of attachment.

The mother is the infant's primary source of stimulation and satisfaction. It is that daily combination of stimulation and satisfaction that forms the basis of the child's emotional attachment to his mother. It is easy to see that if the stimulation is abusive rather than loving, and if there is more frustration than satisfaction, the child's emotional response will reflect such treatment. Nevertheless his attachment is unconditional because he has no choice over it. However, mother love is the appropriate stimulus every human infant requires for healthy growth. This stimulus, in the form of nurturing, cuddling, playing, talking is so vitally necessary to the infant that without it, even though he may be fed, he will develop some very serious psychosomatic disorders. For example, according to Anthony Davids in *Children in Conflict: A Casebook*:

> Frustrated dependency needs lead to stomach ulcers; unfulfilled needs for tactile stimulation and affection lead to dermatitis; and repressed rage against the mother leads to asthma. From the psychodynamic position, asthmatic wheezing is viewed as suppressed crying. The child fears separation from the mother and is angry toward her, but fears rejection and therefore cannot express these emotions directly. Thus emotions gain expression in the form of asthma attacks.[114]

An infant may even die if it is deprived of sufficient maternal stimulus. Ashley Montagu writes in *On Being Human*:

The importance of love in the early social development of the infant cannot be overemphasized. Its real significance can best be understood when we consider a disease from which, but half a century ago, almost all the children hospitalized within their first year of life regularly died. This disease was known as marasmus, from the Greek word meaning "wasting away." The disease was also known as infantile atrophy or debility; today it is known as "hospitalism." When intensive studies were undertaken to track down its cause, the discovery was made that babies in the best homes and hospitals were most often its victims, babies who were apparently receiving the best and most careful physical attention, while babies in the poorest homes, with a good mother, despite the lack of hygienic physical conditions, often overcame the physical handicaps and flourished. What was wanting in the sterilized environment of babies of the first category and was generously supplied in babies of the second category was mother love. [115]

Mother-love is not only necessary for the infant's immediate survival, but also for long-range normal growth, for without it the infant cannot develop the strong emotional attachment to his mother that becomes the prototype of all future emotional attachments. However a strong emotional attachment to mother is not in itself enough to make the child an active lover. As the passive receiver of mother-love he is simply the beneficiary of satisfying physical stimulation and nourishment. As far as he is concerned mother is part of him. It is only when it begins to dawn on him that mother is a separate entity, somewhat beyond his physical control, that the passive sense of attachment is threatened by a growing sense of separateness. The sense of separateness grows as the child becomes mobile, feels the exercise of his own musculature, and can actually separate himself physically from his mother. Because human beings develop mobility while they are still completely dependent, this creates within every human being an acute separation anxiety.

I am inclined to believe that separation anxiety has an instinctual, biological base and is part of our survival reflexes. For the separation from mother in primitive circumstances meant sure death. Without separation anxiety the highly dependent small child might wander too far from mother and be killed. Human beings have a weak sense of smell. We don't run fast. Our muscles are comparatively weak. Our survival depends on strong, intense emotions that link us with other protecting human beings.

Separation anxiety is so intense a psychic pain that most people find it intolerable. The infant deals with separation anxiety by "falling in love" with his mother—that is, changing from a passive receiver of mother-love to becoming an active lover. As a result he develops what psychologists call "attachment behavior," a clinging need to be with mother to dispel the intense psychic pain of separation anxiety. It is the child's first experience of "falling in love," and it is basically a solution to the problem of separation and the unbearable anxiety it causes. Separation anxiety can be so painful that only the most intense attachment behavior can begin to alleviate it. Here is one mother's description of her child's attachment behavior as recorded in *Patterns of Child Rearing*:

> He wants a lot of attention. He wants all my attention. He doesn't let me talk on the telephone—he is climbing all over me, interrupting me, and if I were talking to anyone—even here now—he would resent it terribly. He would have to be climbing all over me and want my attention, and if he can't get it he does something very naughty to get it.

Another mother described her child's intense attachment behavior:

> I try to be understanding about it—I realize he needs an awful lot of security. I try to give him as much as I can, but there are limitations—it gets to the point where I just can't do any more than I have already done. He is very much inclined to say, "You don't love me," and of course it kills me, it breaks my heart, but I really don't know quite what to do about it; and yet I feel that I give him more than his share of love and affection. He gets much more than the other children do, and I really feel that I have neglected the baby terribly for him. I have ignored the baby completely for him, but I think that there would be no limit to what he would want from me. I think he would want me to be around whenever he wanted me, so he could sit in my lap and I could tell him a story, or I could play a game with him, or talk to him. There was one period when he would go out to play and he would suddenly come in the house and throw his arms around me, and he would ask, "Do you love me?"—and then I would assure him I did love him, and he would go out again, but he would keep coming in. He just seemed to feel the need of security, to be assured.[116]

Every normal human being begins developing attachment behavior between eight and twenty-four months of age. But since the problem of separation anxiety only begins with the child's awareness of his separateness, the solution of "attachment behavior" is also only a beginning, for not only is physical separation from mother inevitable but also quite necessary for normal ego development. Therefore the period of "attachment behavior" can be extremely difficult for some children as they try to develop more effective, long-range solutions to separation anxiety.

Attachment behavior is sometimes called dependency behavior, and some parents, assuming that it is a sign of emotional weakness, try to discourage this behavior by not responding warmly to it. This creates in the child an even greater anxiety and sense of dependency because his emotional needs are not satisfied. His frustration may cause anger, in which case anger becomes a part of his attachment behavior. He may deliberately misbehave in order to get the attention he craves, for punishment is preferable to no attention at all. If the anger is internalized, his attachment behavior will take on a masochistic character.

Some mothers are inconsistent in meeting their children's dependency needs. They lavish affection at one moment and show cold indifference at another. This creates unresolved dependency needs in the child, with extremes of tension and relief, so that the child lives on an emotional roller coaster. As Pavlov and other psychologists demonstrated, the erratic, unpredictable alternation between frustration and satisfaction of a need enhances the strength of that need.

The mother who meets her child's dependency needs without fuss enables her child to develop a satisfactory emotional equilibrium that frees him to explore the world. His ego, his sense of self, is enhanced by the satisfaction of *his* needs. Thus the adequate satisfaction of dependency needs encourages the growth of an independent personality. But the mother who alternates between satisfaction and deprivation creates a tense, frustrated, deeply dependent child. Writes Beatrix Tudor-Hart in *The Intelligent Parent's Guide to Child Behavior*:

> The child both loves and hates the person who alternately cherishes him in satisfying his needs, and unaccountably hurts and frustrates him. Often the child will try to resolve the conflict by transferring his rage and hatred to some object accidentally associated with the adult who is causing the frustration. This transference is all the more likely because fear of losing the love of the adult actively inhibits the child from discharging his rage and hate toward its real object.[117]

Unresolved dependency conflicts in early childhood can have serious consequences in later life. Adult alcoholism, for example, can be traced back to emotional problems created during attachment behavior. William McCord writes in *Origins of Alcoholism*:

> We concentrate on dependency conflict, the battle within a person between his intensified need to be loved and his equally strong desire to repress this need. This particular conflict appears prominently in the character of the alcoholic. . . .
>
> From this analysis, a consistent, statistically significant pattern emerges: the typical alcoholic, as a child, underwent a variety of experiences that heightened inner stress, intensified his desire for love, and produced a distorted self-image. . . .
>
> What kind of anxiety is so overwhelming that it causes a person to become alcoholic? We believe that anxiety which results from an internal conflict between a strong "dependency" need and an equally strong desire for independence is one basic source of the disorder. . . .
>
> We believe that a primary characteristic of alcoholics is that they suffer from heightened dependency needs. Maternal alternation between affection and rejection is especially conducive to the establishment of this trait. Maternal affection as well as rejection, in combination with certain other home conditions, might also be expected to have a similar result.[118]

Thus the seeds of alcoholism and other adult emotional problems are planted during the period of a child's attachment behavior and his mother's ambivalent response to that behavior.

The normal solution to separation anxiety is attachment behavior. But, as we pointed out, attachment behavior is only a beginning of a long-range solution as the child grows and develops an independent sense of self and requires increasing separation for that growth. Thus attachment behavior becomes less physical and more spiritual and ends up as feelings of love. Physical separation can then be sustained without any loss of attachment. Love becomes a permanent means of dispelling separation anxiety. But the child who is separated from his mother or loses his mother during the height of attachment behavior before it can be spiritualized, can be permanently hurt emotionally. Some children become hopeless schizophrenics as withdrawal becomes their only means of alleviating the intolerable pain of separation. The adult who loses a wife or husband can look for another mate after the period of grief has passed. But a child cannot actively seek another attachment to relieve separation anxiety. He can only use self-manipulating methods, and withdrawal is the most effective means available to him. Dr. Gerald O'Gorman, discussing schizophrenia in *The Nature of Childhood Autism*, writes:

> It seems that in the majority of cases the child's withdrawal from the rest of the environment is really an extension of his initial withdrawal from, or failure ever to make a normal relationship with, his mother. Nearly always there is evidence of impairment at an early stage in the emotional relationship between mother and child, and this is usually associated with some kind of separation, either physical or emotional. Physical separation may be due to illness of one or the other, or to desertion by mother, or even a prolonged holiday away from the child. [119]

In cases where the child must suffer abusive treatment, attachment behavior is accompanied by stoicism, murderous rage, and cold-bloodedness. The child might become a murderer in later life, having formed no loving attachment but, instead, a cold hatred that leads to criminal, homicidal behavior. The criminal eventually gets to jail, where he is the helpless victim of more abusive treatment. But he has security. Thus he recapitulates his childhood experience. It is to be wondered if perhaps the true but unconscious motive of most criminals is to get into jail, where they can relive the kind of situation they had as dependent children, and thus relieve their separation anxiety. The prison becomes a mother substitute, very much like the abusive, punishing original mother. It is not uncommon for many prisoners, upon release, to commit other crimes that lead them right back to the penal institution from which they just emerged.

However, under normal circumstances a child's attachment behavior develops into love; which is, in reality, the most effective solution to separation anxiety. Assuming that the parent is loving and devoted in return, the child's attachment will remain strong throughout life regardless of other love affairs. In many cases the attachment to mother remains the primary, central attachment throughout life, with all other attachments taking subsidiary place. Many wives complain of their husbands' strong attachments to their mothers. The first loyalties are, in many if not most instances, the strongest, because they are made early in life, under the stress of painful separation anxiety when a child has very limited self-manipulating means of coping with it.

The greatest protection against separation anxiety is the development of loyalty, which becomes firmed and fixed. We develop loyalty because we become aware that the world is full of other attractive people who arouse separation anxiety in us. While love is a defense against separation anxiety caused by growing physical separation between mother and child, loyalty is a defense against the attractions of others who would cause alienation and separation from our primary attachment.

Thus one might say that love is a biological phenomenon, while loyalty is a social one. Two lovers on a desert island do not have to worry about loyalty. Nor do a mother and infant have to worry about loyalty. But when the child is old enough to move about and can develop attachments to people other than his mother, he must develop loyalty to protect his primary attachment. Loyalty is exclusivity. It means deliberately shutting out all stimuli that might arouse separation anxiety.

A child's attachment to his mother undergoes all sorts of modifications and strains required by life. If there are other siblings he must learn to accomodate them in some way. He must adjust to his mother's attachment to his father. He must increasingly satisfy his need to become a separate human being. His attachment, thus, becomes more and more tenuous. Loyalty, or exclusion of threatening stimuli, becomes his chief means of maintaining an attachment through distance and time. Loyalty is the ultimate defense against separation.

When the child becomes an adult, he falls in love. He is once more strongly stimulated, physically and emotionally, by the close, exclusive attention of an attractive person. He recapitulates the intense physical and emotional pleasure of his first attachment. The threat of losing this deeply satisfying, soul-nourishing stimulus creates separation anxiety, which leads to "attachment behavior," which in turn is modified into "love," which then develops into "loyalty" or a monogamous relationship. When we fall in love we recapitulate the entire sequence of emotional development that took place during early childhood. Our principal aim, as in childhood, is to alleviate separation anxiety. In adulthood sexual attraction provides the strong physical stimulus that opens the way to emotional attachment. Loyalty becomes the most essential ingredient in adult love, because the world is full of sexually attractive people who can alienate us from our love attachment. Therefore, as adults, susceptible to the sexual attractions of others, we easily become our own greatest source of separation anxiety.

Every human being has the ability to shut out unwanted stimuli. We do it automatically in a crowded elevator or during the rush hour in a subway train when people are pressed all around us. We withdraw into a temporary fortress and feel greatly relieved when we can get out and move freely. In developing loyalty we undergo the same process but more slowly, recognizing at each encounter with outside stimuli which ones threaten and which ones do not. We tend to reject stimuli that create separation anxiety vis à vis our primary attachment. What we try to do is create an "immovable center," an inviolable attachment that can withstand prolonged separations of time and distance. The maintenance of such an immovable center requires giving up response to much outside stimuli. One learns gradually how to shut out most disruptive, threatening stimuli and to admit only such stimuli as enhance and strengthen our primary attachment.

One attachment can be replaced by another. For example, a woman who is deserted by her husband may fall in love easily with the first man who shows a strong interest in her. We say that she has fallen in love "on the rebound." A new attachment quickly dispels the pain of separation. However there are some people who develop such strong loyalties and whose fear of separation is so great that death is preferable to separation. We often read of a man killing his estranged wife and then himself.

Puritans are so fearful of pleasurable stimuli that they create laws and customs forbidding such stimuli to exist. They are people whose loyalties depend on the use of legal force to guard them against threatening stimuli. They wear clothes that de-emphasize the erotic. They maintain prohibitions against dancing and drinking. One would conclude that Puritans are people who feel themselves easily susceptible to strong outside stimuli and therefore need the organized protection of society to guard them against them.

I know of no scientific studies ever made of loyalty as a psychological phenomenon, yet it is the most effective psychological device human beings use to protect their attachments, to prevent separation, to quell separation anxiety. Loyalty depends not only on the human being's ability to shut out unwanted stimuli, but also to spiritualize emotional and physical attachments. The love of God is the most spiritualized of our attachments. When monks withdraw from the world they do so in order to intensify their attachment to God. They find it too difficult to maintain that attachment in the world of excitement and pleasure, where they are constantly bombarded by strong distracting stimuli. Only by withdrawal can they concentrate on and intensify the attachment that means most to them. The attachment to God easily becomes an "immovable center," because it is not subject to human frailty or inconstancy. God is always there. He does not die. He does not leave you. Only you can leave God. On the other hand, an attachment to another human being can provide strong physical and emotional stimuli, but it is an attachment subject to human inconstancy and mortality. That is why so many people require an immovable center, a source of unlimited, unconditional love, even though they may have strong attachments to other human beings.

Every human being must solve his problem of separation anxiety in his own way. No two situations are alike because no two children and no two mothers are alike. Even the different children of the same mother must solve their separation problems individually. We know of only one category of children who are radically different from normal children in respect to the separation problem: autistic children. They seem to be born without the ability to develop a strong primary attachment to their mothers. They seem to be born with suits of defensive armor against outside stimuli, and it sometimes takes years before an autistic child can be taught to open himself up to emotional stimuli. One would conclude from this that the ability to form emotional attachments is a survival instinct that autistic children are born without. Autistic children survive today because our technical civilization now makes it possible for all kinds of people born with emotional or physical defects and handicaps to survive. But they indicate that it is possible to be born without certain emotional capabilities otherwise necessary for survival.

Every human being requires a certain amount of separation from his mother for normal growth. This is necessary because life requires that we survive our parents. Mothers who discourage such separation because of their own fears of abandonment use all sorts of devices to keep their children dependent, to maintain symbiosis. They practice what is often called "smother love." In such families the children as adults are barely capable of dealing with the outside world. They have simply not been permitted to develop a sense of independent separateness with love replacing symbiosis. They become terribly dependent adults, with weak, fragmented egos.

Most mothers recognize the integrity of their children's separateness and permit normal growth to take place. They supply ample love so that a child can move confidently into the outer world. They retain their child's love and respect because they give their child the freedom to grow and become himself. Independence does not mean loss of attachment. It means a cooperative relationship in which the mother respects the child and vice versa. It means the spiritualization of what was once a physical symbiosis. That spiritualization may sometimes include a fixed loyalty, to compensate for the physical separation, precluding the replacement of that central, primary attachment with another. Thus a Don Juan may have numerous sexual affairs with many women but never fall in love with any of them. Another individual will exclude all sexual stimuli from the opposite sex to guard against disloyalty to his mother. Or a Boston strangler will kill all the women who attract him to prove that his loyalty to his primary attachment, his mother, is inviolate.

Sexual attraction is what leads children out of their families into love relationships with strangers. Thus sexuality is, theoretically, the greatest threat to attachment loyalty unless it can be used to enhance or expand the family. A grandchild is often seen as a gift of loyalty from a loving son or daughter. One's sex life, therefore, will be influenced by the nature of one's primary loyalty. Growth does not depend only on parental permission to grow. It also depends on an individual's willingness to relinquish a strong primary attachment. Some individuals cannot tolerate the loss of such an attachment because it has been such an important mainstay of their emotional equilibrium. But in most cases strong sexual and emotional stimuli from an attractive person permits a transfer of loyalty, particularly if mother has given permission for such a transfer to take place. Not all mothers give their sons permission to fall in love with other women and not all sons will accept that permission even if it is given.

Girls are subject to the same primary attachment to their mothers as are boys. The same separation anxiety develops, the same attachment behavior, the same love and loyalty. In later life girls can recapitulate their primary attachment by becoming mothers themselves and giving their own mothers grandchildren. But first they must find husbands who live up to their parents' standards and are acceptable to them. Loving daughters will have no trouble finding such husbands, but daughters in conflict with their mothers usually do. It is also probable that Lesbianism is the result of a fixed loyalty to mother, proving to mother that no man will ever replace that loyalty.

The need for attachment is the most pressing lifelong emotional need of human beings. With attachment come attachment stimuli, which are necessary for emotional and mental health. Infants cannot live without them; the infants simply waste away and die. Children require a great deal of them, and they will go to great and ingenious lengths to get them. The family provides an ideal situation in which attachment stimuli can be exchanged frequently and strongly. Exchanges of love and affection, as well as arguments and shouting matches are forms of attachment stimuli that make family life as emotionally charged as it is. When parents grow old and children leave, the lack of attachment stimuli creates sadness and depression. One uses memory to relive past experiences of satisfying attachment stimuli.

For an infant, being the passive receiver of nourishment, warmth, love, cuddling, and protection provides it with attachment stimuli. As the child's growing mobility and ego differentiation make him increasingly aware of his separateness, he feels the strong psychic pain of separation anxiety. From being a passive receiver he becomes an active pursuer of attachment stimuli. In most cases he will get what he wants, thus relieving his separation anxiety. By loving he has initiated stimuli that maintain the attachment he has become so afraid of losing. I believe that how a child makes that adjustment, or is permitted to make it by his mother, determines his ability to make love attachments in later life.

With attachment stimuli come attachment benefits, the material comforts of life. In primitive society the attachment benefits for the adult as well as the child came from the family or the tribe. In advanced civilization, unless we are born into wealthy families or dynasties, we must often move outside the family to get attachment benefits. Children receive them from the same source as attachment stimuli until they are ready to go out into the working world. They get a job by attaching themselves to some corporation that, in exchange for labor, dispenses attachment benefits. The emotional jolt that comes with losing a job is often strong, because for the first twenty years or so of our lives we have associated attachment benefits with attachment stimuli. It is hard for many people to separate the two, yet in modern society it becomes necessary to do so. The tendency to seek attachment stimuli from the institutions and corporations that dispense attachment benefits has become one of the more difficult problems of our society. The Japanese have solved this problem by making their corporations giant families where being fired or cut off from attachment benefits is unthinkable. In America, Uncle Sam is assuming more and more the role of dispenser of attachment benefits. In response, more and more Americans are beginning to seek attachment stimuli from their government, which is only equipped to dispense them in a negative way, as for example through the Internal Revenue Service or a penal institution.

When most people leave their families it is to create new families where the generation of attachment stimuli can be continued. But in our society more and more people are leaving their families to live alone or with roommates. As singles they seek "love," but usually wind up seeking attachment stimuli in the form of promiscuous sex. Sex without emotional attachment provides very momentary relief, and the complaint about one-night stands is a common one among singles. If a sexual encounter leads to an emotional attachment, the problem of loyalty and monogamy arises. In a society that bombards people constantly with sexual stimuli, loyalty becomes a difficult problem for some people, particularly when the attachment ceases to provide uninterrupted pleasure and satisfaction. "Love" then becomes conditional, lasting only as long as the satisfaction.

All human beings are subject to sexual vagrancy, and all human beings develop the internal means of dealing with it. The most common method of monogamous people is simply to shut out unwanted sexual stimuli. Single swingers, however, are so responsive to sexual stimuli that it becomes very difficult for them to practice sexual loyalty when an emotional attachment has been established. They must go through the lengthy process of developing the mental means of shutting out unwanted sexual stimuli. This requires a self-discipline that goes against their hedonistic grain. They find it hard to justify such painful self-deprivation, particularly if there is some frustration in their attachment. The result is that their emotional attachments are of short duration and they are forced to suffer the depressions and pains of recurring separations. Suicide becomes one way to end it all. Another is to renounce sexuality altogether and join a religious order where a permanent spiritual attachment to God is made.

Why is a spiritual attachment to God so satisfying to so many people? Because God can be depended on, while human beings can't. Sexual vagrancy, fickleness, emotional instability, jealousy, possessiveness all make human emotional attachments painful, frustrating, and sometimes destructive. But a spiritual attachment to God provides some very much needed attachment benefits and stimuli. First, God provides moral guidance and protection in a dangerous world, something we usually get from our mothers in our first attachment. Second, God provides unlimited, unconditional love, whether we are beautiful or ugly, rich or poor, intelligent or stupid: the same kind of unconditional love we got from mother. Third, God provides a permanent attachment, an "immovable center," that becomes a permanent defense against separation anxiety. Fourth, God provides a tremendous sense of peace, calm, and serenity because the attachment is spiritual rather than physical, based on spiritual faith rather than physical presence.

It is easy to see that in our scientifically oriented world many people cannot establish or accept a spiritual attachment to God. They are therefore deprived of perhaps the most effective solution to the problem of separation anxiety. But belief or faith in God requires a certain inner spirituality, an ability to concentrate, to meditate, to think, to soar beyond concrete reality. Above all, it requires a certain humility and admission of helplessness or defeat. That is why Alcoholics Anonymous is so very effective. The alcoholic, in his utter defeat and helplessness, surrenders to God's will. Those alcoholics who cannot achieve that sense of surrender, that spirituality, wind up dying in the gutters, alone, abandoned, separated from everything that makes life possible.

Surrender is the key concept in the love of God. It is an admission of helplessness. Since we begin life as helpless infants, our solutions to separation anxiety are self-manipulative. As we grow older and find the frustrations of life more and more difficult to deal with, the sense of helplessness returns. We come full circle, seeking peace and comfort in the arms of God instead of our mothers.

So much in modern American society tends to increase separation anxiety on all levels, in all age groups. In childbirth the American hospital intrudes in the mother-infant relationship, causing disruptions in the subtle reflexes and instincts that would establish a satisfying mother-infant attachment from the beginning. Then modern pediatrics, replacing the mother's mother, interferes in child rearing with its artificial feeding and fixed schedules, making mothers insecure and nervous about their mothering abilities. What makes matters even more confusing for young mothers is that pediatricians disagree with one another and have offered different advice to different generations, creating a generation gap in child-rearing practices. Then, when the child finally gets to public school, the educators begin a long process of child-parent alienation, as if the purpose of education were to persuade the child to renounce his parents' values. In addition, the turning away from religion deprives the child of one of the most effective spiritual means for dealing with separation anxiety and achieving emotional equilibrium.

As an adolescent the child is exposed to more ideas that tend to alienate him from his parents, causing conflict at home, emotional confusion within. Girls are encouraged to take the pill and engage in premarital recreational sex before they know anything about love, loyalty, or motherhood. And boys are encouraged to exploit the girls' availability. The result is that few happy attachments are made, but many girls become pregnant, despite the pill, go through the trauma of abortion, take drugs, and become delinquents or even suicides.

And even if marriage does take place, divorce laws are now so relaxed that marriages are dissolved and families broken up without any understanding of the emotional consequences of such break-ups. The temptations of sexual promiscuity and the constant pornographic assault on the senses place additional strains on sexual fidelity and attachment loyalty. Everywhere you turn, attachment values are distorted and ridiculed and all the defenses against separation anxiety are under attack.

The nuclear family itself now excludes grandparents, who are separated from the younger generations by being relegated to special housing for the elderly. There, separated from the rest of the vital world, they live with their psychosomatic illnesses and wait for death. American society makes it difficult for lasting, satisfying attachments to be made. It has created a nation of tense, nervous, unhappy people who seek relief from acute separation anxiety in pills, alcohol, and drugs. Most people are simply too emotionally crippled or confused to be able to create a satisfying, lasting attachment—which is the only

191

cure for separation anxiety. In addition, our society no longer provides the necessary spiritual and cultural preparation for durable attachments. The whole thrust of our culture is toward alienation—between parent and child, young and old, men and women, people and God.

Can we reverse this national drift toward alienation? Possibly. But only if people recognize what is happening to them and their society. Obviously the first place to start is in a new look at motherhood where the whole process of attachment, separation, and love begins. As I pointed out in the previous chapter, modern obstetrics is only beginning to understand its negative influences in the initial mother-infant relationship. In addition, breast-feeding, with the begrudging approval of more and more pediatricians, is a growing phenomenon in this country. These are small but good signs.

In the field of psychology there is a growing understanding of the need for continuity in the mother-child relationship, which will influence our social agencies dealing with disturbed, alienated, and abandoned children. Rita Kramer writes:

> Adoption should take place as early as possible—even before birth where this can be arranged—and with no trial periods, since a succession of temporary placements means the interruption of early attachments that is so destructive for the young child, as well as uncertainty for the adoptive parents, who may hesitate to make a full emotional commitment to the child.[120]

Thus the nature of attachment and separation and their effects on the emotional equilibrium of the child are beginning to be understood. What is also beginning to be recognized is that adults need durable attachments just as much as children. The enormous unhappiness being caused by precipitous divorces is awakening psychiatrists and psychologists to the debilitating effects separations are having on emotional health. Disgruntled mates will be encouraged to stay married and work out their problems, rather than risk the greater pains and depressions of separation. Keeping together is as much of an art to be learned as loving itself. It is assumed that if two people loved each other enough to marry, then there will be enough residual goodwill, in most cases, to permit the attachment to ride out some stormy moments. As José Ortega writes: "True love best recognizes itself and, so to speak, measures and calculates itself by the pain and suffering of which it is capable."[121]

Another good sign is that God is no longer considered to be dead. Many young people are being attracted to religious values—not necessarily organized religion—because they have found secular values to be so empty, so transitory, so unsatisfying. Parents are also rebelling against the alienating influences to which their children are exposed in the public schools. They are beginning to realize that the responsibility for passing their values on to the next generation is theirs and not the educator's. Also there is a growing recognition that the young can enjoy and learn from the old and vice versa, that there is no real conflict of interest between them, and that segregation by age group is both artificial and limiting. And, of course, there is a growing dialogue between the sexes, a recognition that men and women cannot live without one another and that a mutually satisfying modus vivendi is preferable to suicidal warfare.

We are perhaps at the beginning of a new age. It is not easy to be optimistic these days and one should not exaggerate the significance of small signs. But one must always take into account man's inventiveness and resourcefulness. Human beings have an insatiable craving to be happy, and they will go to great lengths to find out how. In their present experiments with moral freedom, Americans are learning all too quickly what doesn't bring happiness. That, in itself, is a good beginning.

12

What Do You Tell Your Daughter?

To the question "What do you tell your daughter?" the answer is painfully simple: "All that you can." Knowledge is power, and the more a girl knows about herself as a human being—which must include the fact that she's a woman—the better she will be able to cope with life and take full advantage of the opportunities both society and nature make available to her. Knowledge is indispensable today, because technology has given women powers they have never had before: the absolute power over the life and death of the unborn. It is an awesome power, which many girls now exercise as if they were choosing a new pair of panty hose. Perhaps I am overstating the case, for I really find it hard to believe that a woman can pass a death sentence on her own unborn child and not live with the emotional ramifications of her decision for the rest of her life. But the danger in technology is that it tends to cultivate insensitivity, a clinical detachment, a deadening of the emotions. And nothing is more dangerous to human survival than that, for our emotions *are* our survival instincts, and when we shut them off we begin to lose our way, to be less than human.

If we murder the unborn while not permitting ourselves to feel that we are committing murder, then we deprive ourselves of the value and function of our emotions. And I am not talking about killing barely visible human embryos; I am talking about the systematic murder of thousands of healthy prenatal infants with arms and legs and eyes and ears. We may think that clinical intelligence alone can prevail. But when we become alienated from our emotions we become merely automatons: computers that occasionally have to go to the bathroom. If people are giving up feeling these days it is probably because we have made life too painful. The result is that we spend most of our resources seeking new sedatives, new anesthetics, new drugs, new techniques of escape and withdrawal to permit us to live as spectators with dulled senses—capable of a minimum of feeling, reacting only to the stimuli of the roller coaster, the horror movie, or the touchdown. So we must continually guard ourselves against the dangers of technology, of intelligence divorced from emotions, of titillations substituting for deep feeling.

When we see widespread unhappiness and discontent amid the chrome and glitter of 20th-century America, when we read that more than five hundred people have leaped off the Golden Gate Bridge since it opened in 1937, we begin to wonder how people ever managed to survive, let alone be happy, in preindustrial times when life was so very harsh—when there were no color TVs, no cars, no electric lights, no central heating. Love made happiness possible under the most primitive conditions of life, and only love can make happiness possible in our technological world.

How do you teach love? By loving. By respecting the integrity of your daughter's own personality. By offering helpful guidance. By permitting her to learn. By being protective, yet having faith in her intelligence. By giving her freedom, but providing knowledge that will enable her to exercise her freedom wisely. By not reacting angrily to mistakes. We all make mistakes, and mistakes are a part of life, adult as well as child.

A daughter's education begins the moment she is brought to her mother's breast for nursing. As mother and daughter get to know one another they start a warm, intimate relationship that will last a lifetime. If there is harmony, understanding, pleasure, patience, tolerance, together with physical warmth, good nourishment, and affectionate stimulation, there is no reason why a child should not see the world as essentially benevolent, friendly, manageable, fulfilling. That there will be some frustration, some conflict, is inevitable. But frustration and conflict will be minimal if the mother gives herself to the maternal role without reservation, without feeling that there is something else she'd rather do, someplace else she'd rather be. Circumstances may force the mother to be elsewhere and to be doing something other than caring for her child, but the child should feel and know that mother would rather be with her. Above all, the relationship should be mutually satisfying. The daughter, needless to say, enjoys having a mother. But mother should enjoy having a daughter.

Should you give your daughter a doll to play with? Or should you follow the current "anti-sexist" trend and get her something not specifically related to her sex? Most little girls will play house and mother-games whether they are given toys or not. The kinds of toys you give denote parental approval or disapproval. If you give your daughter a doll, it doesn't mean that she must forgo a career and become a mother in the future. It means that she has your permission and approval to become a mother if she wants to. However if you studiously avoid giving her dolls, or discourage or prevent her from playing with dolls, then you are telling her that she does not have your permission or approval to become a mother in the future. If you respect the integrity of your daughter's personality, let her choose the toys she will play with. But do not hide your permissions and approvals among the ones you give her. If you give her both a doll and a truck, to see which one she plays with, she will try to guess which one has your permission and approval. She will be asking "Do you want me to be a girl or do you want me to be a boy?" Rather than place your daughter in such a dilemma at such an early, impressionable age, give her toys that are both appropriate to her sex—dolls, dishes, etc.—as well as toys that can be enjoyed by either sex: paint sets, modeling clay, crafts, musical instruments, etc. If you give her toys specifically identified with male behavior—trucks, airplanes, guns, baseball gloves—she will get your message: mother wants me to act like a boy. If you tell her that she has your permission and approval to play with both dolls *and* trucks, then you are telling her that girls can do both. And we know that girls *can* do both. I recently saw a women's professional football game on television. The women were all dressed in full football regalia, and after the game the camera showed one woman joining her children. They seemed to enjoy the fact that mother was a football player. There was no way of knowing, from the report, whether or not mother's interest in football made her a good, bad, or indifferent mother. We don't know if this confused her children. We do know that women can do a lot of things that men do and do them well. But we also know that there are some very important things women can do that men cannot.

Women can have babies. Men cannot. Some women's libbers don't think that this difference is terribly important; but most men consider it of paramount importance. My own opinion is that this difference is the single most important fact of life, principally because it determines the nature of human attachment, and nothing is more important to life and survival than attachment. If, as I believe, a satisfying attachment is the key to happiness, then how one is brought up to find, create, and sustain such an attachment is the most important preparation for life. You prepare a little girl for future maternal attachment by giving her a doll. You don't by giving her a truck.

No matter what the women's libbers say, no matter what the population controllers advocate, the vast majority of women in the world will bear at least one child. For most of these women, the attachment to the child's father and the attachment to the child itself will be the most important attachments of her life. Particularly the attachment to her child. Husbands may come and go. But children are lifelong attachments. How a mother handles that attachment not only determines her child's future happiness but also her own satisfaction at being a mother. We have learned the hard way that mothering is an art handed down from generation to generation, and that, in our technological society where natural reflexes and instincts are easily erased, it becomes even more important to prepare girls for the mothering role. If we want fewer child abusers, fewer tense, insecure mothers, we shall have to teach girls the pleasures of mothering. And before you can teach a girl the pleasures of mothering, you must make her positively disposed toward motherhood.

The trend these days is to make a girl positively disposed toward sex so that she can enjoy plenty of sex with her boyfriends and future husband. The way we do this is to tell her everything she has to know about sex: her sexual anatomy, her responses, her partner's responses, techniques of arousal, etc. The same teaching techniques must be used in preparing a woman for childbearing and the lifelong attachments that come with being a mother. A girl should be told everything she has to know to make the attachment to her child as satisfying as possible—not only for the child's sake, but for her own sake. And so, if you tell your little girl, when you give her a doll, that some day she too will be a mother, you are not lying, because nine chances out of ten she will be. You are not telling her that she may not also be a doctor, a champion swimmer, or even a football player. You are not limiting her horizons; you are simply preparing her for one of the most deeply satisfying and fulfilling experiences a woman can have: an attachment to her own child.

Most women who want careers also want children. Most women do not find any conflict between having children and pursuing a career. They simply have to manage their lives so that they can do both. So you are not committing a sexist sin by giving your little girl a doll to play with. You are simply affirming to her that she has a capability her little brother doesn't have: the ability to become a mother. You make a girl favorably disposed toward motherhood not because you think that she can't do most of the things men can do, but because she can do *one* thing that men can't do: bear children. No boy can become a mother, no matter how much he may want to. But most girls *will*

198

become mothers, whether they want to or not, and that is why girls must be made favorably disposed toward motherhood—so that they don't ruin the lives of the children they bear. The painful fact is that a great many women who don't want children have them. An awful lot of women who don't want to become mothers become them. There is no reason why the children should be made to suffer because of this. We can alleviate much child suffering by making *all* girls favorably disposed toward motherhood; because whether anyone likes it or not, the girls—not the boys—will be bearing the next generation.

To make a girl favorably disposed toward motherhood does not necessarily or automatically make her unfavorably disposed toward anything else. It merely prepares her favorably to accept a role she will most likely have to accept sometime in life. It puts her psychologically in harmony with the basic reproductive and hormonal functions of her body. She becomes less tense and insecure about the business of being a mother. No one says that she has to be a mother, but she is prepared to be one if she has to. Statistically speaking, your daughter will most likely bear a child some day, and when she does she becomes someone's mother for the rest of her life. Nature relies on society to prepare women psychologically for motherhood, to make motherhood more of a joy than a burden, more of a pleasure than a duty.

At one time women regarded sex with their husbands as a duty rather than a pleasure. Now they are being taught what a great pleasure sex can be. The same is true of motherhood. For several generations now the duties and burdens of motherhood have been stressed over its pleasures. Now the emphasis is beginning to shift as more and more women discover the pleasures of motherhood that modern obstetrics has hidden from them for so long. The return to breast-feeding is one of the most significant signs that this shift is taking place. Indeed, the sexual revolution may be superseded some day by a maternal revolution.

It is utter nonsense to tell women that their childbearing capabilities are no longer needed, that their bodies are obsolete because of the population explosion. There has to be a next generation and only today's women can produce it. To say that women's bodies are obsolete is to infer that we don't need a next generation, which is ridiculous, since virtually every human being alive today will be dead in a hundred years. Most women will continue to bear at least one child, regardless of the population crisis, Women's Lib, legalized abortion, or the pill. And since it is impossible to tell while she is a child whether your daughter will become a mother, then all girls should be given a favorable disposition toward motherhood. Probability favors motherhood.

That doesn't mean training your daughter to become dainty and feminine, sexy and helpless. It means cultivating the maternal virtues: patience, gentleness, tolerance, endurance, lovingness, self-discipline, intelligence, responsibility. The maternal virtues are the possitive virtues of life. They stand one in good stead whether one has children or not. So if we train our daughters to be favorably disposed toward motherhood, we are training them to become good human beings with high self-respect and self-esteem.

What do you tell your daughter when she begins to menstruate? You tell her that nature is preparing her to become a mother some day, and you explain to her the entire process of ovulation, how her hormones activate the monthly cycle, and why she has the periodic discharge. Instead of being frightened of the process, she learns to understand and appreciate it. She sees it as a positive sign of her special capability, which in itself is a gift from God. The gift is not merely the baby she may have some day. It is the attachment that will come with the baby, the emotional reward of childbearing and child rearing.

At such times it is always good to acquaint your daughter with the concept of God. No one goes through life without experiencing terrible moments of helplessness and hopelessness. A belief in God can be a tremendously sustaining force. Atheist parents may prefer to give their youngsters purely scientific explanations about the female's reproductive processes. But such cold explanations tend to alienate us from our own mysteries. Science knows very little about the human reproductive system. Sir Charles Dodds, the British biochemist who was the first to isolate the female hormone estrogen, writes:

> We should always be humbled when we think of what we do not know about the female reproductive cycle. We still have no understanding of the mechanism that makes one Graafian follicle in one of the ovaries of a normal woman maturate and ovulate each month. This is a baffling problem. Until we know that mechanism that selects one Graafian follicle, out of perhaps hundreds of thousands, to maturate each month, we still have to proceed with caution on any long-term, hormonal treatment of the human female.[122]

The great scientists have always been humbled by what they didn't know. And wisdom tells any intelligent man that what he knows is only a small particle of what there is to know. Thus, when you tell your daughter about ovulation you are merely shedding some light on one of the mysteries of life. It is a crime to deceive a girl on such matters when we have so little real knowledge to begin with. No girl who menstruates should ever have to feel ashamed about her natural processes and not be as knowledgeable as possible about what is going on within her. She must have this knowledge, anyway, in order to understand the medical technology that has revolutionized women's lives. Nor is it such a bad idea to explain, at the same time, what goes on in the opposite sex to complement ovulation in girls. The human reproductive system is intricate, ingenious, and awe-inspiring. Why not let young people know its details? Technology is now providing them with many dangerous ways to interfere with these natural processes. How can they be expected to make intelligent decisions about using this easily available technology if they are not aware of how it interferes with their normal body functions?

The trouble with modern medical technology is that it tends to separate our body functions from their emotional payoffs. This leads me to believe that the intricate relationship between our body functions and our emotional responses is not well enough appreciated by our medical technicians. I suppose the truth of the matter is that our scientific knowledge is simply insufficient. As advanced as we may think we are, we are still only on the threshold of knowing what human life is about.

As your daughter matures and starts going out with boys, you may want to tell her something about sex. With the so-called New Morality about, with its rampant premarital promiscuity, venereal disease, and unwanted pregnancies, you may want to give her the benefit of your wisdom and warn her about what can happen if she is careless. I don't believe that any one of us has an easy recipe for happiness that we can pass on to our children. But if we know what does *not* bring happiness, then we ought to impart at least that information to our daughters.

First, I would advise her against having sex before marriage. I would advise this not in order to deny her its pleasure, but to enable her to have it when she can most enjoy it. There are several good practical reasons for advising against premarital sex: to guard her from unwanted pregnancy, to guard her against venereal disease, to guard her against an emotional attachment that may be of short but painful duration, to guard her against the awakening of a sexual appetite that may lead to promiscuity and make it difficult for her to establish a loyal attachment. I believe that the key to happiness is a durable, loyal attachment to someone you love. If you study the lives of the most successful, happy people, you will invariably find at the center an emotionally satisfying and strongly vital attachment. Thus the advice I would give a daughter is to find a young man with whom she can have such an attachment.

If she does find such a guy, should she have sex with him before marriage? Again I would advise against it, on the grounds that she may become pregnant, thereby forcing marriage before they are ready for it. Marriage is a conscious commitment to loyalty, and unless they are ready to make it they ought not to do what should only be done in the context of that commitment. If an abortion is required, that certainly will throw a pall over a good relationship. The pill, theoretically, is supposed to make such eventualities impossible. But not even the pill

201

is 100 percent effective. Besides, the pill is known to cause over fifty different side effects—from blood clots and strokes to depression and irreversible sterility. Barbara Seaman writes in *The Doctors' Case Against the Pill:*

> The estrogenic and progestational components of oral contraceptive drugs, as we know them today, are extremely active hormonal agents which have effects on many biological systems within the body . . . in fact, the contraceptive effects of these drugs may be merely incidental to many other pharmacological effects. . . . Using the pill is like tinkering with nuclear bombs to fight off a common cold. . . .
>
> The amount of medication that some doctors hand out to counteract pill side effects is staggering. To name just a few: diuretics for water retention; tranquilizers for irritability and nervousness; thyroid preparations for fatigue and lethargy; blood thinners for women who have developed clotting disorders; anti-nausea preparations; pain killers; remedies for indigestion. Since the pill changes the balance of hormones and bacteria in the vagina, vaginal fungus infections (and attendant "screaming" itching) have become so common that one drug company has advertised a powerful local antibiotic in medical journals with the slogan, "If she's on the pill, she may need the tablet."

Thus, if your daughter is contemplating taking the pill, you will be doing her a great service by making her aware of the risks involved. A woman's complex hormonal system is delicately balanced and connected to all the organic systems of her body. The pill creates organic disequilibrium. It has only been in use since 1961, and we have no idea what its long-range effects will be on the millions of women who have used it. Dr. John H. Laragh, professor of clinical medicine at Columbia University, states: "I wouldn't use it if I were a woman. Women think it's magic, but there is no magic. Look at cortisone. It was once thought to be a magic drug. Now a lot of users have no spinal column left."[123]

No, your daughter and her intended need not engage in premarital sex. If they intend to spend a lifetime together, they will have plenty of sex after marriage. Of course your daughter may not take your advice, but at least give it—with the reasons for the advice you give. Let her know that the advice is based on human experience and not some arbitrary moral code reflecting your personal idea of virtue.

There is an art to giving advice. Advice is not an ultimatum or an order. It is wisdom generously imparted to help someone else make a difficult but intelligent decision. People don't need advice to make easy decisions. They need it when the choices at hand are difficult to make. For example, it may be difficult for a girl to resist sleeping with the guy she is going to marry. But a difficult decision can be made easier with additional knowledge. The best knowledge, of course, is the knowledge we get from our own experience. But that can be painful and costly. The second best source of knowledge is from those who've had the experiences and are willing to talk about them. There is plenty of that knowledge around, available at little cost and no pain.

Warnings are stronger than advice, but you should not have to give warnings to a daughter who loves you, trusts you, and values your guidance. Daughters need guidance, especially now when girls are placed in the position of having to make difficult moral decisions that may effect their entire lives. If you have brought up your daughter to have a favorable disposition toward motherhood, then she will have a sense of responsibility about any emotional attachment she has with a man, knowing full well what premarital sex can lead to. You will find that most of the girls engaging in coed promiscuity today have a generally negative attitude toward motherhood, and therefore make no connection between sex and maternal attachments. Their orientation is limited to the arena of male-female sexual interplay, in which the guys are out for sexual pleasure and conquest and the girls think they are out for the same. The girls, I am convinced, really are looking for a guy to love them, but are searching among the most irresponsible males they can find. The result: emotional mutilation, plus a trip to the abortionist if they get pregnant.

Abortion. I am amazed how little college girls know about prenatal life and what doctors actually do to it when they snuff it out. Yet they all have opinions on the subject, and the overwhelming stand among college girls is for legalized abortion. One university girl to whom I spoke strongly favored abortion on demand right up to the day of the child's birth. Her knowledge of prenatal life was totally lacking. I wondered how she was able to reach her strongly opinionated state of female liberation with so little knowledge about anything except her own impulses. But the truth is that the vast majority of women who favor legalized abortion do so on emotional grounds only. They are like the millions of women who take the pill and haven't the faintest knowledge of the hormonal system they are tampering with.

I think, therefore, that every high school girl should be given a thorough, detailed course in prenatal life now that she has been given the power by medical science and the courts to snuff out that life on demand. The power is too great to be exercised without knowledge; and if our society has deemed it proper to give that power to every female, responsible and irresponsible alike, then it has a moral duty to see that she makes her decisions on the basis of knowledge, and not merely emotion or convenience. Since the prenatal infant is defenseless and cannot speak in its own behalf to save its own life, society has a moral duty to present its case to the mother before she makes her decision. If all girls were thus educated and informed, I think the rate of abortions would decline drastically because there would be fewer unwanted pregnancies. Girls would begin to realize that careless behavior involves more than themselves and their boyfriends. They would have greater respect and appreciation for the lives they might inadvertently create.

All talk of female liberation is phony and hypocritical if the women do not assume the responsibilities that must go with their newly acquired powers. Female liberation cannot mean liberation from responsibility, otherwise it is not real liberation at all. It cannot be a moral blank check drawn on society's unlimited tolerance. Freedom makes far more demands on a person than does dependency. That is the first lesson learned by anyone who wants to be independent. Therefore I would give a girl a course in prenatal life before I would teach her such "useful" subjects as trigonometry, anthropology, or medieval poetry. I would give her this course in high school, to balance those courses in sex education that encourage premarital sex by telling her all about those wonderful easily available contraceptives and her so-called natural right to abortion.

These days there is great emphasis in the media on the sexual revolution and the new spirit of sexual freedom that the young are supposed to enjoy; but no emphasis is put on the responsibilities that must go with freedom if freedom is to be of any value. Since most people are no longer influenced or deterred by Biblical admonitions, we need the knowledge science has given us to counter the forces of irresponsibility. The last ten years have seen a tremendous increase in the knowledge we have about prenatal life. There is no reason why this knowledge should not become part of the modern high school curriculum. Nor would it be a bad idea for boys to be given this knowledge too. Since every unwanted pregnancy also involves a male, it is time that we awakened a sense of responsibility in the boys as well as the girls. Simply because medical science has developed more efficient means of abortion does not mean that we must encourage or tolerate behavior that leads to unwanted pregnancies. Knowledge of prenatal life may take some of the "fun" out of promiscuity. But an unwanted pregnancy is no fun for the girl who has one, no matter how efficient the abortion, and the abortion is no fun for the fetus.

Another way to help your daughter gain a favorable disposition toward motherhood is to introduce her to the concepts of natural childbirth and breast-feeding by giving her books on these subjects to read. Many girls get their ideas about childbirth and infant care from old wives' tales or hearsay. They may have deep fears about the pains of childbirth and some vague, erroneous notions about breast-feeding. Books on natural childbirth and breast-feeding would replace fear and uncertainty with knowledge and a sense of personal security. A girl would be able to help her future husband understand these things and she would be able to face her obstetrician with knowledge instead of the usual ignorance. It is so very important to build up a girl's self-confidence with knowledge. I am convinced that a girl who knows about ovulation, her hormonal system, prenatal life, natural childbirth, and breast-feeding will find drugs and promiscuity of little interest. She will realize that drugs and premarital "recreational" sex are in direct conflict with the maternal values her knowledge has made her appreciate.

Drugs and sex are the major preoccupations of today's youth. But they are used only as a means of making up for the lack of attachment values in their lives. By encouraging behavior that makes the creation of durable, satisfying attachments virtually impossible, we make drugs, alcohol, and sexual vagrancy the only means to alleviate painful separation anxiety. Sedation makes life without loyalty tolerable but not happy. It permits a lot of people to live through one day and go on to the next. And since the continued use of drugs, alcohol, and promiscuity makes it increasingly more difficult to attain the satisfactions of attachment, it also increases the pain that must be sedated by ever-increasing doses of pain killer. Thousands of young people get caught up in this vicious, self-destructive cycle. Only those whose lives are firmly anchored to attachment values are spared such emotional agony.

What are the attachment values? Patience, tolerance, love, loyalty. The most important, of course, is loyalty. A commitment of loyalty requires sacrifice. You cannot be loyal and enjoy sexual promiscuity at the same time. Those who think they can simply wind up making themselves unhappy by undermining their attachments. Loyalty is the most effective defense against separation. Therefore you should advise your daughter to find a man to whom she can be loyal, without equivocation. Premarital sexual promiscuity not only makes it difficult to find such a man, but it also makes it difficult for a woman to remain sexually loyal to her husband. Once she has acquired a taste for promiscuous sex, she will find herself flirting with temptation, which often means flirting with marital disaster.

It is perhaps requiring too much of a woman to be sexually faithful to one man during her entire life. Certainly there are situations in which divorce is justified. But the alternative to a basic commitment to fidelity is either betrayal of a trust or an inability to be loyal at all. In an earlier chapter we cited the example of a woman who had found a man who was sexually more satisfying than her husband, yet she did not want to give up her husband just for that. What it illustrates is that no one person will ever have all the qualities we may want or admire in a mate. But we must realize that if our mates are not perfect, neither are we; and if we expect them to be loyal to us—as imperfect as we are—we must be loyal to them. The wife who cheats on a loyal husband would be appalled if he retaliated in kind.

A human being may be limited in attributes and qualities, but each human being is a world in himself. One of the deepest pleasures in attachment is getting to know another human being as well as one knows oneself. It often makes one know oneself better. When José Ortega defined love as "an intense affirmation of another being, regardless of their attitude toward us" he was saying that there had to be something in that other human being that could evoke from us that intense affirmation. In that affirmation is a focusing of our emotional attention. The person we love stands out in the crowd, as if surrounded by an aura. We are dazzled by his or her presence. Without him the house is empty; with him the house is full. Some women are lucky to find a man whom they can love so completely. Margo Albert, describing her actor-husband Eddie Albert, once said in an interview: "When you find a man you absolutely adore, you are so lucky you have to walk around on your knees all day."[124]

How do you inculcate the attachment values? By explaining to your daughter what they are. *Patience.* We need patience to guard ourselves against rash emotional actions that can hurt others and destroy what it is we are trying to build. We need patience to let growth take place. *Tolerance.* We need tolerance because everyone is different, and no one is perfect. If you would have others accept you with all your faults, you must be prepared to do the same for others. *Love.* There is no attachment without it. But it is only a beginning. Unless it leads to loyalty, love can be undermined. Loyalty arises out of the need in every human being to create an "immovable center" in his life. In a world of endless choice, variety, temptation, and shifting values, loyalty is the most difficult value to inculcate. Loyalty represents the most personal and complete of commitments. It is the key to happiness. Because it requires sacrifice and emotional self-discipline, the young find it too hard to accept. So instead of demanding loyalty of themselves, they seek someone who will demand it of them. But loyalty can never be obtained on demand. It can only be given freely, for loyalty is a gift, the greatest gift one human being can give another.

Thus there are many ways to give your daughter a favorable disposition toward motherhood, thereby instilling in her a sense of maternal responsibility. It simply takes concern and interest, a desire to do what can be done, a determination to see that the knowledge she should have gets to her. If it doesn't, she will more easily fall under the sway of her peers, and peers can be pretty dangerous. For example, one study made by the New School for Social Research reported that friends, not drug pushers, lead most innocent youngsters to hard drugs.[125] Another interesting study, made by two professors at Johns Hopkins University, estimated that 75 percent of American teenage girls who get pregnant for the first time are unwed when they conceive.[126] Which means that when teenage girls engage in premarital sex, they don't seem to have much concern for the possible consequences. The report, published by the Planned Parenthood Federation, was intended not to discourage premarital sex among teenagers but to elicit greater support for making contraceptives and abortion more easily accessible, thus encouraging premarital sex. We live in a peculiar society, where an organization devoted to Planned "Parenthood" bends over backwards to make irresponsible teenage behavior easier for teenagers to "enjoy." And so, if *you* don't give your daughter a favorable disposition toward motherhood, no one else will.

Where do we go from here? Much depends on what people learn from the last ten years of experience. As of this writing, January 1975, the retreat from motherhood is still in full swing. The birth and fertility rates for 1973 were lower than those for 1972. In fact, in 1973 there were fewer births in the United States than in any year since 1945. The 1973 fertility rate was the lowest in our history. Yet, surprisingly, up through 1973, the number of marriages continued to rise. In 1974, however, the marriage rate in the U.S. declined for the first time since 1958 by 2.5 percent. The declining rate merely reflected the fact that in 1974 more couples were living together without the benefit of matrimony than in previous years. Which merely means that young people are getting married and living together not necessarily because they want children, but because the need for attachment has not diminished and never will.

But what is this declining birthrate going to do to America? It is already creating a lot of empty classrooms in our primary schools. It is also forcing manufacturers of baby products to change their lines or go out of business. And it means that in thirty years a diminished young population will be heavily taxed to pay the retirement benefits of the aging majority. It also means that we will have a society of many "only children," that is, a lot of people who won't know what it's like to have a brother or sister. The rich, overflowing attachment stimuli that came with large families will be missing from our national experience. Parents will have fewer children, but more emotion will be invested in each one of them. People in general will have fewer blood relatives, making the loss of one of them a severe loss indeed. Family gatherings will be shadows of their former selves. Will this be good or bad? Will the quality of mothering improve as the number of children decrease? Who can say? But I have a feeling that a lot of our present childless couples are going to produce a lot of late children when they've had all the fun and games they can take and then decide that a future generation is not such a bad idea after all.

The future generation. I venture to say that they will look at us in ways we can scarcely envisage now, perhaps with sympathy at our

207

unhappiness, perhaps with contempt at our insensitivity to basic human values. The retreat from motherhood is perhaps inevitable for a nation retreating from its basic belief in the sanctity of human life. Technology has dehumanized us. It has made us believe that machines have more validity than human emotions, that pills are better than hormones, that sex is better than love, that a "career" is better than a baby. A nation in that frame of mind, denying en masse that it needs a future, is headed for dissolution. We have not yet reached the point of no return. Other nations, decimated and ruined, have made their comebacks.

But our enemies are unlike any that other nations have had to face. Our prime enemy is a scientific conceit that permeates our society from top to bottom and asserts that the human race needs nothing but a good social engineer right out of Harvard or MIT. Since we no longer put our trust in God, we now put it in the hands of scientists, and they are a very mixed bag indeed. They go where the grant money is, and their idealism is about as real as their financial independence. The dedicated are a small minority. They put some of their human concern into their work. But the majority run the show, and they are bedazzled by their own machines, their own computers, their own technology. For the moment the nation is bedazzled with them, expecting continued "miracles" from this new class of high priests. That childbearing and its prevention should be the prime focus of so much research indicates that scientific conceit cannot tolerate being anything less than Godlike. That, I believe, is the chronic disease of our age. Can we survive it? Only if science can be made to serve human values. Perhaps the future generation, small as it may be, will be forced to discover the means to do exactly that.

References

1. *New York Times*, April 16, 1974, p. 1.
2. *U.S. News & World Report*, April 22, 1974, p. 43.
3. Caroline Bird, "Gearing Up for Near Zero Growth," *Signature* magazine, March 1973.
4. Ellen Peck, *The Baby Trap* (New York: Bernard Geis Associates, 1971), pp. 8, 9.
5. Garry Wills, "What? What? Are Young Americans Afraid to Have Kids?" *Esquire*, March 1974.
6. Sara Davidson, "At Last! Help for Child-Abusers," *Woman's Day*, March 1973.
7. *Boston Sunday Herald Advertiser*, May 19, 1974.
8. *Houston Post*, August 14, 1973.
9. Lester David, "Are You Runaway Prone?" *Seventeen*, April 1974.
10. Lincoln and Alice Day, *Too Many Americans, Tomorrow's Issue* (Boston: Houghton Mifflin, 1964), p. 2.
11. Garrett Hardin, editor, *Population, Evolution and Birth Control: A Collage of Controversial Ideas* (San Francisco: W. H. Freeman and Company, 1964).
12. Robert W. Kistner, M.D., *The Pill* (New York: Delacorte Press, 1968), p. 268.
13. Robin Morgan, editor, *Sisterhood is Powerful* (New York: Vintage Books, 1970), p. 28.
14. *Ibid.*, p. 220.
15. Hal Evans, "Epidemic of Child Abuse is Sweeping America," *National Enquirer*, September 23, 1973.

16. Robin Morgan, editor, *Sisterhood is Powerful, op. cit.*, p. 486.
17. *Ibid.*, p. 488.
18. *Ibid.*, p. 489.
19. Lisa Hobbs, *Love and Liberation* (New York: McGraw-Hill, 1970), p. 4.
20. Miriam Schneir, editor, *Feminism, The Essential Historical Writings* (New York: Random House, 1972), p. 78.
21. *Ibid.*, p. 38.
22. *Ibid.*, p. 113.
23. *Ibid.*, p. 145.
24. Caroline Bird, *Born Female* (New York: David McKay Company, 1968, 1970), p. 41.
25. Kate Millett. *Sexual Politics* (New York: Doubleday & Co., 1969, 1970), Equinox Books edition, p. 189.
26. Betty Friedan, *The Feminine Mystique* (New York: W. W. Norton and Company, 1963), Dell paperback edition, p. 14.
27. *Ibid.*, p. 21.
28. *Book Review Digest*, 1953.
29. *Saturday Review*, February 21, 1953.
30. Betty Friedan, *op. cit.*, p. 351.
31. Marge Piercy's essay, "The Grand Coolie Damn," in *Sisterhood is Powerful*, describes the SDS scene where women did the "shitwork." This aptly descriptive word is used by Ms. Piercy on p. 424.
32. Robin Morgan, editor, *Sisterhood is Powerful, op. cit.*, p. xx.
33. *Ibid.*, p. 35.
34. *Ibid.*, p. 521.
35. *Life*, December 12, 1969.
36. Robin Morgan, editor, *Sisterhood is Powerful, op. cit.*, p. 309.
37. *Ibid.*, p. 489.
38. *Ibid.*, p. 488.
39. Germaine Greer, *The Female Eunuch* (New York: McGraw-Hill, 1971), Bantam paperback edition, p. 251.
40. *Ibid.*, p. 233.
41. *Ibid.*, p. 233.
42. *Ibid.*, p. 233.
43. Kate Millett, *op. cit.*, p. 25.
44. *Ibid.*, p. 45.
45. *Ibid.*, p. 28.
46. *Ibid.*, p. 46.
47. *Ibid.*, p. 58.
48. Robin Morgan, editor, *Sisterhood is Powerful, op. cit.*, p. 225.
49. Simone de Beauvoir, *The Second Sex* (New York: Alfred A. Knopf, 1953) Bantam paperback edition, p. 26.
50. Desmond Morris, *The Naked Ape* (New York: McGraw-Hill, 1967), Dell paperback edition, p. 52.
51. *Ibid.*, pp. 53-54.
52. Philip Wylie, *Generation of Vipers* (New York: Rinehart & Company, 1943, 1955), p. 58.
53. Diana Lurie, "Empire Built on Sex," *Life*, October 29, 1965.
54. Helen Gurley Brown, *Sex and the New Single Girl* (New York: Bernard Geis Associates, 1970), Fawcett paperback edition, p. 15.
55. Barbara Seaman, *Free and Female* (New York: Coward-McCann & Geoghegan, 1972), Fawcett paperback edition, p. 18.
56. *Boston Sunday Globe*, May 19, 1974, p. 76.

57. Barbara Seaman, *op. cit.*, p. 41.
58. *Playboy,* September 1973, p. 92.
59. Barbara Seaman, *op. cit.*, pp. 294-95.
60. Robin Morgan, editor, *Sisterhood is Powerful, op. cit.*, p. 254.
61. Eric Berne, M.D., *Games People Play* (New York: Grove Press, 1964), paperback edition, p. 13.
62. Garrett Hardin, *op. cit.*, p. 249.
63. Lincoln and Alice Day, *op. cit.*, pp. 125-26.
64. Robin Morgan, editor, *Sisterhood is Powerful, op. cit.*, p. 246.
65. *Ibid.*, pp. 341-42.
66. *Ibid.* This is a composite quote drawn from pages 487, 488, 490, 492.
67. Lisa Hobbs, *op. cit.*, pp. 85-86.
68. Jane Beckman Lancaster, "In Praise of the Achieving Female Monkey," *The Female Experience,* from the Editors of *Psychology Today,* 1973, p. 9.
69. "An Obstetrician Teaches Dad to Deliver His Baby Himself," *People Weekly,* January 20, 1975, pp. 40-43.
70. *The Female Experience, op. cit.*, pp. 23, 24.
71. Shulamith Firestone, *The Dialectic of Sex* (New York: William Morrow and Company, 1970), Bantam paperback edition, pp. 198-99.
72. *Ibid.*, p. 199.
73. *Ibid.*, p. 72.
74. *Ibid.*, p. 85.
75. *Ibid.*, p. 87.
76. *Ibid.*, p. 91.
77. *Ibid.*, p. 104.
78. Gordon Bermant, "A Conversation with Alice Rossi," *The Female Experience, op. cit.*, pp. 92-93, 94.
79. Eleanor Roberts, "The Story Behind Our Soaring Divorce Rate," *Boston Sunday Herald Advertiser,* January 13, 1974, Section Five, p. A7.
80. Stuart A. Queen and Robert W. Habenstein, *The Family in Various Cultures* (Philadelphia: J. B. Lippincott, 1952), pp. 177-78.
81. Germaine Greer, *op. cit.*, p. 234.
82. *Ibid.*, p. 238.
83. *Ibid.*, p. 239.
84. *Ibid.*, pp. 244-45.
85. *Ibid.*, pp. 248-49.
86. Shulamith Firestone, *op. cit.*, p. 212.
87. *Ibid.*, p. 231.
88. Robert E. Hall, M.D., *A Doctor's Guide to Having an Abortion* (New York: New American Library, 1971), p. 57.
89. David R. Mace, *Abortion, The Agonizing Decision* (Nashville: Abingdon Press, 1972), p. 47.
90. *Ibid.*, p. 92.
91. Robert E. Hall, M.D., *op. cit.*, p. 50.
92. Nicholas Von Hoffman, "Abortion; The Right to Life," *Playgirl,* August 1974, p. 55.
93. Carole Klein, *The Single Parent Experience* (New York: Walker & Co., 1973), p. 116.
94. Robert Bluford, Jr., Th.D., and Robert E. Petres, M.D., *Unwanted Pregnancy* (New York: Harper & Row, 1973), p. 94.
95. *Ibid.*
96. *Ibid.*
97. *Ibid.*, p. 56.

98. *Ibid.*, p. 56.
99. Geraldine Lux Flanagan, *The First Nine Months of Life* (New York: Simon & Schuster, 1962), p. 55.
100. Group for the Advancement of Psychiatry, *The Right to Abortion: A Psychiatric View* (New York: Scribner, 1970).
101. Marion Steinmann, "Behind the Drama of Saving Babies in Trouble," *Today's Health,* June 1974.
102. Rita Kramer, "Parent and Child: A New Approach to Adoption and Custody," *New York Times Magazine,* October 7, 1973, p. 10.
103. Rita Kramer, *op. cit.*
104. *Today's Health*, February 1974.
105. Barbara Seaman, *Free and Female, op. cit.*, p. 157.
106. Elliott H. McCleary, *New Miracles of Childbirth* (New York: David McKay Company, 1974), p. 51.
107. *Ibid.*, p. 222.
108. *Ibid.*, p. 225.
109. *Ibid.*, p. 229.
110. Virginia E. Pomeranz, M.D., *The First Five Years* (New York: Doubleday & Company, 1973), p. 4.
111. La Leche League International, *The Womanly Art of Breastfeeding* (Franklin Park, Ill. 60131, 1958), p. 13.
112. Dana Raphael, *The Tender Gift: Breastfeeding* (Englewood Cliffs, N.J.: Prentice-Hall, 1973), pp. 125, 126.
113. José Ortega y Gasset, *On Love* (New York: Meridian Books, 1958).
114. Anthony Davids, *Children in Conflict: A Casebook* (New York: John Wiley & Sons, 1974), p. 5.
115. Ashley Montagu, *On Being Human* (New York: Hawthorn Books, 1966, 1950), p. 55.
116. Robert R. Sears, Eleanor E. Maccoby, and Harry Levin, *Patterns of Child Rearing* (New York: Harper & Row, 1957), p. 168.
117. Beatrix Tudor-Hart, *The Intelligent Parent's Guide to Child Behavior* (New York: Delacorte Press, 1963), p. 62.
118. William McCord and Joan McCord, *Origins of Alcoholism* (Stanford, California: Stanford University Press, 1960). This is a composite quote drawn from pages viii, 54, 87.
119. Gerald O'Gorman, *The Nature of Childhood Autism* (New York: Appleton-Century-Crofts, 1970), p. 64.
120. Rita Kramer, *op. cit.*, p. 70.
121. José Ortega y Gasset, *op. cit.*
122. Barbara Seaman, *The Doctors' Case Against The Pill* (New York: Peter H. Wyden, 1969), p. 146.
123. *Ibid.*, p. 23.
124. *Boston Herald American,* August 21, 1973.
125. Pamela Smith, "Keeping Up With Youth," *Parade,* August 18, 1974, p. 18.
126. *Ibid.*

INDEX

213

216

220